TEACHING WITH A PURPOSE

© 1984 by Houghton Mifflin Company

TEACHING WITH A PURPOSE

Doug Hunt
University of Missouri, Columbia

Instructor's Guide and Resource Book for

Writing With a Purpose

James M. McCrimmon

Eighth Edition

by

Joseph F. Trimmer   Nancy I. Sommers

HOUGHTON MIFFLIN COMPANY   BOSTON

Dallas   Geneva, Illinois
Hopewell, New Jersey   Palo Alto

Printed in the U.S.A.

ISBN: 0-395-34247-3

ABCDEFGHIJ-A-89876543

CONTENTS

TEACHING WITH A PURPOSE

INTRODUCTION: A NOTE TO NEW TEACHERS

The problem with one-size-fits-all clothes, as a friend of mine once pointed out, is that so few people have one-size-fits-all bodies. Similarly, trying to give general advice to new teachers is that so few of us who teach composition have typical goals and teach typical students in a typical college. Good teachers always find methods to suit their circumstances, and some of the best are no more likely to adopt each others' practices than they are to borrow each others' toothbrushes. Nonetheless, some beginners might find it helpful to hear about the pits I have fallen into over the last decade and the ladders by which I've tried to climb out of them. For this reason (and certainly not because I'm confident that I do things right), I'll spend this introduction describing my own approach to managing a composition class, including my experience teaching with pre-publication page proof of the Eighth Edition of <u>Writing With a Purpose</u> in the fall of 1983. I'd feel more comfortable describing someone else's practices, but as Thoreau puts it, "I should not talk so much about myself if there were anybody else whom I knew as well."

I don't want to give the impression at the outset that teaching composition is hopelessly idiosyncratic. In the past fifteen years, professionals have published many useful articles and books; likewise, such organizations as the Conference on College Communication and Composition continue to lessen the isolation of the individual teacher and move the profession toward consensus. Those of you who intend to become professional composition teachers should be familiar with the recent litera- ture. A good beginning is the bibliography that concludes this book, a thoughtful and eminently useful collection of sources chosen and annotated by Barbara Weaver of Anderson College. Others should at least know that the general drift in the field is toward "student-centered, process-oriented" teaching. These rather ugly terms mean that today's composition teachers don't stand at the lectern, pulling tools (semicolons, topic sentences, etc.) out of the toolbox one at a time, explaining their func- tions, and then telling the student to build a term paper. In- stead they work at the student's elbow as he or she progresses stage by stage through a writing project. They explain the process as it evolves and introduce tools as they are needed.

The shift from lectern to elbow is a goal that can never be completely achieved in the daily reality of teaching, but the pursuit of it dramatically affects the teacher's role.

1

THE TEACHER'S ROLE IN A COMPOSITION CLASSROOM

In the typical classroom, the teacher dispenses knowledge and students receive it. Ideally they receive it tentatively, with critical faculties fully alert, but after twelve or thirteen years in the system, undergraduates have learned that receiving is their business. To a distressing degree, they see college as a series of spiral notebooks filled with transcribed lectures. If composition teachers walk home at the end of the day with shoulders sagging, it is largely because they have struggled all day against the traditional current that rushes from teacher to student. When you step into your composition class, your first duty is to turn the tables, to make the students into producers rather than consumers, to convince them that they can find something worthwhile to say.

This reversal of roles is hard for everyone. Your students will very likely be taking four other classes with clearly defined subject matter and definite criteria for rightness and wrongness. While the subjects are sometimes hard to learn, they are not very threatening. They don't demand that students make judgments in gray areas or expose their personal convictions. In fact, professors in some areas will tell their students (quite correctly) that they don't know enough about the subject to form judgments or have convictions. When you tell them that they must discover subjects and purposes that will be interesting and significant, they will naturally be uneasy. They've been told over and over that they can't swim, and you are telling them that by semester's end, they'll be doing laps in deep water.

You, meanwhile, inherit a class structure designed with the other courses in mind. The semester is made up, typically, of forty-five "lecture" days. The classroom has thirty or so seats, bolted to the floor, perhaps, facing the front. The students come in at 9:00, in transit from an 8:00 biology lecture to a 10:00 history lecture. They sit down and open their spiral notebooks at the second divider. The pressure is almost irresistible, but if you are wise you <u>won't lecture</u>. You won't let your students fall back into their roles as receivers of knowledge you dispense.

The most obvious alternative to the lecture is the class discussion, but most discussions I have seen in composition classes have been flaccid things. I pass by a doorway and hear the teacher ask, "Joanie, how would you define a thesis statement?" Joanie flips through a couple of pages in the text until she finds the answer, which she reads almost verbatim. "Good!" the teacher says, glad for any response. "Now, John, . . ."

Ultimately, the goal of class discussion is <u>real</u> discussion, exchange of ideas, collaborative learning, but the students in my classes are rarely attuned to this sort of learning. As the semester progresses, they will get better at discussions, but to get them started, I lay out some ground rules. On every discussion day, students will receive a participation grade: 3 points for an excellent recitation, 2 for adequate knowledge of the reading, 1 for attendance. Sometimes that participation grade will be determined by performance on a quiz; whether there is a quiz or not, students should come prepared to discuss their reading assignment <u>with their books closed</u>. This may strike you at first as a harsh step back to the teacher-centered classroom. In fact, it is a pragmatic way to get myself off center stage. In a graded discussion, students know that they can't get the answer from the book or from me, so they are thrown back on their own devices, just as they will be when they write. And since we discuss a question until we've reached a consensus on it, the students' comments become short persuasive speeches--excellent practice. (For an example of a discussion quiz, see page 29. Notice that the questions move from mere recall to application and interpretation.)

In a typical semester, we will spend perhaps twenty-five days in class discussion (including the discussion of many student essays). Another ten or twelve will go to workshops (discussed below). Occasionally, I will lecture on those few topics in grammar, usage, punctuation, and rhetoric about which objective knowledge can be dispensed. In general, though, students end the semester feeling that much of what they learned about writing, they learned on their own or from conversations with their classmates. I was a faintly helpful presence. This is progress. When I first started teaching, I made a stronger impression on my students, but they learned less.

If composition teachers aren't dispensers of knowledge, what are they? Fortunately, <u>Writing With a Purpose</u> tells us in its first chapter, by observing that the teacher's role is essentially like that of an editor--not a copy editor, of course, but an editor-in-chief, someone who has a stake in the success of the writer. You have the ultimate authority and burden of grading, of course. But your main responsibility is to work with your writers as a senior collaborator and encourager. You may have trouble (particularly after the first paper) imagining yourself as a Harold Ross or a Katherine White managing the remarkable group of young writers who created <u>The New Yorker</u>, but give it a try. It is a healthier exercise than seeing yourself as a Mr. or Mrs. Gradgrind pouring knowledge into twenty empty vessels.

It is only as an editor that I try to make a strong impression on my students. At the end of the semester--unless they have listened very carefully, indeed--they won't know whether I am a Republican or Democrat, a Jew or Gentile, a feminist or a male chauvinist, but they will know I am a very attentive reader. If a student chooses a word brilliantly, I'll notice. If a student strains a metaphor in a good cause, I'll comment on both the worthiness of the effort and its limited success. The new edition of <u>Writing With a Purpose</u> gives teachers a tremendous tool for showing the sharpness of their editorial eye. Throughout the text, but particularly in the first four chapters, there are many examples of student writing that you and your class will read together. If in your discussion of these you leave an impression of how sensitively and intelligently you read student essays, you'll give your students a strong motive for good work. You will, of course, want to strengthen this impression by occasionally duplicating a worthwhile essay from your own class and leading a discussion of its merits (loudly proclaimed) and its weaknesses (politely insisted on).

Seeing yourself as an editor has implications you must be ready to accept. Center stage, as in every writer/editor relationship, is now occupied by the essay-in-progress, and the rhythm of the semester becomes the rhythm of drafts and deadlines. When I lay out my syllabus, I begin by marking the due dates for essays, making sure that I don't make one fall due on the last day of class when it will be too late for it to be commented on and "published" to other class members and that there is adequate time between essays for all the planning, drafting, and revising I expect my students to do. These deadlines set, other things begin to fall into place: dates when preliminary drafts will be due, days when students will divide into workshop groups and critique one another's papers, days when we will examine successful essays from the last assignment. Next I arrange readings from <u>Writing With a Purpose</u> and from the reader, always choosing the chapters, exercises, and essays that will best prepare students for their own upcoming essay. When I first started teaching, I felt the semester flapping around me like an oversized poncho. My problem was always filling up the days between essays. The solution, surprisingly, turned out to be paying <u>more</u> attention to the essays. Now I am always trying to find room to squeeze in one more sentence revision exercise between the preliminary draft and the final draft, or trying to get to the discussion of logical fallacies before the workshop groups begin to critique persuasive papers.

But your editorial role demands more than management of deadlines. There is also the encouragement of your writers, who because of their inexperience are likely to find the process of producing a significant and interesting essay daunting. A great morale booster is to talk with your students about your own composing processes. If your students don't see that you, too, are a writer, they may assume that you are "talking from the book" with no real sense of their difficulties. You have enough writing experience to be able to add significantly to the discussion of process in <u>Writing With a Purpose</u>. If you dislike getting started and have to create an artificial deadline to keep yourself going, say so; you will relieve the anxieties of your students who are fellow sufferers. If you never use formal outlines, confess and explain what you do instead. Give your students an idea of how long and hard you have to work on a paper and how much revision you usually do. Anecdotal information about your practices will add interest to your class and depth to the discussion of the writing process.

If you have time, you might carry this teaching strategy a step further and write at least one of your assignments along with the class. Show them everything--including the brainstorming, the journal writing, the drafts, the notes on revision. Let them see how much time you "waste" on false starts. Show them (if your drafts are like mine), the insertions and deletions, the theres for theirs and the it'ses for itses. All of this will probably reassure your class, and you will gain in credibility more than you lose in dignity. You will also get a clearer picture of what your assignment actually asks students to do. But most importantly, you will be setting an example by showing the purposeful process you go through in producing an essay.

Eventually, like every editor, you will have to judge the final copy, but even here you shouldn't forget your role as motivator. The easiest thing to write on a paper is a proof-reader's mark, and every week in our writing lab I see a few papers on which the teacher's reaction is limited to a handful of these marks and a sentence at the end. I spent an enlightening hour last year handing tissues to a student who brought in such a paper, on which she had gotten a B. The tears weren't for the grade; they were for the energy and ego poured into a paper she didn't feel had been really read. On the next paper, I'm sure, she didn't try as hard. To avoid such scenes, be as energetic in your search for accomplishments as you are in your search for weaknesses. You needn't gush: "a clever word choice" will do nicely, or "a fine example." If you praise honestly, you will get good mileage from a short compliment.

Your efforts to recognize a paper's strengths should extend beyond individual comments to an overview of the paper given in the end comment. Point out that even an F paper is not (ordinar-ily) a uniform disaster. You may have failed it, regretfully, because its subject wasn't narrowed to manageable dimensions and its sentences were ungrammatical. But you noticed that it had the fairly clear sense of purpose and audience that you expect to find in good papers, and that the diction was often precise and amusing, and that, other things being equal, it might have earned an A or B. Students who get comments of this sort may not be good company for a few hours, but will probably come round to seeing that their situation is not hopeless.

Part of the problem of getting your writers motivated is the artificiality of their situation. Phoniness is built into the composition classroom where the teacher is the only reader of students' papers. Students may see the teacher as a microscopic critic or as a friendly collaborator, but they will find it hard to see through him or her to the "primary" or "wider" audience mentioned in Chapter 1 of Writing With a Purpose. As a result, they will too often write grotesque parodies of "what the teacher wants to hear." In my first year of teaching, I apparently looked like someone who wanted to hear about parties "characterized by a congenial atmosphere that is conducive to intimate interpersonal relationships," about "daffodils dancing lazily on sweet breezes in the shimmering sunshine of a hazy summer day," and about intriguing sexual experiences. I don't think that the students who wrote these papers meant to be dishonest, but they had been put in the false position of looking for a hole in my particular armor. The artificiality of their situation had weakened their resolve to write in good faith, and they had begun to search for a short cut.

The most practical way out of this situation is to bring your students into the process of reading and critiquing. Whenever preliminary drafts fall due, I have the students bring in their originals plus three copies, and then break the class into groups of four. Here they can read one anothers' drafts and offer reactions and advice. When the chairs are bolted down, the students must crane their necks to talk to one another, or risk injury by sitting on the writing surface of their chairs, or dirty their jeans by sitting on the floor, but these inconveniences give the occasion an air of freedom, almost of rebellion. This setting is ideal, especially when students read their papers aloud and hear how they "play." I've not yet met a student hardened enough to read the "congenial atmosphere" line in front of three lounging classmates. To make the workshops effective, though, you must spend some time training your students in the art of pleasant, frank criticism and you must (at least in the early sessions) draw up critical agendas. You can teach the proper critical attitude by leading class discussions of a few student drafts. Writing With a Purpose provides you with possible critical agendas in the reading strategies (pp. 124-126) and revision agenda (pp. 126-128) of Chapter 4.

Group work bears unexpected fruit. In my early days as a composition teacher, I tried to comment copiously on ever preliminary draft. By working every waking hour, I could just keep up with the class and could be, in effect, everyone's private tutor. But as the fatigue built up, my comments became less and less productive and the class grew more and more burdensome to me and the students. Eventually it occurred to me that I was hopelessly outnumbered, and I began to tell the students that they would just have to tutor one another. My comments on preliminary drafts became almost exclusively questions, very much like the questions posed in the guidelines of Chapter 1 of Writing With a Purpose. The students dealt with these questions in their groups so far as possible, but I soon noticed that as class broke up, there would be a flurried exchange of phone numbers and some agreements reached to get together in a couple of days to look at new drafts. Since that time, I've encouraged the peripheral class, the class of phone calls and meetings at the student union, in every way I can. In the first week of class, I make it very clear to the students that I will not grade their papers relative to the other's, but relative to fixed standards. If

everybody writes well, works hard, and solicits help from classmates if necessary, we could conceivably have a class of all As
and Bs. If they don't, we could have a class of Ds and Fs. I
pass around a ditto master for people to put their phone numbers
on if they don't mind being called by classmates who want some
help, and I put my home number on the sheet so that I will become
a part of the network.

Some of you will be reluctant to give out your home number,
and understandably so. But it has worked out well for me. I've
done some of my best teaching with a dishtowel in my hand.
Students usually call me after they have talked to one or two
classmates about a problem, after they've become fairly articulate
about their dilemma. I offer only tentative opinions, remind
them that only they can ultimately tell what will work in their
papers, and try not to be mistaken for an authority. At any
rate, the network takes shape without my playing too active a
role in it, and I soon find that in conferences students begin to
cite each other as authorities. "Julie said that the thesis
statement sounded too mechanical. What do you think?" "Ray
looked at this last night and thought that _guy_ wasn't too informal
in this paper. I think he's right, but I thought I'd check with
you."

I got a phone call last spring from a former student of
mine who had transferred to U.C.L.A. He was taking an exposition
course and had just written an introductory paragraph he thought
was very clever, but teetered on the brink of being too clever.
So he read it to me, I asked him a few questions about where the
paper was going, and we generally talked the thing over. Just
before he hung up, he apologized unnecessarily for having called
me at home and said that he wouldn't have bothered me if he could
have reached Neil. Neil, you see, was his classmate the year
before and his most reliable critic. I was the second choice.
Wonderful.

SOME PRACTICAL HINTS

Begin the semester with a short moratorium on grades.

Few of your students will be experienced writers, and many
will begin the semester with more anxiety than they can put to
productive use. As Mina Shaughnessy noted, the very weakest will
see their writing as "a line that moves haltingly across the
page, exposing as it goes all that the writer doesn't know, then
passing into the hands of a stranger who reads it with a lawyer's
eyes, searching for flaws."[1] If you require an early paper and
give out richly deserved Ds and Fs, you may literally scare such

---

[1] _Errors and Expectations_ (New York: Oxford University
Press, 1977), p. 7.

students out of their wits; you may kill their desire to take chances in their writing, to have fun with it, to invest a little of themselves in it. This is not to say that you should avoid all writing assignments in the early days. On the contrary, you should get your students writing as early and as often as possible. The second and third chapters of Writing With a Purpose discuss planning or prewriting activities appropriate from the very beginning of the semester: brainstorming, freewriting, journal writing, discovery drafts, and so forth. Some of this writing could be handed in, with the understanding that it will not be graded (though credit may be given), but that you intend to make a few marginal comments to help the student toward a full-dress essay. These comments should be as positive as possible: you are running along behind the student, keeping one hand on the fender while he or she gets up to speed.

Important as this moratorium is, it is a disservice to students to let it extend too long. At my university, they need a graded paper under their belts by the fourth week (before the add/drop deadline) so that they can take stock and get help if necessary.

Choose topics for which your students can find a purpose.

The worst student essays are often written in response to topics that could be proposed only in a composition class. As an undergraduate teaching assistant, I once had to grade thirty-two responses to the question, "Does the arrow point up or down?" The teacher who set the question was inspirational, but the question was terrible and got wretched answers. Nearly as bad are papers responding to broad topics with which few students (and very few freshmen) feel personally engaged--"Freedom" or "American Political Parties." You will do both your students and yourself a favor if you assign topics that will produce lively papers rather than rewrites of fossils from fraternity files.

In the early part of the semester, a good practice is to let students develop topics that grow naturally out of the planning exercises in Chapter 2 of Writing With a Purpose. You might, for instance, have them hand in their journals along with a note that proposes three topics and explains how these arose from the journal writing and why they think they would be interesting. (See "Guidelines for Selecting Your Subject," pp. 17-18). But if you feel that a composition class should prepare students for writing in other college courses and in the professions, you will eventually want them to write on assigned topics so that they can learn the art of finding personal angles, voices, and tones when they must write on topics that seem at first imposed and alien.

Some students will get lost in the switch. That is, some students will never be good at maintaining an individual tone and perspective when they address a topic that grows out of anything but personal experience. You can help them greatly, though, if

8

you will give your assignments early and create a context for them. Suppose, for instance, that you want their final paper to be on the general topic "1948 and 1984." If you assign this topic very early in the semester, assign some readings about the postwar years, and urge students to bring copies of newspaper and magazine articles from 1948 to class as a basis for discussion, you may help one student find a "personal" angle in contrasting views of women, another in the history of race relations, another in the accuracy of Orwell's political vision, another in the professionalization of college basketball. Some of your students might discover such topics quickly, but many will need weeks of brainstorming, journal writing, and class discussion to prime the pump.

Explain your standards as a grader.

Both students and teachers are sometimes bewildered by the ambiguities of the teaching and grading system we work within. If we are going to help the student while the paper is in process, we need to be an ally--almost a lawyer for the defense--accentuating the positive and extenuating the negative, looking through the murkiness of what a draft actually is to see what it might be. Our students need to understand this and to understand that when we grade final drafts, we have to leave this personal involvement behind and become neutral judges, evaluating according to fixed standards. We have to abandon our role as teacher/editor and read on behalf of the "primary" audience mentioned in Chapter 1--the audience of strangers.

You can remind your students of your detached attitude in grading by giving them a written set of standards. Here is mine from fall 1983:

Typical Characteristics of the A Paper

The paper never strays from its purpose or mistakes it audience. The subject is focused, significant, interesting, manageable.

Not only is the paper correctly organized, but the organization doesn't seem mechanical or imposed.

Each topical paragraph has a controlling idea, solid detail, smooth transitions.

The sentences are varied in length and structure according to the author's purpose and emphasis.

The word choice is almost uniformly good. Words are chosen for precise denotation, connotation, tone.

Mechanically, the paper is correct except for excusable errors of inadvertence and violations of extremely technical rules.

Typical Characteristics of the B Paper

The paper has a firm purpose, but may not always affect the audience as the writer expects it to. It is focused and interesting.

The organization is correct, but transitions are sometimes strained.

Each topical paragraph has a controlling idea and good supporting detail.

The sentences are usually varied to suit the writer's purpose and indicate the writer's emphasis.

The word choice is generally correct. The writer goes beyond the automatic word to find one more precise and effective.

The paper is generally correct mechanically, though there are some problems with complex grammar and punctuation traps.

Typical Characteristics of the C Paper

Though the paper has some interesting parts, the interest is not uniformly maintained. The purpose is not always clear.

The organization is acceptable, though some parts may be slightly awry. The essay has a clear thesis or principle of organization.

Each topical paragraph has a controlling idea and some support, though the support is sometimes a bit vague or weak.

There are very few errors in sentence structure, but the sentences are not varied in length and structure.

The word choice is generally correct, but the range of words is limited, so that the diction is sometimes imprecise and monotonous.

Though the paper contains few major errors, there are mistakes in niceties of spelling, grammar, and punctuation.

Typical Characteristics of the D Paper

Only in a few places does the paper find its purpose and audience. Too often it seems an unfocused exercise rather than an interesting essay.

Some principle of organization is apparent, but it isn't successfully followed.

The paragraphing is rational, but the topical paragraphs are underdeveloped--often a series of generalizations.

Errors in sentence structure are frequent enough to distract the reader, but are not pervasive.

Words are occasionally misused. Attempts to go beyond everyday vocabulary go awry.

The sentences conform well enough to the grammar of English as spoken by educated, but not fussy people. They often fail to conform to written conventions.

Typical Characteristics of the F Paper

The paper seems to be a mechanical exercise without a purpose or an audience.

There is no apparent principle of organization.

There is no apparent rationale for the paragraphing.

There are frequent sentence structure errors of the gravest sort.

Words that should be within the range of college students are misused or confused.

Some errors indicate a failure to understand the basic grammar of the sentence. Simple words are frequently misspelled.

Remind your students that you grade by merits rather than demerits.

Students often have the notion that their essays start out in a sort of Platonic heaven as As and then fall, error by error, to a more mundane grade. This view partly explains their tendency to complain that they get Cs, even though "hardly anything is marked wrong." You can save your students some confusion if you tell them that a blank page starts out as a zero and works its way up to a certain level more by a display of strengths than by an avoidance of weaknesses.

I used to explain this distinction to students via a sports metaphor. Writing a paper is not like playing golf, where your main job is to keep the ball safely in the fairway, avoid the rough and the traps, and keep your score <u>low</u>. It is more like softball, where you swing at the ball lustily and tries to put some points on the scoreboard. My golfing students told me I had misunderstood their game.

Be clear on the extent to which you are grading on form rather than content.

I sometimes hear a teacher tell students that they will be graded entirely on form because composition is the study of <u>how</u> a thing is said rather than <u>what</u> is said. This is a perfectly

sensible position, but one that will certainly be misunderstood.
The teacher probably means, "Don't worry about whether I agree
with the position you take in a paper. The final issue in this
course is not whether your position is right or wrong, but that
you find a position and present it clearly." What some students
will hear is, "I don't care what you say so long as you spell and
punctuate correctly." Even if you make yourself generally clear
on this slippery form/content distinction, you may need to add a
couple of warnings: first, that essays involving required
reading must show an understanding of that reading; second, that
some topics invite bad writing. I doubt that I have had a dozen
students in nine years who could have written creditable papers
on abortion or religious conversion, topics that offer the
student an armor of impenetrable cliché and stylized expression.
An attack on the armor will probably be interpreted as an attack
on the writer, so you will want to discourage your students from
writing on topics appropriate for street-corner harangues.

Take a sensible stance on error.

The last decade has seen such controversy on the subject of
error that you should be acquainted with the views of both sides.
The "liberal" view, best stated in Mina Shaughnessy's Errors and
Expectations, is a reaction to the persnicketiness that many
people have come to associate with English teachers:

> This emphasis upon propriety in the interest
> not of communication but of status has narrowed
> and debased the teaching of writing, encouraging
> at least two tendencies in teachers—a tendency
> to view the work of their students microscopically,
> with an eye for forms but with little interest in
> what was being said, and a tendency to develop a
> repugnance for error that has made erring students
> feel like pariahs and allowed teachers of mediocre
> talents too many easy victories. (p. 113)

The "conservative" view is best expressed by a professor in our
journalism school who used to call me every couple of weeks to
ask just what the hell we imagined we were teaching students in
composition classes, since we had clearly left to him the job of
telling juniors and seniors what sentences were—or the duty of
failing them for their ignorance.

Sympathy with both of these views has driven me into a
position of uneasy moderation. First, I try to convince my
students that error is an important consideration but only in the
final stages of the composing process. The new edition of
Writing With a Purpose makes the stages of the process very clear
and so provides a platform from which to preach this message.
Second, I never use a student paper as the butt of a usage lesson
(though I occasionally draw isolated bad sentences from the
papers of very good students). Third, I mark all the errors that
draw attention to themselves in the final draft of a paper,

unless the student makes so many errors that a thorough marking job would be cruel and superfluous. Fourth, I make correctness one factor among many in determining the paper's grade. Fifth, after each graded paper, I give students a chance to hand in a correction sheet that will itself be graded (at about 1/10 the weight of an essay). A student who makes ten errors on the paper thus has a chance of nailing all ten on the correction sheet and earning a minor A. Students who have proofread well will have fewer errors and an easier time earning correction points.

Some of you will feel that this system is cumbersome (the grading of the correction sheets obviously takes extra time) and that it makes error too much of an issue. I have been able to use it in recent years principally because my students have done a good job of proofreading their own papers and one another's on preliminary drafts. One semester, before my classes reached this happy state, I compromised by marking the first ten errors and then drawing a line across the page to indicate that from that point on I would concentrate on other matters. This had a healthy psychological effect on my students, who used to call writing a paper with fewer than ten errors "clearing the bar." Another alternative, used by many good teachers, is to put students on notice that certain errors will be marked on a set of papers, explain how those particular errors can be avoided or corrected, and mark them only.

Even if you decide to mark all outright errors, you should avoid being overbearing. Every semester in our writing lab I see papers red-penciled sentence by sentence until they are written in the teacher's style. The student writes "Johnson was a proud man," and the teacher changes "proud man" to "arrogant person." The student can't understand why the change is an improvement and is forced to conclude either that the teacher is playing the petty tyrant or that this whole business of prose style is cloaked in mysteries he or she will never penetrate. If you're confident about your ear and are teaching very good students, you may find it worthwhile to attack sentences that are clear, economical, and unesthetic. But with average freshmen, you will probably want to restrain yourself. When you find a sentence that you wouldn't have written because it sounds too much like Time magazine or National Geographic, lift up your pencil and let it go. Don't consider a variation from your style an error.

Use conference time wisely.

Most composition teachers post office hours and encourage at least some of their students to come in for individual conferences. I find that I need to set aside an hour a week per fifteen or twenty students and tell students whose schedules conflict with mine that I can arrange special appointments. Individual conferences are probably most beneficial to your very worst students and your very best. Some of the most enthusiastic will come in as often as they can because they really do want to talk about their writing. Count your blessings and spend what

time with them you can. Some of your weakest students will have
to be encouraged to come in. I often arrange a conference with a
student when I return a paper with a disappointing grade. The
conference allows me to point out all the things he or she did
well and to suggest some steps that may strengthen the next
paper. I always arrange a conference when I find myself tempted
to write an end comment accusing a student of plagiarism, laziness,
insincerity, or some other heinous crime. Such accusations,
reduced to writing, quickly build a barrier between student and
teacher. But the plagiarist sometimes comes to the conference
with a disarming confession, and the "lazy" student may turn out
to be learning disabled.

As a teaching tool, the conference has the advantage of
allowing instruction tailored to the individual student, and I
have sometimes set up a series of conferences for students who
needed special instruction in grammar, punctuation, essay exam
strategies, and so forth. But preparing individualized instruction
is very time-consuming, and the new teacher should approach it
warily. In fact, it may be best to view the conference more as
an opportunity to learn than as an opportunity to teach. Did the
last paper go awry because you assigned a topic too far outside
this particular student's experience? Do the sentences that so
confused you make perfect sense when the student reads them aloud
or explains them? Does the absence of examples come from lack of
thought or from an assumption that "you already know all that
stuff anyway"? Does the weakness of the conclusion indicate an
inability to generalize or an inability to stay awake after
working the night shift? Showing an interest in these things may
improve a student's performance more than making a few more
observations on dangling modifiers.

I don't want the preceding paragraph to be misunderstood,
so let me make my first warning about conferences be that they
should be kept businesslike. Students coming straight from high
school may have had very few individual conferences with teachers
that were not strictly disciplinary. They may be so befuddled by
your kindness and attention that they will misconstrue them. A
student who begins to unfold his or her personal life sometimes
needs to be reminded that your main interest in it is that it not
interfere with his or her work. A student who begins to cry amy
need a few words of consolation and an invitation to leave for a
few minutes to regain enough composure to continue productively.
My other warning is that you should not overload yourself by
having every student come in routinely. This practice creates
scheduling problems for everyone and often leaves the teacher too
exhausted to offer any sensible advice.

Be realistic about your students' interest in their grades.

I have known some idealistic teachers who regarded their
students' "obsession" with grades as a disease to be eradicated.
Unfortunately, their cure was to refuse to discuss exactly how
semester grades would be assigned: "You'll hand in papers and

talk in class, and in the end I'll know very well who deserves
what grade. Don't worry about it." Students who are confident
of their abilities and who have no fear of failing out of school
or losing scholarships may not be troubled by such a system. But
by the end of the semester, others, weaker and less confident,
may be paralyzed by anxiety. One way to spare them this needless
worry and spare yourself several "how am I doing?" conferences
is to develop a simple point system and encourage them to total
their grades as they go. In freshman classes, I usually assign
points for everything I expect students to take seriously and
even make something of a production of noting a daily discussion
grade on my seating chart. With older and better motivated
students I loosen up a bit.

Be realistic about your workload, especially in marking papers.

Some experts in composition argue that time spent commenting
on papers is essentially wasted. I can't agree. I know that
word for word the comments conscientious teachers wrote on my
papers were the most instructive reading of my school years, if
not the most pleasant. And I know that on end-of-semester
evaluations, my students almost uniformly suggest that more
comments would be useful. I don't deceive myself or my students
by claiming that I limit my comments for their sake; I limit them
for my own.

My typical grading process is to read through a paper once
to see and appreciate the good things in it, my pencil idle
except to make an occasional check mark where I know a comment is
needed. I then give the paper a thorough reading, using proof-
reader's marks and brief comments in the margin, and perhaps half
a dozen times writing a longer comment on the back of a page.
The longer comments are numbered, and numbers are written in the
paper's margin to show where they apply. All this commentary
naturally distorts my view of the paper, so I give it a quick
rereading before I make an end comment and assign a grade. Over
the course of an afternoon, with fidgeting included, I can get
through papers of moderate length (three pages) at about fifteen
minutes per paper. This means that a set of forty papers (two
sections) will take me about ten hours. Some teachers with more
efficient mental equipment or larger coffeepots seem to be
quicker.

Ten hours of intense labor added to a week's other work is
quite a strain, and I have learned to keep that fact before me
while I am marking. It helps me fight off the guilt when I have
to limit my comments on a paper that shows prodigious labor and
great potential for improvement. Being frank with your students
about the limitations you work under can be a still better salve
for the conscience. You can tell them that you will do the best
job you can in fifteen or twenty minutes and that in many cases
it won't be enough. Encourage those who want more help to see
you during office hours. Remind them that they can make up for
some of your shortcomings by commenting carefully on one anothers'

work during workshops, and spend a class period after each major
paper discussing two or three representative papers at length.

The paper load is not limited to weeks when final drafts
are due. Preliminary drafts logically deserve more time because
the student has a more immediate opportunity to respond to
advice. As a practical matter, though, I must limit my marking
time to a few minutes per paper. I now spend this few minutes
noting questions the student and the student's group should
consider. Journals, quizzes, and short paragraphs require very
little grading time, but each adds a little weight to the burden.
If the load gets too heavy, shed a few hours with regret, but
with a clear conscience. Avoid if possible practices that add
work: accepting nearly illegible papers, allowing rewrites of F
papers, letting papers come in at the student's convenience
rather than according to your schedule. You can probably get
some time-saving hints by talking with other teachers and by
consulting the National Council of Teachers of English booklet,
Classroom Practices: How to Handle the Paper Load.

Use your textbook to full advantage.

Writing With a Purpose is virtually an encyclopedia of
composition. It contains enough professional examples to fill a
small reader and enough student examples to make up an anthology
of the various types of student writing. The sentence chapter
alone contains enough information and enough exercises to amount
to a mini-course. The handbook is comprehensive. If you get to
know the text, you'll find that it can save you hours searching
for and duplicating supplementary material.

Unit I, newly added in the Eighth Edition, is particularly
useful and exciting, and has made this my most successful teaching
year ever. If you invest class time heavily in it in the early
weeks it will pay rich dividends. Much that I have tried unsuccess-
fully to tell my students is clearly articulated and amplified
here. Too often in the past, despite my homilies about revision,
students continued to imagine the essay as something that springs
fully formed from the writer's head. Their planning amounted to
a few minutes of head scratching at the start, and the first
draft was intended--with some cosmetic revision, of course--to be
the last. The Eighth Edition hasn't eliminated this attitude
entirely from my class, but it has made it distinctly the minority
view. Most of the students begin planning their papers very
early: I sometimes detect the germ of a paper in a journal entry
dated a month before the discovery draft. Students produce stout
preliminary drafts for discussion in their groups, fully anticipat-
ing that much of the material won't appear in the final draft.
The day before I wrote this page, I entered one group just in
time to hear a writer responding to one of his classmates who had
criticized the wording of a sentence: "I think you're right,
Tom, but I'm a couple of drafts from needing to worry about
that." Another student approached me rather sheepishly after
class to say that her group had liked her draft very much and

that she was afraid that most of the changes she made as she
worked toward the final essay would be minor: "There won't be
much of what you guys call revision."

Teach from personal conviction about good writing.

In the introduction to The Elements of Style, E. B. White
presents a memorable portrait of the man who taught him composition
at Cornell in 1917--William Strunk, Jr. Strunk exemplifies
everything the modern "student-centered, process-oriented"
teacher rejects. His idea of a textbook was "seven rules of
usage, eleven principles of composition, a few matters of form,
and a list of words and expressions commonly misused." He taught
from the lectern rather than the elbow: "Sergeant Strunk snapping
orders to his platoon." I don't think I could name a teacher
whose methods are more opposed to my own, but I'm sure I can't
name half a dozen whose classes I would rather attend. I'll let
White give my reason:

> The professor devotes a special paragraph to
> the vile expression the fact that, a phrase that
> causes him to quiver with revulsion. The expres-
> sion, he says, should be "revised out of every
> sentence in which it occurs." But a shadow of
> gloom seems to hang over the page, and you feel
> that he knows how hopeless his cause is. I
> suppose I have written the fact that a thousand
> times in the heat of composition, revised it out
> maybe five hundred times in the cool aftermath.
> To be batting only .500 this late in the season,
> to fail half the time to connect with this fat
> pitch, saddens me, for it seems a betrayal of the
> man who showed me how to swing at it and made the
> swinging worthwhile.[2]

I read this paragraph at least once a year, and it always
gives me a lift. Composition is a large subject, and I don't
suppose a teacher can claim to have mastered it until he or she
has mastered grammar, rhetoric, pedagogy, and the intricacies of
the writer's psychology. But mastery isn't necessary to success.
People teach composition (even those who regard it as conscript
labor) because they are hooked on the written word. They are
convinced that good writing is important and that the best
teachers are not the ones who subscribe to this or that pedagogi-
cal theory or have polished this or that lesson, but the ones who
let their conviction show. Count yourself a success if you can
convince a few of your students that the swinging is worthwhile.

----

[2] New York: MacMillan, 1979, p. xiv.

CHAPTER 1 TOWARD PURPOSEFUL WRITING

The main goal of Part 1 of <u>Writing With a Purpose</u> is to change the student's image of the writing process. Through simple inexperience, most students confronted with an essay assignment immediately focus their attention on the finished product. They are like travelers who hope to take off in New York, recline their seat for a long nap, and wake up in San Francisco. The text attempts to redirect their attention to the terrain between a paper's beginning and the final draft. It reminds students that most writers travel overland, take occasional wrong turns, retrace their routes, have breakdowns, repair the damage with the tools readiest to hand, and--if they are good-- somehow manage to press on. Eventually it reminds them that the alert writer sees unexpected sights along the way and sometimes, mid-route, decides to change destinations.

The Hemingway passage on p. 6 presents the process through the eyes of a consummate professional. Your students should notice that the theme of the passage is not the final triumph, but the "good and severe discipline" that a writer exercises along the way. It gives students a glimpse of the soundest of writing habits: "I always worked until I had done something, and I always stopped when I knew what was going to happen next. That way I could be sure of going on the next day." It also introduces the theme of revision: "I found I could cut out that scrollwork and ornament and throw it away and start with the first true simple declarative sentence I had written." Above all, it emphasizes the faith in oneself that experience brings: "You have always written before and you will write now."

THE WRITER'S ENVIRONMENT AND HABITS

This section encourages students to redirect their attention, to think for a while about how they write rather than what they write. Notice that it is not at all prescriptive. Throughout Part 1, the authors avoid telling students what specific things they must or must not do in the writing process. The important thing is that they learn to recognize their processes and have faith in them.

19

Exercises (p. 9)

These questions might be the basis of a journal entry or might be discussed in small groups. They are such good interview questions that you may want to bring a writer (journalist, technical writer, business executive, historian) to class for an interview. If you don't find time for this exercise early in the semester, it would probably work well later, when the students have shared writing experiences to talk about.

THE STAGES OF THE WRITING PROCESS

By the time they finish Part 1, students will be thoroughly familiar with the stages of the writing process. The important note here is the nonlinear nature of the stages. Students should anticipate frustrations in drafting and revising that will force them back to the planning stage. The students who enjoy writing classes most and do best in them are often those whose journals are filled with false starts and insightful comments on excursions that failed.

In addition to reminding students that different writers use different processes, the Thurber interview and the Woolf excerpt reinforce the themes of revision and confidence. Thurber is sure that "it'll work out all right" in the seventh draft. Though considerably less cheerful, Woolf has faith in the process of revision. Even if she scratches a day's work out entirely, she has "examined the possibilities." Here is the great and hard lesson. For most student writers, writing is recording a conclusion. For Woolf, it is examining the possibilities.

MAKING DECISIONS IN THE WRITING PROCESS

The three critical elements of every writing situation introduced here are the pillars on which the entire text is based, so you will want to be sure that your students begin, at least, to understand their significance and their relation to one another. The student who properly considers subject, audience, and purpose should produce a paper as stable and sure-footed as a three-legged stool. The reader, of course, will not have to think of the legs one at a time, testing the solidity of each, but the novice writer will.

SELECTING YOUR SUBJECT

Students with limited writing experience may not understand that writers almost always choose their own subjects. When the history teacher assigns a paper on Jacksonian democracy, one very able student who has thought about the dangers of demagoguery will emphasize the irrational forces that swept Jackson into office. She will stress the success of the Jackson machine in portraying its sometimes ungenerous candidate as a friend of the common man, and may present vividly the havoc wreaked in Washington

by drunken backwoodsmen who came to celebrate Jackson's inaugura-
tion. Another equally able student more sympathetic with populism
may begin the paper with an unsympathetic portrait of the pre-
Jacksonian system of Eastern power elites and limited suffrage.
He can then offer as a welcome contrast the post-Jacksonian
system of "frontier" politicians who appealed directly to the
people, including many newly enfranchised voters. Decisions
about subject are inevitable, and students will be better off if
they learn to make these decisions consciously and systematically.

A NOTE ON SIGNIFICANCE, INTEREST, AND PERSPECTIVE

Some of the text's considerations on choosing a subject are
logistical--finding a subject on which the writer is knowledgeable,
and being sure that the subject is manageable in the form and the
number of pages allowed. In these areas of practical management,
students will improve with practice. But students often have
trouble finding "a special or unusual perspective" on their
subject (Guideline 1) and finding a topic that is "significant"
and "interesting."

To give them a concrete picture of what these terms can
mean in an essay, I introduce two more terms into the discussion:
foreground and backdrop. A writer achieves significance, interest,
and perspective by showing a specific incident, episode, or
example against backdrops of more general meanings. In "Brandon's
Clown," the foreground incident is Wally's first experience of
painting for a commission. Unlike many freshman "first experience"
papers, though, this one has a set of well-defined backdrops that
give the incident significance. One of these backdrops is
introduced by Wally's father: "Son, you have a special talent.
Be smart, use it to make money." In the first paragraph, this is
an effective gag line, but it articulates a question that dominates
the whole paper: how willing we should be to compromise our
integrity, our special talents and callings, to make money. A
second backdrop appears in Wally's thesis statement: "Creating
artwork for a client, I soon discovered, demands much more than
talent and a lust for money." The "much more," we find out,
includes a sensitivity to the audience and an ability to blend
its purposes with the artist's own. This second backdrop is, of
course, a special case of the first, so that the whole situation
might be seen schematically this way:

Everyone's Problem of Compromising Integrity

The Problem of Art on Commission

Wally's Experience

The Reader

The reader is encouraged to see the <u>significance</u> and <u>interest</u> of Wally's experience against these larger backdrops, and the essay now, in the most literal sense, becomes an opportunity for the reader to see the problem of compromise from Wally's <u>perspective</u>.

The distinction between backdrop and foreground can be reinforced in the discussion of every essay in <u>Writing With a Purpose</u>. In Chapter 4, for instance, you will find one student's essay presenting the Washington monument against the backdrop of human foibles and another presenting ownership of a wood-burning stove against the backdrop of human fanaticism. At the end of Chapter 5, you will find an E. M. Forster essay that presents his experience of owning land against the larger backdrop of the effect of property on the character. In Chapter 14, you will find a research paper that presents the history of telephone advertising against the backdrop of America's shift from a rural to a technological society. Very often teachers complain that students choose subjects that have no "depth," a term that sounds mysterious and snobbish. By teaching your students the backdrop/ foreground distinction, you can demystify this criticism and give your students a tool with which they can gauge the depth of their own papers.

ANALYZING YOUR AUDIENCE

<u>Writing With a Purpose</u> eliminates a common source of tension in the writing class by facing the problem of audience frankly. Yes, students should write partly to please themselves; writing that the author is unenthusiastic about rarely excites anyone else. Yes, students should write to please the teachers (or editors); it is foolish to deny their expertise or their authority. But ultimately, students must learn to write for an audience of strangers, and it is on that audience that all eyes are trained. This discussion in the text helps me explain to my students why, although I am personally sympathetic with them, I <u>must</u> comment and ultimately grade as a stranger.

Beginning writers have a hard time envisioning this audience of strangers, so you may do them a favor by encouraging them to think very hard about the audience they intend to address-- picturing the faces in the crowd. Even public figures sometimes need this reminder. I am writing this page, for instance, the week after James Watt made his notorious statement before a meeting of Chamber of Commerce lobbyists that he had appointed a coal-leasing commission with "every king of mix you can have . . . a black, a woman, two Jews, and a cripple." Apparently, Watt pictured his audience too narrowly. He remembered the lobbyists, who were perhaps overwhelmingly male, white, Protestant, and able-bodied, and who laughed heartily at the joke. But he forgot the cameras, the reporters, and 220 million Americans, many of whom were certain to find the remark offensive. On some papers, you may want your students to pick a very narrow audience, but I generally advise my students not to imagine an audience that is uniform in age, race, religion, or sex.

A NOTE ON AUDIENCE IN THE ESSAY, THE LETTER, AND THE REPORT

The very phrasing of the guidelines on p. 22 should give
your students a hint of the creative tension that makes the
essay. Always it is "the readers" of "my" essay. At this point,
you might offer your students a stipulative definition of an
essay: an essay is a personal statement that is interesting to
an audience of strangers. In the personal letter, there is no
difficulty reconciling the personal and the public; the reader is
primarily interested in the writer and only secondarily interested
in the larger-than-personal significance of what the writer has
to say. In a letter to a friend, we can chat idly, complain
bitterly, gossip maliciously, and still expect a sympathetic
reading. In an essay, we had better have something to say and
generally will find it better to keep our personalities and
prejudices from getting too much in the way. On the other hand,
an essay is not a report, a mere objective presentation of
information akin to the tax form or the encyclopedia article. It
always contains a personal view, one shared neither by the whole
human race nor by every objective observer.

"Brandon's Clown" nicely balances Wally's personal view
with his need to present a subject of larger-than-personal
significance. Both the statement the essay makes and the voice
it makes it in are distinctly his: the humorous portrait of
himself as a self-conscious artist "proud of the dark maelstroms
of anxiety" he can create on his canvas, the disparaging view of
his client--"a pleasant young woman whose only exposure to art
was probably the Sunday funnies," the enthusiasm over the apparently successful compromise. But Wally doesn't forget the audience
of strangers and carefully alerts them to the more "public"
aspects of the subject: the general problem of compromising
one's integrity and the more specialized problem of the artist's
struggle to preserve integrity.

DETERMINING YOUR PURPOSE

If you have used previous editions of Writing With a
Purpose, you'll notice the addition of two new terms in this
section: hypothesis and discovery draft. Both terms are gentle
reminders to the student that purpose is not fixed at the beginning
of the writing process, that it emerges as we write. In effect,
these terms tell students to form the clearest idea of their
purpose that they possibly can and they to try to shape a thesis,
"but don't think you have really arrived at a thesis until you
have tried it out in writing. Call it a hypothesis to remind
yourself of its tentative nature, then use it to write the best
draft you can of your paper, but don't assume you have produced a
solid draft when you are done. You have only produced a discovery
draft, one that may help you find a truer purpose and thesis."
The new terms, like much of the new material in the Eighth
Edition, encourage the students to keep the paper a little longer
in its plastic state, encourage them to spend more time rethinking
and revising. Traditionally, composition books have treated

essays as problems of arrangement. Before students wrote, they
were to have a firm thesis and outline, and once the composition
started, they general direction of its progress (or decline) was
fixed. The essay was like a pen-and-ink drawing, each stroke of
which is necessarily final. The Eighth Edition treats the essay
as an oil painting, which can be worked and reworked in
successive layers.

With each layer the purpose should be clearer, but purpose
itself is an elusive concept. On p. 23, the text gives two
definitions:

> In effect, purpose directs and controls all the
> decisions writers make throughout the writing
> process. It is both the <u>what</u> of that process and
> the <u>how</u>: that is, the specific subject the
> writer communicates and the strategies--from
> establishing organization and point of view to
> perfecting tone and word choice--that the writer
> uses to communicate the subject most effectively.

> [It is] what you want to accomplish in your
> writing, the impression you want to make.

If students don't take in the full import of these definitions at
once, encourage them to turn back to them from time to time.
Layered over by experience, they may prove to be pearls. Students
should, however, see at once that finding a purpose is not merely
a technical accomplishment and that they are not likely to
succeed at it if they view their essays as exercises in avoiding
error.

The metaphor of the three-legged stool is perhaps sound
enough that we can stand on it once more. Since all three legs
will eventually join at the top, students having trouble finding
their purpose can always turn their attention to subject and
audience and work upward from there. When they make a personal
statement that will interest an audience of strangers and when
they show their foreground subject against a backdrop of general
interest and significance, they will very likely have found their
purpose.

Review Exercise (pp. 29-32)

1.   Wally seems to be a methodical worker. He works in his
college studio, does preliminary sketches in a sketchbook to
which he can later refer, and seems positively affectionate about
the tools of his craft: the "arts" (paints) are "inviting" and
he has a "favorite brush." Once he begins the project, he goes
"every morning" to examine the work he has done the night before.
Apparently, he sketches areas in the evening and fills in the
detail in the mornings, when he is full of energy. He, like
Hemingway, quits for the day only when he knows "what is going to
happen next."

2.   Wally's _planning_ process is delineated in the ninth and tenth paragraphs. He spent "hours" over the next "several weeks" filling pages of his sketchbook with quick drawings of circus subjects. Notice that this is a very active bit of planning, rather like the freewriting, codewords, or journal writing a student might do while trying to narrow from a general subject to a specific subject. The _drafting_ is the evening sketching. The _revision_ is the morning painting, where he will "reappraise" the draft/sketch before bringing it into a more finished form.

3.   Wallys' situation is typical of the situation in which most academic and professional writing takes place. The general subject is assigned by Mrs. Hobbs. She isn't as general as the bank manager or as specific as the Patton imitator in paragraph 2, both of whom are given as examples of the problem of trying to paint for patrons who are indifferent to the artist's need to please others without abandoning a personal vision. She wants something that will fit into a blue nursery with a circus motif, "something happy and cheery." His specific subject is a brilliant (though not altogether successful) blend of his patron's cheeriness and his gloomy vision. Consider how it fits the "Guidelines for Selecting Your Subject."

(1)   _What do I know about my subject_? We can probably assume that he knows the subject from direct observation.

(2)   _What is the focus of my subject_? From a sketchbook full of circus drawings, he has selected one image that can carry his theme.

(3)   _What is significant about my subject_? The subject raises a large issue that is on Wally's mind very strongly and that all humans face almost daily: the conflict between our need to put on a false face and our desire to maintain our honesty and our pride. On this subject he has much to say because of his experience with painting for commissions, a situation that puts unrelenting strain on the artist's integrity.

(4)   _What is interesting about my subject_? Wally is no doubt interested in the subject. Clowns are a special case of the "screaming" faces that he has found consistently interesting. There is, unfortunately, no reason that Mrs. Hobbs, equally uninterested in art and in Wally and not particularly attuned to the eternal note of sadness, should find the subject interesting.

(5)   _Is my subject manageable_? From the moment Wally conceives this subject, it seems manageable on a small canvas: a clown's face and two balloons, rendered in enough detail to hint at underlying sadness.

4.   All three audiences mentioned in Chapter 1 have representatives in "Brandon's Clown." The primary audience is (_in ovo_) Brandon, but more immediately Mrs. Hobbs, whom Wally analyzes in

unflattering terms. She is "a pleasant young woman whose only
exposure to art was probably the Sunday funnies," and who asks
for the usual "happy and cheery" stuff. Wally's comment that
their interview takes place "between snatches of dialogue from
General Hospital shows that he considers her to to be a Philistine.
The intermediate audience--the equivalent of the writer's editors
and teachers--is represented by Wally's mother, who gives the
painting a remarkably terse review: "It's black." He is alarmed
by this review, but defends the painting and notes that his
mother is reading Reader's Digest (which presumably allies her
with the Philistines). Wally is clearly aware of himself as an
audience he must please, and paragraphs 8, 9, and 10 show the
process by which he learns how to please himself within the
confines of his commission. Clearly he paints Brandon's Clown
primarily to please himself, and it is only in paragraph 14 that
he begins to see this as an error: "the expression on the
clown's face suddenly seemed harsh and scolding." Consider how
Wally followed (or failed to follow) the "Guidelines for Analyzing
Your Audience":

(1) Who are the viewers that form the primary audience for my
painting? Wally's primary audience is a young, middle-class
mother-to-be who seems to spend more afternoons watching
soap operas than she does reading existential philosophy.
She is commissioning a painting for a nursery, which means
that she is looking for something that fits her view of a
child's world, a view exemplified by the circus animals and
the stroller and the little rocking horse on the top of the
dresser.

(2) What do my viewers know or think they know about my subject?
Wally can probably assume that Mrs. Hobbs knows about
clowns from observation, but can't assume that she has
thought much about their blend of happiness and sorrow. In
a painting destined for her child's nursery, she will
probably react positively to a clown painting only if she
sees it as cheerful.

(3) Why will my viewers "read" my painting? Mrs. Hobbs will
not expect to learn anything from this painting, and she
certainly will not want to be persuaded (in a nursery
painting!) that life is a sad business, even for clowns.
She expects to be amused in a rather predictable way, and
wally knows this, though he refuses to act on it.

(4) How can I interest my viewer in my subject? This question
doesn't occur to Wally, who doesn't take the trouble to
interest himself in Mrs. Hobbs's interests. Why the circus
motif? Is it only that she imagines children like
circuses, or does she like them herself? Is her interest
in the animals, really, rather than in the circus itself?
If the circus does interest her, is it because it is exotic
or because it is familiar? If Wally had been more curious
about Mrs. Hobbs's interests, he might have pleased her
more and been more satisfied with himself.

(5)   How can I help my viewers "read" my painting? This may be
another question Wally has paid too little attention to.
Is it likely that Mrs. Hobbs will understand the statement
Wally is making in the painting?

5.   Wally has at least three purposes. One is to satisfy his
patron: "to compromise my pride for a buck." Another, in
obvious conflict with the first, is to live up to his artist's
reputation and express his private vision, stated with some
exaggeration as "man's inability to overcome despair." A third,
which seems to be largely unconscious till the end, is to express
his rejection of the "pleasant" middle-class world of General
Hospital, Reader's Digest, and the Sunday funnies. His hypothesis, that clowns conceal "their real pain behind their painted
masks" looks at first like a brilliant reconciliation of his
purposes. But his mother's reaction prompts him to reassess this
purpose. Just as a writer will ordinarily resist criticism by a
teacher or editor, Wally defends his painting, but begins a
process of reappraisal: "perhaps it was a bit dark—for a
nursery painting." Consider how Wally follows the "Guidelines
for Determining Your Purpose":

(1)   What are the requirements of my painting project? Wally is
painting to fulfill an assignment. By the end of the
essay, he suspects that he has flubbed it by forgetting
that his painting should be appropriate to a child's world.

(2)   As I proceed in this project, what do I need to know?
Wally probably has all the information about his subject
that he needs, but he has not considered all his audiences.
Brandon, "fresh and innocent," is not clearly in his mind
until the painting is complete.

(3)   What hypothesis can I use as my working purpose? See
discussion above.

(4)   What purpose have I discovered for this painting project?
See discussion above.

(5)   What is my thesis? Unfortunately, Wally doesn't see the
flaw in his thesis until the painting is finished. It
might be interesting to have the class speculate on a new
thesis for Wally. How would this do? "Beneath the grease
paint that gives him features of grotesque despair, a clown
enjoys the comedy of his bad fortune." Not very well, I'm
afraid. Should Wally have avoided faces altogether?

6.   Wally introduces two general topics in the first two
paragraphs—"words of wisdom passed from father to son" and types
of painting commissions. These two build a solid pedestal for
the specific subject: one instance of Wally's difficulty in
following his father's advice to paint for money.

7.   From the introductory information that precedes "Brandon's
Clown," we can assume that the essay was written for class. The

intermediate audience would, therefore, be the teacher. About
the primary audience there might be some dispute. The
informality of some passages suggests that Wally is writing with
his classmates in mind: "I am known on campus as 'the guy who
paints screaming faces,' a tag I am quite happy with," "all the
enthusiasm of the only girl in the eighth grade not chosen for
the pompom squad." But Wally does not rely on information or
perspectives he shares exclusively with his classmates; the paper
may have been written by a college student at Ball State
University, but there is nothing in it that would confuse an
intelligent milliner in Santa Barbara. Wally appears to be
writing for a hybrid audience, a cross between his classmates and
"the general reader." He assumes that this hybrid reader has:

a.   A sense of humor and a desire to be entertained

b.   A vague interest, at least, in how artists work

c.   An awareness that General Hospital and The Reader's Digest
      are not the finest flowers of American culture

d.   An ordinary interest in the problem of preserving personal
      integrity while making money

He does not insist that this reader have:

a.   Special knowledge of art or artistic technique

b.   Knowledge of him or his previous paintings

The opening paragraphs catch the reader's attention partly by
establishing the playful tone Wally will use as he pursues a
serious subject ("Son, you have a special talent . . .. Use it
to make money"). These paragraphs also introduce the reader to
the artist's quandary, and so allow Wally to follow that ancient
bit of narrative advice--get your protagonist into trouble
immediately.

8.   Wally's purpose in the essay ties together a great many
purposes, of which we might make a partial list:

a.   To make a good grade

b.   To amuse the reader

c.   To inform the reader about the difficulty of creating art
      on commission

d.   To rethink an incident in which he overreacted to a
      challenge to his integrity.

These various purposes are united in the thesis, but I don't find
a thesis statement in the paper. The first sentence of paragraph
2 hints broadly at a thesis: "Creating artwork for a
client . . . demands much more than talent and a lust for money."

Illustrating the "much more" is the real purpose of the essay.
Had Wally written out a more explicit thesis it might have read,
"Creating artwork for clients demands humility and an ability to
merge your vision with theirs." "Brandon's Clown" is so well
focused that it doesn't need this explicit statement.

QUIZ

I sometimes begin class discussions of text chapters with a
quiz--rarely collected and graded, sometimes given orally, and
always discussed immediately. The quiz gives students some
slight incentive for keeping up with their reading, but its main
purpose is to help the class focus its attention on the chapter's
key concepts and to avoid the sort of deadly open-book group
reading that sometimes passes as class discussion.

Recall questions (with answers in brackets)

1. What are the three stages of the writing process?
   [planning, drafting, revising]

2. In what sense are these stages not fixed "stages" at all?
   [Not a "simple linear sequence"; even in the process of
   revising, writer may need to loop back for additional
   planning--see Writing With a Purpose, p. 12]

3. What are the three elements in any writing situation?
   [subject, audience, purpose]

Quotations to put into context (with guidelines for answers in
brackets). Students should try to comment on both the source of
the quotation and its significance.

4. "Goddam it Thurber, that's highschool stuff" [comment on a
   Thurber draft by his wife. Thurber's answer--that it would
   work out all right in the seventh draft--shows the importance
   of rewriting in Thurber's composing process.]

5. "Is it significant? Is it interesting? Is it manageable?"
   [questions that news magazine editors ask about potential
   stories and students should ask about potential essay
   topics]

6. "the general reader' [Writing With a Purpose, p. 20]

7. "the junk food addict" [potential special audience--see
   text, p. 20]

8. "hypothesis" [working purpose--see text, p. 23]

Quotations from student essay to put in context (open-ended
discussion questions)

9. "'I want a portrait,' he says, 'that makes me look like General Patton.'"

10. "For my hours after leaving the easel, I will walk about with my shoulders stooped and head down, frowning, lost in reflections on man's inability to overcome despair."

11. "'You know, something happy and cheery,' she said between snatches of dialogue on <u>General Hospital</u>."

12. "Resolved to compromise my pride for a buck, I began gathering my paints, brushes and canvas with all the enthusiasm of the only girl in the eighth grade not chosen for the pompom squad."

13. "Clowns had screaming faces, even though they concealed their real pain behind their painted masks."

14. "a beautiful, tiny wooden rocking horse swayed peacefully on the dresser top."

15. "It's fine. Will you take a check?"

CHAPTER 2 PLANNING

Not all your students will be happy to hear the central
message of Chapter 2: that the writer will ordinarily do much
thinking-in-writing before settling down to write a serious
draft. Many of them would prefer to believe that essays spring
up overnight, like Jack's beanstalk, and they will be reluctant
to see that the essay's slow evolution is an advantage. You
might point out that few of us are quick enough to be really good
conversationalists. When we don't have adequate planning time,
we forget our nuggets of information or our funny anecdotes until
the moment for them has passed, and then we must sit silently
while other discuss the country we haven't visited, the movie we
haven't seen, or the book we haven't read. But if we are given
time to prepare, we can say something interesting on a great many
subjects. Writing in this sense, stands in about the same
relation to conversation that badminton does to tennis. The
shuttlecock slows down so that we nonathletes have time to run to
it.

The chapter details several strategies students can use to
take advantage of the time writing allows for gathering material.
It is so large and diverse that you may want to break it into two
or three reading assignments. The exercises on p. 47 and p. 62
are basic sources of information. Even if you break the chapter
into thirds, though, you're not likely to have time to discuss
everything in it in class and to have your students do every
exercise, so I would encourage you to treat the chapter as a
smorgasbord. Urge your students to look over all the planning
strategies so that they can select ones appropriate to their own
situations and habits. Give them enough practice with a few of
the strategies so that they learn how much more material they can
generate by thinking-in-writing rather than indulging in the sort
of slack-jawed daydreaming that often disguises itself as
planning a paper. If you are going to restrict your discussion
to only a few of the exercises or discussion sets, you may want
to consider the following:

1.   The discussion questions on Laurie's freewriting (p. 44)
      may be particularly useful in classes that use workshops
      extensively. Laurie's problems of finding a purpose
      involve some difficult questions of tone: she has to
      decide whether she will write about her father from the
      perspective of a rejected, bitter daughter or that of an
      understanding, saddened daughter. A good discussion of

this essay can help your groups deal sensitively with the
difference between a writer's persona and a writer's
personality. Question 4 is the critical question and could
be made more intriguing by asking students what they would
say to Laurie about her hypothesis and attitude if this
were a draft discussed in a group.

2. Jenny's planning activities occupy a large portion of the
    chapter, and students may wonder how much good they did
    her. You can probably make a good case for planning
    activities as a prod to the subconscious if you discuss
    questions 5 and 6. Note that all of Jenny's scouting,
    mapping, and speculating activities have prepared her to
    appreciate the atmosphere of the Varsity Barbershop.

3. The Hogarth exercise (pp. 76-80) is back by popular demand
    from the previous edition of Writing With a Purpose. It is
    such a provoker of class discussion and participation that
    teachers who need to get their students actively involved
    in the class may want to be sure to use it.

4. The journal exercise (pp. 80-82) probably takes less time
    than any of the others mentioned above. It is obviously a
    must in classes that emphasize journal writing.

You should also notice that the authors weave into Chapter
2 a couple of threads that tie together exercises through Chapter
4. Following either of these threads can help students overview
the whole writing process. One thread is Mary's essay on wood-
burning stoves, which first appears on pp. 67-74 of this chapter,
continues as drafting exercise 1 in the next chapter, and culminates in a revising exercise in Chapter 4. By following this
thread, you will allow your students to look closely at the
evolution of a solid and amusing essay of about 1,500 words--one
that incorporates some research without losing the personal
voice. The second thread has the student build an essay. It
begins with writing exercise 4 of this chapter, which starts with
mapping and moves through other planning activities. These in
turn produce a draft in writing exercise 4 of Chapter 3, and this
draft is revised in writing exercise 4 of Chapter 4.

SOURCES AND STRATEGIES

USING MEMORY IN WRITING

Code words, brainstorming, freewriting and journal writing--
the strategies discussed in this section--are usually associated
with writing from personal experience, and you may want your
students to experiment with them as preliminaries to a personal
experience paper. All, however, can be useful in papers of other
types. You'll find in Chapter 13, for instance, a journal entry
that begins a student's planning of the research paper featured
in Chapter 14. To develop the habit of planning in writing, I
require that all students keep a journal in which they make some

sort of planning entry (approximately 150 words) for each class
day of the semester. I collect the journal periodically, tally
the entries, and make a few marginal comments, but I never grade
for correctness. Some start out resenting this "busy work," but
most are converted by the semester's end. One of my favorite
journal entires, from the third week of class, begins, "This
thinking-in-writing thing really works. It's like writing a
letter to yourself."

Questions for Discussion (pp. 43–44)

1.   I think that Laurie identifies her frustrated relationship
      with her father as the most interesting and significant
      aspect of her subject, but the freewriting touches on
      several other themes worth considering:

      a.   the ways that sex roles were imposed in Laurie's
            family (and, by implication, in others like it)

      b.   The way in which Laurie's father (and, by implication,
            other working men) uses sports as a drug to escape the
            bitterness of the working day

      c.   The contrasting difficulties of father-daughter and
            father-son relationships

      d.   A portrait of Laurie's father as an embittered man

      I personally favor the last of these. It should be interest-
      ing to Laurie, not only because she is interested in her
      father, but because she knows something about bitterness
      ("still makes me angry"). It should be interesting to
      readers, particularly to students, who are usually at an
      age when they look back on their families and forward to a
      life they hope will be satisfying. It is significant
      because it raises the important issues of how people deal
      with frustrated ambition and how we try to see through
      people's hard shells to the life inside. And it raises
      these issues by showing a particular man that Laurie knows
      well. Still, as teacher or classmate, I would not push
      Laurie too hard to see things my way. She clearly is on
      the track to seeing them her own way.

2.   These are very difficult questions. If Laurie is going to
      pursue the question of her relationship with her father,
      baseball is likely to diminish in significance. It may
      finally dwindle to a paragraph. We probably need to see
      more about the father, particularly about the more attractive
      side of his nature that made her want to be close to him.
      But will she have space to develop both sides of her
      personality adequately and still be able to describe her
      frustrations in dealing with him? Certainly the bulk of
      the initial freewriting is being left behind—no Yogi Bear
      in sight, no violence (or violins) on television. The

character sketch seems more manageable in a short paper because it would save Laurie the difficulty of probing both her father's psychology and her own.

3. A sympathetic reader might not be disturbed by the harsh tone at the freewriting's end, but a neutral or hostile reader would surely notice that Laurie seems at last to reject her father and his beloved baseball as harshly and unfairly as he ever rejected her. It may be that Laurie is oversimplifying her feelings at the end ("Beyond that now . . . Don't try anymore.") and would seem more sympathetic if she though more deeply about her feelings. If she feels this much bitterness, she'll have to give a more convincing account of her rejections so that the reader is prepared to feel some of the same bitterness. As the freewriting stands, it gives us readers enough reason to sympathize with the father that we are not ready to give up on him.

4. I think that Laurie's hypothesis (though it could be stated more delicately) is that her father rebuffed her approaches because he was bitter, sexist, and hidebound. I think that her attitude toward her subject is at times equally bitter and borders on the hidebound. She seems at times to be justifying her rejection of her father. But the freewriting has other dimensions. She seems sometimes to be attempting a sympathetic explanation of her father's character. Other possible hypotheses are:

    a. May father is so locked up in a masculine world of unhappy labor and "manly" sports that he can hardly see daughter.

    b. No one can understand my father without understanding his disappointments.

    c. Baseball, which was once my father's window on the world, has become a door slammed against the disappointments of life.

USING OBSERVATION IN WRITING

The strategies in this section are the most innovative the the chapter, which means that they will be received with the most skepticism by your students. In class discussion, I found that mine were least enthusiastic about mapping, so--remembering my duties as a manual writer--I decided we simply must do a mapping exercise.

Because my first assignment asked students to use as a source their own experience between the ages of ten and fourteen, the map became a "memory map." One student mapped the sawmill where he worked one summer for his brother; his paper on the

importance of heroes in early adolescence included this nice bit
of description:

> We pulled up to the edge of the log yard and I
> looked around. There was a sea of mud surrounded
> by huge ranks of logs. Scattered at random
> throughout the log yards were a few stumps, the
> remnants of what was recently a stand of mixed
> oak and hickory. Huddled on the far side of the
> log yard was a cold-looking jumble of machinery
> that was patiently waiting to chew up logs or
> men, whichever fell into its steel processes.

This description serves the writer's purpose of showing the bleak
environment in which the brother's virtues shone brightly. I can
look at the memory map and see the origins of the details.

Another student drew a map of the house she grew up in in
Bogota, Columbia, complete with a maid, cook, and gardener. When
she described the map to her classmates, they were naturally
curious about the issues of class and wealth the domestic arrangement suggested. As it turned out, the student didn't use the map
at all in constructing her first paper, but her classmate's
reation to it provided a topic for the next paper: an explanation
and justification of the class structure in Latin American
countries.

Exercise (pp. 62-63)

1. Some of the subjects your class may discover are:

    a. The barbershop as a male institution

    b. The barbers as performers

    c. The peculiar etiquette and protocol of the barbershop

    d. The barbershop compared with the beauty shop

    e. The barbershop as community crossroads

    f. Everett as the "personality" of the barbershop.

2. The third speculation ("Varsity Barbershop as Network") is
    surely the most interesting. It is significant because it
    shows us the barbershop performing an unexpected and
    important function. Everett is "the media" pared down to
    one man who can be manageably discussed in one essay.

3. We'd have to lift up Jenny's skull and have a look around
    to be sure of our answer here, but she probably has done
    enough field research to write her paper. She may have a
    hypothesis now and be ready to move on to the drafting

stage. She may, of course, have to loop back for some subsequent planning.

4. The text suggests two possible audiences: men (who are familiar with barbershops) and women (who are not). The first speculation (as object) could conceivably be interesting to women who have an outsider's curiosity about barbershops. The second (as action) and particularly the third (as network) might be interesting to men as well as women because they give a fresh perspective on a familiar place.

5. Starting with Jenny's earliest scouting exercises, we can see at least the following hypotheses:

    a. A college campus is a bewildering mixture of people and activity.

    b. A laundry room is harshly utilitarian, unsoftened by any considerations of comfort or pleasure.

    c. People waiting for busses reveal the protocols of American behavior in the presence of strangers.

    d. The physical layout of the barbershop gives it an air of masculinity.

    e. Haircutting at the Varsity Barbershop sometimes seems to be a sideline; the principal product is talk.

    f. The character of the Varsity Barbershop is an extension of Everett's gregarious personality.

6. If we examine the string of hypotheses above, we can see Jenny's purpose gaining strength. Her planning activities have helped her think about the personal and impersonal elements of her city. She is now prepared to write a paper that will show Everett's ability to overcome impersonality, to orchestrate gossip, to help the community be a community. The sixth hypothesis above is a likely thesis, though it might be more sharply focused: "The Varsity Barbershop has become a community center because of Everett's gregarious personality." Though much of her planning will not appear directly in the paper, we can imagine how some items will fit. The description of the drab uninviting intersection might be used in contrast with the lived-in appearance of the shop (magazines, coat rack, comfortable chairs). Even the contrasting sounds might prepare us for the more intimate atmosphere (honking horns and grinding gears versus the snip and whir of haircutting). Certainly, some bits of dialogue will be useful: "Hi, how are you?" "I'm waiting for Everett," the dialogue with the insurance man. Several of Jenny's observations—the silence of the barbers before customers arrive, Everett's hello being the biggest, Everett as switchboard operator, the custom of

saying goodbye to everybody--could obviously have a place
in the paper.

Planning Exercise (pp. 76-83)

1.   If you ask your students to write about "Beer Street," you
will want to give them some information to save them
eyestrain and frustration:

    a.   The larger sign at the upper left shows men and women
dancing around a stack of grain. The sign's caption
reads "Health to the Barley Mow." With a little
prodding, students might be able to guess that the
smaller sign is an advertisement for gin and that the
painter has suspended the bottle to serve as a model.

    b.   The peculiar-looking object held up near the signpost
is a hindquarter of mutton.

    c.   The boardsheets on the table are The Daily Advertiser
and a copy of the king's speech to Parliament.

    d.   The manuscript held by the women to the right of the
table is "A New Ballad to the Herring Fishery" by Mr.
Lockman.

    e.   The titles of the books at the lower right are now too
obscure to be worth noting, but the attached tag says
"For Mr. Pastern the Trunkmaker in Paul's Ct. Yd."

A.   General impression: Generally speaking, this scene gives
an impression of health, prosperity, and cheerfulness.

B.   Major landmarks, activity centers, focal points: The major
focal points are the artist on his ladder and the group of
workers below him in the foreground. This group is the picture's
major activity center. Less important activity centers are the
building in the background with workers on and in it. The group
of men around the sedan chair in the background, and the pawnbroker's house in the middle distance.

C.   Specific Details:

    1.   The poorly dressed artist on the ladder is painting a
small advertisement for gin beneath the much larger
one for beer.

    2.   Below him are a group of people drinking beer. Each
carries something besides a flagon of beer. The man
smoking a pipe holds a leg of mutton aloft and has a
punch or awl hanging from his belt. The man with his
arm around the girl carries a singletree (piece of
harness). The girl herself carries a key and has a
basket of vegetables beside her. The two women

looking at the manuscript carry baskets of fish. The man to their right carries a basket of books destined for "Mr. Pastern the Trunkmaker."

3. On the table are a copy of The Daily Advertiser and "His Majesty's Most Gracious Speech to the Houses of Parliament."

4. The two women to the right of the table appear to be singing "A New Ballad to the Herring Fishery."

5. Scaffolding has been erected against the largest building in the background, and four men are on the roof, drinking beer and waving their hats. Another man stands at a fourth-story bay as a barrel is lowered to the street.

6. Porters carrying a sedan chair in the street below take a break. The one in front mops his brow while the other drinks a beer.

7. From the steeple in the background flies Britain's flag.

8. The house of "N. Pinch, Pawnbroker" is propped up by a pole. His sign, the traditional three balls, sags from the wall. A boy carrying several mugs hands him a small one through the wicket in the door.

D. Hypothesis: Students' hypotheses are almost certain to be variations on the theme of beer's good effects. It is consistent with health, which the eighteenth century associated with plumpness. It is consistent with labor, since the people of Beer Street all show signs of employment. It is consistent with prosperity, since only the pawnbroker and the artist painting the gin sign seem to be poor. It encourages fellowship and fun (hat waving, singing, and flirtation, at any rate). And it is conducive to patriotism, since the beer-drinking citizens read the king's addresses and fly their country's flag.

Students who see that the picture leads inevitably to these remarkable conclusions may be tempted to the further conclusion that Hogarth was an eighteenth-century pitchman hired by some brewery. They may be interested to know that his purpose in the two companion pictures was moral and serious. They were part of a series of didactic prints on the vices of the lower classes. Intended for wide distribution, these prints can be seen as early precursors of Alcoholics Anonymous ads and surgeon generals' warnings.

After your students have worked with the exercise, you many want to compare their conclusions with Hogarth's intent. Hogarth composed verses to accompany each print. For "Gin Lane" he wrote:

Gin cursed Fiend, with Fury fraught,
 Makes human Race a Prey;
It enters by a deadly Draught,
 And steals our Life away.

Virtue and Truth, driv'n to Despair,
 Its Rage compells to fly,
But cherishes, with hellish Care,
 Theft, Murder, Perjury.

Damn'd Cup! that on the Vitals preys,
 That liquid Fire contains
Which Madness to the Heart conveys,
 And rolls it thro' the Veins.

For "Beer Street" he wrote:

Beer, happy Produce of our Isle
 Can sinewy Strength impart,
And wearied with Fatigue and Toil
 Can cheer each manly Heart.

Labour and art upheld by Thee
 Successfully advance,
We quaff Thy balmy Juice with Glee
 And Water leave to France.
Genius of Health, they grateful Taste
 Rivals the Cup of Jove,
And warms each English generous Breast
 With Liberty and Love.

Fortunately, his prose is less dreadful, and he has
left us an explicit explanation of his intent:

When these two prints were designed and
engraved, the dreadful consequences of gin-
drinking appeared in every street. In Gin Lane,
every circumstance of its horrid effects is
brought to view in terrorem. Idleness, poverty,
misery, and distress, which drive even to madness
and death, are the only objects that are to be
seen; and not a house in tolerable condition but
the pawnbroker's and Gin-shop.
Beer Street, its companion, was given as a
contrast, where that invigorating liquor is
recommended, in order to drive the other out of
vogue. Here all is joyous and thriving.
Industry and jollity go hand in hand. In this
happy place, the pawnbroker's is the only house
going to ruin; and even the small quantity of

porter that he can procure is taken in at the
wicket, for fear of further distress.[1]

2. Thoreau keeps his journal, as he might put it, "deliberately." As several scholars have pointed out, many entries
are polished as if for publication, and Thoreau often
addresses the reader in second person: "Associate as
reverently and as much as you can with your loftiest
thoughts." One might easily conclude from such evidence
that Thoreau's journal is not a journal at all, but a
collection of essays. I don't think this is true, but
Thoreau does habitually write entries that he can later
read as if he were a stranger. The entries are to be
objects of contemplation at some later time. Notice the
second-to-last sentence, where Thoreau pictures himself
juxtaposing journal entries as a researcher might juxtapose
sources.

Woolf's method is obviously quite different. She says
that she writes her diary entries "faster than the fastest
typewriting" and utterly without polish. While Thoreau
works deliberately, she sweeps up her thoughts "accidental-
ly." Her theory, surely influenced by twentieth-century
pyschology, is that slower, more self-conscious writing
might uncover fewer "diamonds." She writes so fast that
her editorial "censor" hardly has time to interfere, just
as the sluggish superego hardly has time to censor the
powerful images of a dream. Obviously, her journal entries
are very much like freewriting.

At first glance, Didion's method seems even more sharply
opposed to Thoreau's than Woolf's does. She considers and
rejects the idea that she writes the notebook as a
storehouse for facts on which she can later reflect--slices
of life stored up for a rainy day. Thoreau, of course,
does see his notebook as a storehouse and a source of
inspiration. But their methods are not precisely opposed:
neither sees the journal primarily as "an accurate factual
record," and Thoreau would find the entry "shopping, typing
piece, dinner with E, depressed" just as useless as Didion
does. Both writers use their journals to record not the
world, but a view of the world. Thoreau (at least the
early Thoreau) is habitually a philosopher and moralist,
and his journal writing strengthens this habit. Didion, in
her notebook and essays, is habitually an instrospective
commentator on the passing scene.

----

[1] Quoted in John Bowyer Nichols, Anecdotes of William
Hogarth (London: Cornmarket Press, 1970).

CHAPTER 3 DRAFTING

Like Chapter 2, this chapter uses student writing to
exemplify stages of the writing process, but with a surprising
twist. Larry's essay, which we follow throughout the chapter,
wobbles along the path and never quite finds the sure footing we
sensed in Wally's (Chapter 1) or Jenny's (Chapter 2). The
progress it makes is solid but unspectacular, and it allows you
the chance to discuss the progress of an average essay striving
to realize its above-average potential. If you intend to have
your students do peer critiques of drafts, this should be a very
useful chapter. You may want to concentrate your discussion on a
few important stages of Larry's work, perhaps the discovery draft
(pp. 96-97), the comments that follow the descriptive outline
(pp. 100-101) and the second evaluation of the formal outline
(pp. 108-110).

Just as Chapter 2 laid out more planning strategies than a
student is likely to use in a particular essay, Chapter 3 lays
out a variety of drafting strategies. Eventually students will
have to decide which they find most useful, so some class time
could be productively spent discussing the relative merits of the
various strategies.

Spending time on the discussion problem on thesis
statements will save you much tedious correction on the first
essay. I like my students to have the three criteria for a good
thesis (restricted, unified, and precise) hanging at their sides
like the workman's tools in Hogarth's "Beer Street."

Drafting Exercise 1 (pp. 111-113) is a link in the Mary
sequence discussed in Teaching Strategies for the previous
chapter. Students will almost inevitably cluster Mary's information to produce an outline on the costs of a wood-burning stove,
and so will be surprised in Chapter 4 to discover that Mary's
revision is a re-vision, indeed.

Writing exercise 4 continues the chain of "process" assignments also mentioned in the notes on Chapter 2.

Questions for the Sarton Passage (p. 86)

These questions don't occur in the text, but might help you
prepare your class discussion.

1. Sarton describes the art of arranging flowers as "play" and
    as "engrossing work." What causes the "joy" to become
    "arduous and complex"? The joy becomes arduous and complex
    for two reasons. The first is that Sarton is taking the
    arranging seriously--a person indifferent about the result
    could not invest enough energy in flower arranging to find
    it arduous. The second is that if the art is taken
    seriously and the material is abundant, the arranger must
    make careful choices, an exhausting enterprise.

2. What does Sarton mean by the art of choice? How does it
    apply to both arranging flowers and drafting a piece of
    writing? How does the discovery of an abundance of
    material complicate the art of choice? In one sense, the
    answers to these questions are terribly obvious. But you
    may want to remind your students that writing, like flower
    arranging, involves the art of choice because there are no
    foolproof blueprints or formulas. At every step, the maker
    must rely on his or her own critical judgment. Obviously,
    abundant material makes the choice harder, since the maker
    must entertain more possibilities and reject some that have
    merit.

3. Sarton says that arranging flowers and writing are alike in
    that one is constantly trying out new combinations
    (drafts). Does she see this arranging and rearranging as
    an ordeal or an opportunity? Sarton obviously sees
    "redrafting" more as an opportunity than an ordeal, but she
    doesn't claim that it is easy. Notice how nicely chosen
    the word engrossing is to express both the difficulty and
    the pleasure.

4. What problems occur "when you think the thing is finished"?
    Sarton lists three problems that occur in arranging
    flowers. What comparable problems occur in composing
    essays? Sarton says that the finished arrangement may (1)
    topple over, (2) look too crowded, or (3) look a little
    meager. Each of these has its analogue in writing. You
    will undoubtedly read some essays this semester that are
    unbalanced by uneven development, some crowded with
    superfluous details, some that haven't enough detail to
    keep the assertions decently covered.

5. What does Sarton mean by "seeing energy"? How long does it
    take for her to use up her seeing energy arranging flowers?
    How long when she is drafting a piece of writing? How long
    can you sustain your seeing energy when you are writing?
    This question is closely related to question 2. "Seeing
    energy" is the strength artists need to step back from the
    mechanics of what they are doing and examine the results
    with a critical eye. Sarton reports that she loses the
    necessary "fresh eye and steady hand" after about an hour
    of flower arranging or after about three hours of writing.
    I wish I had as much endurance. A good class discussion of
    seeing energy may discourage your students from staying up

all night to produce drafts, a practice so common when I
was an undergraduate that at 3:00 a.m., the dormitories
were lit up like ballrooms.

THE SCRATCH OUTLINE

The text's discussion of the scratch outline is fairly
detailed, as it should be, since many students will never have
constructed one. It describes the most common method of
outlining, the one you will probably want to recommend to those
who have not found their own systems. Since the scratch outline
is for private consumption, though, I wouldn't discourage
students who have discovered their own peculiar methods so long
as these methods get results. A computer science student I had
in class some years ago was so used to flow charts that his
outlines looked like the sketch on the next page:

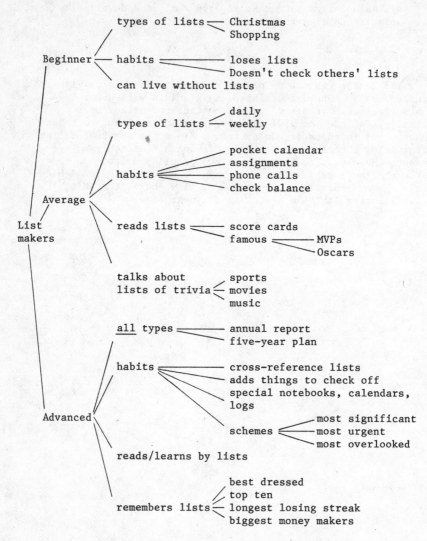

Beginner
- types of lists — Christmas / Shopping
- habits — loses lists / Doesn't check others' lists
- can live without lists

Average
- types of lists — daily / weekly
- habits — pocket calendar / assignments / phone calls / check balance
- reads lists — score cards / famous — MVPs / Oscars
- talks about lists of trivia — sports / movies / music

Advanced
- all types — annual report / five-year plan
- habits — cross-reference lists / adds things to check off / special notebooks, calendars, logs / schemes — most significant / most urgent / most overlooked
- reads/learns by lists
- remembers lists — best dressed / top ten / longest losing streak / biggest money makers

List makers

Book of Lists at top of reading list

His papers were, as you might guess, meticulously organized.
Some students will find that after they have lived with their
topics for a while they needn't write long scratch outlines
because a single word can become shorthand for many details and
arguments. The scratch outline is probably the most
idiosyncratic part of drafting, but I would encourage those who
have not developed their own system to begin by experimenting
with the one described in the text.

DRAFTING A HYPOTHESIS

Some of you may be uneasy to find the drafting of the
hypothesis listed after the construction of the scratch outline,
but others of you would have been uneasy had they come in the
reverse order. The hypothesis and scratch outline evolve
together, of course. Students can't construct useful scratch
outlines without having some sense of purpose, some inkling of a
hypothesis. Nor can they have a real hypothesis until they have
some sense of how the paper can be developed, a hint of an
outline. By presenting the two stages in this order, the text
protects students from the error of seeing the scratch outline as
a fixed road map.

THE DISCOVERY DRAFT AND THE DESCRIPTIVE OUTLINE

These terms may be new to both you and your students.
Calling the first draft a discovery draft is really a bit of
propaganda for the text's underlying emphasis on writing as a
process through which the writer discovers a purpose. It makes
the first draft sound more experimental and adventurous, more
like the downhill skiing of the Canfield quote. If students come
to think of the first draft as primarily an opportunity to
experiment, they will feel less obligation to preserve it. I've
known many freshmen who drowned trying to pull a leaden first
draft to shore. The descriptive outline is yet another reminder
that the discovery draft is "something to work with" rather than
something suitable for framing.

COMPOSING AN EFFECTIVE THESIS

If you read many professionally written essay in class, the
subject of the _implied thesis_ is certain to come up. You
certainly don't want to claim that writers must always express
their theses in single sentences, but I think you can argue that
good writers always have theses that _could_ be so expressed.
Whenever my class discusses a professionally written essay in
class, we reach a consensus about what the thesis is, whether it
is stated or implied. That bit of business out of the way, I can
tell my students that they should always compose a restricted,
unified, and precise thesis statement—even if they decide the
essay will be more effective if this thesis doesn't appear in the
final essay.

Discussion Problem (p. 105)

1.   The statement is not precise. It could mean that the royal
     family is important to the British as:

     a.   A symbol of their heritage

     b.   A model for family life

       c.   A target for gossip

       d.   A source of humor

       e.   Any number of other things.

2.   This one looks okay. Some would object that "almost every person" lacks restriction, but the tone of the statement tells us that we should give the writer some latitude for comic generality.

3.   Not unified. The paper could divide into a discussion of weaknesses and a separate discussion of inability to prevent war. Better would be: "The United Nations has many weaknesses that destroy its ability to prevent a war between major powers."

4.   A wonderfully bad thesis. It makes two separate assertions. It is so unrestricted that the author seems obliged to discuss both the beginning and the end of the universe and the beginning and the end of a football game. And its diction is imprecise: "beginnings of <u>things</u>."

5.   Not unified. The author might choose between two assertions, each quite large enough to fill a short paper.

6.   Not precise. Even if we knew what the American Dream was, we'd have to guess what the author means by the metaphorical "snows of yesteryear." The author might mean:

       a.   Social historians agree that the American Dream of nearly uniform affluence is unrealistic in today's world.

       b.   Social historians agree that the American ideal of rugged individualism is a longing for a mythical past.

7.   Okay.

8.   Not unified.

9.   A good thesis. Some students might feel that it lacks unity, but note that the first assertion (about the gorilla's image) is grammatically and rhetorically subordinate to the second. We can see that this is really a paper about the gentleness of gorillas.

10.   Not restricted or precise. The twentieth century is not going to fit tidily into three pages, and <u>exciting</u> is a vague word.

CONSTRUCTING A FORMAL OUTLINE

Evaluation and Discussion Problem (pp. 108-110)

First Evaluation

1. Some common elements of the scratch outline and the formal outline are:

    a. The tripartite division of list makers

    b. Some information about the frequency, number, and kinds of lists each type prefers

    c. The mention of The Book of Lists under the third type

    Some things that appear in the scratch outline but are eliminated in the formal outline are:

    a. The original names of the three types (beginner, average, expert)

    b. Some details about the second type (the pocket calendar, the scorecard, and the list of MVPs, for example)

    c. Some details about the third type, including the list of organizational principles (most significant, most urgent, most overlooked)

2. Larry's attempt to balance his outline has led him to make these additions:

    a. Sections on how much each type needs lists (the Cs under each Roman numeral heading)

    b. Sections (Ds) on the casual and careful list makers' attitude toward The Book of Lists, added to give continuity and heighten contrast

    c. A section on the occasions when the compulsive list maker makes lists, added to parallel observations about the other two types

    d. Miscellaneous small additions to the "casual" and "careful" sections to keep the paper from being unbalanced by the amount of detail under the "compulsive" type

3. Larry has integrated into his new outline all the conclusions he drew after creating the descriptive outline except number 2 (which involves the introductory paragraph and so lies outside the scope of the outline).

4. The new outline matches Larry's new perception of his
    subject because it focuses on the psychology of list
    making, which he has found to be the most significant and
    interesting aspect. It matches his perception of audience
    because it adds detail that will amuse the reader and
    organizes this detail in a pattern that will help Larry
    inform the reader about the distinctions between the types.
    It matches his emerging purpose by allowing him to present
    his list makers as characters in the human comedy of excess
    and delusion. The match in these three respects may not be
    perfect (see comments below), but the outline shows great
    progress.

The Second Evaluation

1. Although the thesis is improved, it is lifeless and doesn't
    reveal Larry's purpose, which is not merely to show that
    there are three types of listmakers. If we examine the
    evolution of Larry's thinking, we see the paper moving away
    from a list of details about list makers and toward a comic
    observation on human nature. Should his thesis be
    something like, "Our ways of using lists would shock those
    philosophers who define man as a wise, tool-using animal"?)

2. I see two possible weaknesses in relations among the parts:

    a. On entry I, B, 4, I can't see how reading and
        remembering other people's lists is necessary to
        knowing how to use a list. Entry II, B, 4 creates the
        same problem

    b. I have trouble distinguishing entry II, C, 1 from
        entry II, C, 2. Wanting to control one's life and
        wanting to organize it sound like much the same thing.

    I don't know that these are important objections. An
    outline represents only a fragment of what is on the
    writer's mind, and Larry might have anticipated these
    problems and thought of solutions.

3. I see two possible problems with order:

    a. The A, B, and C sections under each Roman numeral
        entry don't seem to be in the most logical order. In
        the case of the casual list maker, for instance,
        wouldn't it be most logical to say that he doesn't
        really need lists, then that he does make them on rare
        occasions, then that when he does make them, he
        doesn't know how to use them? This would be C-A-B
        order according to the present outline.

    b. The transition from the A, B, and C sections (which
        treat general characteristics) to the D sections

(about The Book of Lists) will be difficult, particularly in the case of the casual list maker. The
detail just appears, inexplicable as an overnight
mushroom.

4. We could, of course, come up with a dozen other types of
list makers: the erratic, the illegible, the cryptic, the
abbreviated, etc. But these would have nothing to do with
Larry's scheme of classifying list makers by their level of
interest in lists. Within that scheme, he seems to have
exhausted all likely possibilities. His subdivisions,
likewise, could be multiplied indefinitely, but the ones he
has chosen seem sufficient for his purpose.

5. On the face of it, Larry's outline seems designed for a
three-paragraph body like the one in his discovery draft.
The capital letter entries could conceivably be developed
into full paragraphs in a longer paper, but some would be
hard to develop: consider entry I, D. An attempt to
develop the Arabic numeral entries into full paragraphs
would almost certainly fail: imagine entry II, B, 3 as a
full paragraph.

Drafting Exercises (pp. 111-116)

1. One clustering would be types of cost:

Purchase Cash Costs	Maintenance and Operating Cash Costs
purchase price	chimney cleaning
installation	chain saw
reflecting shield	wood splitter
fireproof rug	wheelbarrow
polish	wood crib
chimney cap	truck and gas

Related Cash Costs	Labor Costs
window fans	installation
carpet cleaning	guard duty
drape replacement	sharecropping

Worry and Nuisance Costs
"hernia panic"
fear of improper installation
lost weekends
stoking
fear of fire
weariness of stoves as a topic of conversation

A hypothesis for this clustering would be that the total
cost of a wood-burning stove is unacceptably high.

2. The Jordan essay should be easy for your students to
outline. It reminds us that professional writers can

follow textbook methods of organization. The essay
contains two literary allusions. The first, to Caesar's
comment on Casius in Julius Caesar (act I, scene 2), will
be familiar to everyone. The second, from a song in
Browning's "Pippa Passes," is hidden in paragraph 6.
Jordan tells us that the fat "know very well that God is
not in his heaven and all is right with the world."
Students who don't catch the allusion may mistake this for
a theological statement. In fact, it is a refutation of
Pippa's optimism:

> The lark's on the wing:
> The snail's on the thorn:
> God's in his heaven--
> All's right with the world!

Almost any sentence from the first paragraph might be
called the thesis, though any one in isolation seems vague.
In an expanded form, her thesis is that thin people are
less congenial than fat people because they are too
energetic, too hard, too logical, and ultimately
oppressive.

Different people will outline the essay differently, but
the contrast pattern is unmistakable. This outline tidies
up the organization a little artificially.

Thesis: Thin people are less congenial than fat people.

I. Thin people are too energetic.

    A. They've always got to be adoing.
       1. Give them a coffee break, and they'll jog.
       2. On an evening off they fix the screen door or
          lick stamps.
       3. They say, "There aren't enough hours in the
          day."

    B. Fat people think the day is too long already.

    C. Thin people have speedy metabolisms that make them
       bustle.
       1. They nervously rub their hands together.
       2. They look for new problems to tackle.

    D. Easygoing fat people will put things off till
       tomorrow.

II. Thin people are psychologically hard.

    A. They don't like gooey soft stuff.
       1. They don't like hot-fudge sundaes.
       2. They are crunchy and dull, like carrots.

B. They go straight to the heart of the matter.
1. They want to face the truth.
2. They say, "The key thing is . . ."

C. Fat people are nice, if not jolly.
1. They are not neurotic, as some people say.
2. They realistically see things as hazy and vague.

III. Thin people are too logical.

A. They say, "If you consume more calories than you burn, you will gain weight. It's that simple."

B. Fat people realize that life is illogical and unfair.
1. They grin at the comment on gaining weight.
2. They know that in a fair world they would be able to eat all the doughnuts they wanted.

C. Thin people keep lists of logical statements that lead to happiness.
1. "Get a grip on yourself."
2. "Cigarettes kill."
3. "Cholesterol clogs."
4. "Fit as a fiddle."
5. "Ducks in a row."
6. "Organize."
7. "Sound fiscal management."

D. Fat people don't think such programs lead to happiness.
1. They know happiness is elusive.
2. They wouldn't want regimented happiness.
3. They prefer cheesecake.
4. The story of the jigsaw puzzle shows how fat people play things by ear.

IV. Thin people are oppressive.

A. Their perfectionism is a reproach to the fat.
1. They sit on the edge of the sofa, neat as a pin, discussing rutabagas.
2. Fat people remove their coats and shoes and put their feet on the coffee table.

B. They look down on other people.
1. They like math and morality.
2. They like to reason on human limitations.
3. They have their acts together.
4. The expound, diagnose, probe, prick.

C. Fat people are convivial.
1. They like you despite your faults.
2. They excuse your failings.

3. They sympathize with your problems.
4. They help you.
5. They gab, giggle, guffaw, etc.
6. They will take you in.

It's easy to see that Jordan's thesis doesn't represent her purpose exactly: this essay is surely not a serious attack on thin people. But students may have trouble saying just what her purpose is. Some will say that the purpose is to amuse the reader, which is not a bad answer but not a terribly good one. Why amuse the reader on this subject rather than another? The real purpose is to define a type of person our culture consistently presents as an ideal—the thin, efficient, analytical, ambitious type—and to subject it to humorous criticism. Henry Fielding said that his purpose in Tom Jones was "to laugh mankind out of their favorite follies and vices." In this short essay, Jordan takes on one type of folly.

CHAPTER 4 REVISING

Chapter 4 is my favorite of the entire book. After some useful opening comments, including the introduction of three reading strategies to help students be objective in their revisions, it moves through four drafts of Rod's essay on the Washington Monument. These drafts and Rod's revision agendas give students a case study of dozens of important issues of audience, voice, purpose, diction, tone, and research. Such a case study is surely the best way to round out the overview of the writing process and encourage students to "go and do likewise." Actually, the chapter manages to bring a second case study to a close in revision exercise 2, a return to Mary's wood-burning stove essay. The composite picture of the writing process given by these two studies teaches some valuable lessons. Both writers do a great deal of thing-in-writing before they reach their final essay. Both end up "throwing away" the bulk of this prewriting, but having it enrich the final product. Each faces the problem of balancing personal vision with an attempt to address a larger than personal topic. Rod solves the problem by moving from a personal narrative to an informative and carefully researched paper and then reintroducing his personal vision by adjusting the tone and using his experience indirectly. Mary starts with an objective question about the cost of wood-burning stoves, does research that appears to be leading to a strictly informative and possibly dry essay, and then surprises us with a shift in subject and purpose that presents an amusing personal view. The case studies lead so naturally to good discussions that you should find this chapter a pleasure to teach.

The Eudora Welty interview (pp. 120-121) introduces the major themes of the chapter and is worth pausing to discuss. Her scissor-and-pins style of revision gives students a concrete image of the global revision most professionals practice, and her experience of not recognizing a proof page of her own manuscript is a memorable example of a writer examining her work "with the eyes of the cold public." Your students will want to remember this objectivity when they read to revise.

LOOKING TO REVISE, READING TO REVISE, REVISION AGENDA

Horace, in the Ars Poetica, advises a young writer to submit his manuscript to severe critics and then to lock it away for nine years before considering whether to publish it. Many

student essays would be better if they could age in a desk drawer
for a few weeks, at least, between drafts. But even this pace,
hasty as it is by Horace's standards, is too leisurely for the
semester-long composition course. The reading strategies in the
text amount to catalysts, designed to speed the process of
disengagement that makes writers capable critics of their own
work. They may strike you at first as slightly silly, but my
experience with them convinces me that they are one of the text's
moments of inspired whimsy. Some of my students have thrown
themselves into the imaginary situations with gusto and good
results.

The revision agenda is an effective tool because it forces
the student to make an objective statement of the paper's goals,
strengths, and weaknesses before thinking-in-writing about
changes in the next draft. When my students hand in papers, they
also turn in preliminary drafts and revision agendas so that I
get some insight into their revision process. The real gain of
insight, though, is theirs, and one student, knowing I was
writing this manual, particularly asked me to tell you how
helpful she had found the revision agenda as a tool.

REVISING: A CASE STUDY

Reading through Rod's revision radically altered the view
some of my students had of the revising process. One day when
the class was divided into groups, I eavesdropped on a conversation
in the far corner. The group had just finished discussing the
last of their preliminary drafts. Feeling slightly disappointed
with their papers, they began to talk about Rod: "you know, he
makes me so mad! I don't know why, but every time I think about
those drafts, I get mad!" There followed one of those lively
discussions that tells a teacher the class is working. The other
students were also mad at Rod, mad because he had taken the time
to get through four drafts, mad because he had started with a
draft inferior to theirs but had ended with one they feared they
couldn't equal, mad because he had convinced them that the
success of their papers depended on a course of exhausting
rethinking about their subjects and their relations to them.

Questions About Rod's Revising (p. 146)

1. Rod's focus changes almost completely from first draft to
    fourth. It's tempting to say that it narrows, but this
    tells only part of the truth. In the second draft, there
    is a narrowing, since Rod eliminates the section about
    preparing for the trip, the section on the trip itself, and
    the details of other sightseeing in Washington. In subse-
    quent drafts, though, after he has decided that the history
    of the monument is the most significant and interesting
    part of his subject, Rod broadens his chronological scope
    dramatically. It isn't simple that Rod has narrowed the

beam of his spotlight; he has also shifted it to a different portion of the stage.

2. One of my favorite passages among Rod's revision agendas is his realization that when he writes <u>bummer</u>, <u>lousy</u>, and <u>stuff</u>, he sounds like a high schooler. We might call this a discovery about voice or persona, but it is as sensible to call it an awareness of audience. Who could he imagine himself reading the paper in front of that wouldn't find this diction a little childish? Other high schoolers, perhaps, if they cared only about being amused and didn't imagine they were listening to an expert. In his second revision agenda, while he is busy kicking himself for the childishness of the "greenie-meanie" passage, Rod discovers that he <u>is</u> a sort of expert and that he needs to stop viewing his audience as a collection of kids and broaden it to include people like the couple from Indiana. He finds in the next draft that he overdoes the expert's voice, that he sounds "like a tour guide--a dull one" and that he has produced a paper that his friend (a cartoon watcher and punk rock fan) finds boring. In the final draft, he struggles to find a voice that will work before a broad audience that includes punk rockers and middle-aged farmers. He very nearly succeeds, though he suspects (quite rightly) that his flippant references to "old George" might offend some readers. As he moves from draft to draft, Rod begins to see himself less as a teen-ager on holiday than as an informed and amused observer.

3. In the first draft, Rod's purpose is "to describe our junior class trip." He sets about this in a literal and straightforward fashion, beginning with the story's beginning and ending with its climax--the sight of the Washington Monument. He adds a dash of humor here and there, but he wants primarily to give the reader a sense of what the experience was like from his perspective. The second draft shortens the narrative and refines Rod's attempt to tell the story from his perspective: we see one afternoon through his eyes--the middle-aged couple, the "hard-to-get" girls, the view from the top of the monument. In the third draft, Rod's purpose changes dramatically. He decides that his purpose is to inform his reader about the history of the monument. The fourth draft keeps this informative purpose, but merges it with his earlier purposes. It is not enough to inform the reader about the history of the monument: the reader should also be entertained and given a "you are there" sense of the impressiveness of the monument.

4. Rod can't find a thesis in his first draft; neither can I. The first sentence announces the subject, but it is merely a statement of fact and gives no sense of purpose. At this point Rod is merely telling a story. The second draft has a likely looking thesis: "But for simple beauty nothing I saw in Washington could compare with the Washington

Monument." Unfortunately, this thesis does not control the writing, and Rod decides to talk about "greenie-meanie" fights and his conversation with two middle-aged tourists. The thesis of the third draft comes closer to controlling the paper: "The story behind the monument is in many ways as interesting as the story behind Washington himself." Rod accurately sees that the one problem with this thesis is that it isn't sufficiently restricted. The reader is left with an indistinct expectation that the essay will say more about George Washington that it does.

5. An exhaustive answer to this question would require much space and time. A few observations:

    a. A block of statistics about the monument's height, weight, cost, and period of construction appears toward the middle of the second draft as part of the park ranger's talk. In the third draft, where Rod concentrates on the history of the monument rather than its impressiveness, the statistics shrink into a single sentence in the introductory paragraph. In the fourth draft, they are expanded and used at the very outset to give an initial impression of the grandeur of the place.

    b. As a special case of the use of statistics, look at the 898 steps and the thirteen-second elevator ride. These, too, make their first appearance in the second draft, where they lie side by side, as presented by a park ranger. In the third draft, they vanish entirely. In the fourth draft, with its emphasis on curiosities and the tourist's-eye view, these two statistics separate. The number of steps is introduced as part of the story of Edna Rousseau, the seventy-six-year-old who managed 307 round-trip climbs. The thirteen-second elevator ride is saved for the conclusion, which depicts the ordeal the tourist must endure to see the monument.

    c. The carnival atmosphere of tourism is mentioned in drafts one, two, and four. In the first draft, it is simply there, uncommented on—in the Lincoln Dogs and Congressional Burgers, Uncle Fred's list of Redskin draft picks, the difficulty of keeping order on the bus trip, and the running from museum to museum to stay in the air-conditioning. In the second draft, Rod has developed an attitude toward this atmosphere, and he presents the indiscriminant sightseeing of the middle-aged couple and the high jinks of his friends at great length, contrasting them with the dignity of the monument. The narrowed focus of the third draft drives the issue out, but it reappears in the conclusion of the fourth draft, where Rod emphasizes the need for historical perspective on the monument to help counteract the distracting effect of the tourist atmosphere.

5.   I, too, am happiest with Rod's fourth draft. It does the best job of balancing a public subject with a personal view—a feat I greatly admire and believe to be at the heart of a liberal education. It also appeals to the broadest audience, not just to the adolescent who might like the tone of the second draft or the factmonger who might like the third. The other drafts have merit, of course. The high school's preparation for the trip could be an interesting paper in itself, and the sketch of the middle-aged tourists in the second draft is amusing. Draft three, though its style is in Rod's words "kind of flat," contains some interesting facts and is well-organized. One lesson students can learn from this exercise is that the process of revision requires the rejection of material that is good in itself, but inconsistent with the purpose of the final essay.

Revising Exercises (pp. 147-152)

1.   Examining the architechtural drawings requires some straining of the eyes and use of the imagination.

   a.   The first plan is a sort of cathedral tower
        containing a statue of George Washington (in uniform,
        I think, judging from the cape) instead of an alter.
        The shield over the door is decorated with stars and
        stripes. In a sense, three subjects are combined,
        patriotism, religion, and war. The second plan is
        Robert Mills's National Pantheon, which Rod briefly
        describes in his third and fourth drafts. At the base
        of its obelisk is a "temple," with Washington standing
        over the entrance as the driver of a triumphal chariot.
        Inside the colonnaded temple would have been statues
        of other founding fathers. We could say that it
        suggests two subjects: the stature of the founding
        fathers and Washington's preeminence among them. The
        third plan baffles me, as a good sphinx should.
        Perhaps it can be viewed as a discovery draft by J.
        Goldsborough Bruff: if the print were larger, we
        could see a penciled annotation, "hurriedly drawn."
        I'm sure that this design would suggest no particular
        subject to me if Bruff hadn't noted that the sphinx is
        "symbolic of lofty aspirations . . . valor and immortal-
        ity." The present monument is essentially Mill's
        conception without the temple and the statuary.
        Towering over the city, it suggests both Washington's
        historical stature and the simple strength of his
        character.

   b. The imagined audience for the first design must be
       people who respond to religious imagery and see no

conflict between religion and patriotism. The architect
also assumes that the audience likes Gothic architecture (much more popular in the nineteenth century than
in Washington's time), and perhaps likes its association
with the civilization of Western Europe. Mills's
audience would be people with an admiration for the
classical world and architecture, and with enough
sense of history to want to remember Washington in the
context of other great men. The designer of the
sphinx clearly imagines an audience with a taste for
allegory and enough knowledge of sphinxes to respond
to them as symbols of "lofty aspirations, keen fore-
sight," etc. The present monument is so simple that
it requires nothing of the audience but an ability to
associate grandeur and simplicity with Washington
himself.

c. The purpose of a national monument to Washington
    should surely be to inspire Americans by presenting
    him as a hero and a model. The first design attempts
    to do this by presenting him as a Christian soldier--
    notice how the statue of Washington below is echoed by
    the statue of the angel on the pinnacle. I think this
    message is too complex and that Washington's straight-
    forwardness and honesty get lost in the complexity of
    arches, windows, and spires. Mills's attempt to
    inspire Americans by presenting not only Washington
    but the other founding fathers as Olympian gods is
    more promising, but it is also a bit complex. J. G.
    Bruff's purpose is, I assume, to honor Washington by
    associating him with classical antiquity and superhuman
    mystery. But his monument is small and inscrutable at
    best. For reasons Rod has described well, the simple
    design--"the rugged individual"--seems to make the
    strongest impression.

2. Mary's essay, like Rod's, has undergone quite a
    sea-change.

    a. The subject at the beginning was wood-burning stoves.
        In the final draft, the subject is the monomania of
        "woodies."

    b. Mary began by imagining readers in her own situation:
        people who were contemplating buying wood-burning
        stoves and who needed information that would help them
        decide whether to do so. Her new conception of her
        audience includes this old audience, but encompasses
        as well people who are interested in or amused by the
        human inclination toward zealotry. She definitely
        assumes an audience with a lively sense of humor and
        enough knowledge of church matters to recognize the
        allusions that are sprinkled through the essay.

c. In the planning stage, Mary seemed to be headed toward
a thesis having to do with cost. This was her search
question at the outset, and it was clearly on her mind
when she made the list on pp. 111-113. But the new
thesis, best stated in the second sentence of her
essay, touches on cost only indirectly by portraying
woodies as "a highly principled and dedicated cult of
true believers." True believers are not likely to
count nickels, of course.

d. Once again, this is a large question, and I will give
only a partial answer.

   (1) Mary <u>keeps</u> her roughly chronological order, her
first-person narration, and her sense of humor.
As a result, she maintains her informal relation
with the reader.

   (2) She <u>deletes</u> a tremendous amount: the details of
her interview with George and Susie, her attempt
to calculate the "true cost" of the stove by
figuring "the amount of . . . life required to
be exchanged for it," and most of the technical
data she gathered from her reading.

   (3) She <u>reduces</u> markedly the cost data she gives and
reduces the comparison of stove models subordi-
nate clause.

   (4) She <u>enlarges</u> her observations on the irrationality
of Bill's behavior and adds more to humor to her
account of it.

   (5) She <u>rearranges</u> in several subtle ways. Notice,
for instance, that the "B.T.U." she found so
confusing in her reading of <u>Wood for Home
Heating</u> now appears at the end of paragraph 8
amidst a discussion of the Saturdays spent
cutting wood, a subject that Susie complained
about in the interview and that Mary soon
experienced for herself. <u>Stoking,</u> which was a
new term for Mary when she read the <u>Mother Earth
News</u> article, appears four paragraphs after
"B.T.U." and gives a "woodie" flavor to her 3
A.M. conversation with Bill.

QUIZ

For comments on the use of quizzes, see pp. 2-3 of this
manual.

CHAPTER 4

Recall Questions

1. What setting do the authors suggest you imagine yourself in when you are reading to revise for subject? [A dentist's waiting room--looking at magazines]

2. What imaginary setting do they propose when you are revising for audience? [A banquet hall--listening to an after-dinner speech]

3. What imaginary setting do they propose when you are revising for purpose? [Attorney's office--signing contract]

4. What three questions should you ask yourself in preparing a revision agenda? [What did I try to do in this draft? What are its strengths and weaknesses? What revisions do I want to make in my next draft?]

Quotations from student Essay to Put in Context

5. "Lincoln Dogs" [Served in the school cafeteria as part of the preparation for the Washington trip--Rod's first draft]

6. "bummer" [Adjective used to describe the bus trip in the first draft--Rod decides to cut it out because it makes him sound like a high schooler]

7. "We seen your bus pull in just a minute ago." [Comment by the middle-aged Indiana woman in the second draft-- deliberately ungrammatical to heighten the reader's sense that she and her husband are the sort of uninformed tourists who won't appreciate this monument]

8. "The story behind the monument is in many ways as interesting as the story behind Washington himself." [The faulty thesis from Rod's third draft--insufficiently restricted, since Rod does not intend to discuss Washington's life]

9. "Know-Nothings" [Political group that steals the monument in the third and fourth drafts]

10. "He solved this problem by killing a pigeon." [Sentence from the fourth draft--Rod's attention-getting introduction to the anecdote about Colonel Casey's method of getting a rope to the top of the monument]

11. "Burn Again" [Mary's clever title for her wood-burning stove essay--introduces the analogy between "woodies" and religious zealots]

12. " . . . I saw a sinful gleam from his eyes shine through the darkness." [A part of Mary's concluding sentence about Bill's failure to stoke at 3 A.M. one morning--labels the

gleam "sinful" because it indicates Bill is backsliding
from the "Woodies" faith]

CHAPTER 5 COMMON METHODS OF DEVELOPMENT

Students are very often confused about the relation between purpose and method of development. A semester never passes in our writing lab without some such discussion as this:

Tutor: What's your purpose in this essay, Jerry?

Student: To compare McDonald's and Burger King.

Tutor: I'm sorry, I must have asked that question stupidly. I mean, what are you trying to show your reader in this essay? What are you getting at?

Student: I'm trying to show how the two restaurants are alike and how they are different.

Tutor: Yes, but why? What's your reader supposed to get from this comparison?

Student: He's just supposed to get an idea of how one place is different from another. I mean, that's the point, isn't it? Our teacher told us to compare two places.

Tutor: Un-huh. Let's look at it a different way. What's your thesis her?

Student: It's right at the end of the first paragraph: "While McDonald's and Burger King are alike in some ways, in many ways they are different.

One semester, frustrated with this sort of impasse, I began comparison-paper tutorials by putting a three-by-five inch card face down on the table and announcing that it contained the key to the success or failure of the essay. If the student and I could read through the paper together and then answer the question on the card, the essay probably had merit. The question: "So what?"

The methods of development discussed in Chapter 5 are powerful heuristics. As the text points out on p. 158, they translate into a set of questions that can help students discover their purposes. But you must be sure that your students don't confuse purpose with method.

Like Chapter 2, this chapter is a smorgasbord. If you give paper assignments by method of development, you may not want to assign it as a block, but rather in sections whenever they are pertinent to an upcoming essay. If, like me, you don't specify in your assignments what method of development is to be used, you may want your students to read through the entire chapter at once so that they will be able to use it as a resource as they decide what methods best fit their purpose in an essay. However you use the chapter, you'll want to remind your students that professional writers rarely limit themselves to a single strategy. The E. M. Forster essay in the review exercise illustrates this point well.

The passages used to illustrate methods of development amount to an anthology within the text. They are all excellent in their own right and deserve discussion, not just as examples of an essay type, but as examples of the professional writer's control over subject, audience, and purpose.

NARRATION

Because narration seems to be the most natural mode of discourse, the one students have the most experience with in day-to-day conversation, teachers often choose to start their semester with narrative papers. If you follow this plan, you'll want to warn your students that although narratives <u>seem</u> easy, they present perilous difficulties of audience and purpose. Too often the student approaches the narrative as an attempt at total recall, mechanically recording events as they happened to produce a sort of robotic accounting:

> I woke up that morning feeling a little stiff because I had played tennis the evening before. My mouth tasted funny, so I immediately brushed my teeth. While I was brushing them, I noticed a daddy long-legs in the bathtub, so I picked him up with a piece of toilet paper and flushed him down the toilet. I couldn't decide what to wear. It was a little chilly now for shorts, but I knew if I wore jeans, I would be too hot by the time classes were over. After thinking about it a while, I decided to wear shorts. I might be a little cool at first, I thought, but by noon I'd be comfortable enough. So I put on my khaki shorts.

The text advises that a narrative essay must make a point and in the writing exercise on p. 162 instructs students to "anticipate how your readers may relate to your experience and call their attention to your purpose for telling them about it."

You might remind your class that both Wally's essay (pp. 29-31) and Mary's (pp. 148-152) use narrative successfully.

Discussion Questions (p. 162)

1.   Your students' attempt to answer this question may help them see the difficulty of finding a single subject for a narrative. Like Rod's early narrative drafts in Chapter 4, this short passage has many subjects. Besides the three suggested in the questions, students might find the following:

a.   The effect of fear on learning.
b.   The ineffectiveness of regimented learning.
c.   The hidden guilt children often feel.
d.   What it was like to be Garrison Keillor at twelve.

The difference between Keillor's successful narrative and Rod's unsuccessful one is that all Keillor's subjects are reconciled in a larger purpose. See #3.

2.   Keillor assumes that his story will interest anyone curious or nostalgic about the process of growing up. He does not assume that his readers will share his knowledge of the geography of Minneapolis or that their introduction to swimming was as traumatic as his. He does assume, though, that they had enough childhood experience with fear and guilt and isolation to respond to his story.

3.   Once again, this _is_ a narrative, so there may be some dispute about the purpose. If your students flounder, you might direct their attention to the last two sentences of the story. Ask them why Keillor finally found learning to swim "so quick and so simple." I think that the purpose of the story is to remind the reader that many things, particularly in the process of growing up, can't be forced. They come in their own sweet time.

DESCRIPTION

Like narrative, description seems easy but poses great problems of purpose. A friend of mine, an able teacher with a style very unlike my own, once described to me a favorite in-class exercise. He would bring a soft-drink can to class, put it on his desk, and ask his students to describe it as they saw it. When they read out the results, he would criticize students for making assumptions that went beyond observation: "You say that the can says Coca-Cola on the side, but from where you are sitting, only the _la_ shows." I was surprised that he found this exercise productive, so I asked him if its purpose was to show his students what a narrative essay should be. "No, sir," he answered. "It is to show them what it _should not_ be." His point was that aimless description, description as an end in itself, is boring and purposeless. He would follow this negative lesson

with the reading of an essay (like Bogan's) in which description
serves a purpose.

Discussion Questions (p. 165)

1.   The connection between the change in seasons and peoples'
behavior in response to the change, is the notion of retreat--
retreat indoors and finally retreat into the two heated rooms.
The second paragraph helps establish that connection by juxtaposing
the warm smells of the kitchen and the wild weather outdoors.

2.   Obviously, Bogan assumes an audience with some experience
of autumn and winter in northern latitudes. A Fiji Islander
might be confused about the lighting of lamps at 4 P.M. She also
assumes an audience acquainted with a world that grows a little
less familiar year by year: a world in which people who could
afford pianos and padded books hung laundry to dry and heated
with wood stoves, a world in which people knew what cold plaster
smelled like. The advent of central heating hasn't made the
passage inaccessible. We still feel the change in the seasons,
see the slanting sunshine of autumn and blowing leaves. But I
suspect that the passage is richer for those who have childhood
memories like Bogan's.

3.   It would be unfair to the passage to deny that Bogan finds
the sensory description worthwhile in its own right. Still, she
does focus the experience on psychological impact of the change
in seasons--the shutting down and turning inward that winter
inevitably brings. In the last sentence, she is no longer
running along with the blowing leaves, seeing the sunlight
reflected off windows, she is alone in the sitting room, listening
to the leaves and the "low secret voices" of the women.

ILLUSTRATION

Illustration is probably, as the text points out, the most
common method of development and presents the fewest problems
with purpose.

Discussion Questions (p. 167)

1.   King Solomon's Ring is a book about animal behavior, which
is Lorenz's broadest subject. Here he narrows to the behavior of
birds, still further to the behavior of birds reared in isolation,
and further yet to the mating behavior of birds raised in isolation.
Two subjects raised in the opening paragraph, but not pursued in
their general form, are the inability of isolated birds to
identify their species and their tendency to interact socially
with the species they are raised by.

2.   Lorenz does not assume that his audience has special
knowledge of animal behavior, though he does assume that they

will understand some biological terms: <u>avian</u>, <u>ingestion</u>, <u>pharynx</u>. He assumes that he is giving the reader new information, and so he words his general point very clearly in the first paragraph and avoids the technical language of ethnology. (Ethnologists talking among themselves would use the word <u>imprinting</u> to describe the process Lorenz describes here.)

3.   Lorenz first develops the thesis by giving us an "easy" example, one that doesn't strain our imagination and is presented in comically human terms ("fell head over heels in love with our handsome Rhode Island cock"). He then gives us the "hard" example of the peacock fixated on the giant tortoises, an example that reminds us that the type of behavior Lorenz is describing is <u>not</u> a familiar variation of human behavior, but is something alien and wonderful. The third example shows us this peculiar behavior in greater detail. It is the strongest example because it is so graphically presented: the reader can hardly forget the "minced worms and jackdaw salivia" being crammed into Lorenz's mouth and ears.

COMPARISON

For a discussion of purpose in the comparison paper, see the general note at the head of this chapter.

Discussion Questions (pp. 170-171)

1.   Auden restricts his subject by dealing exclusively with American and European attitudes toward four questions about money: its origins in the exploitation of others, its general availability, its relation to merit (and self-worth), and its proper uses (for the European, the purchase of power and freedom). He doesn't, for example, discuss how much money is thought to constitute real wealth or how people feel about taxation. These restrictions of his subject give the essay a moral focus that leads almost inevitable to some expansions: the question of Indians and slaves, the generosity of rich Americans, the psychological problems of Americans who inherit fortunes.

2.   That Americans are mentioned first in the thesis may be happenstance, but the shift in order for the body paragraphs serves a clear rhetorical purpose. Auden was, as all students of literature know, British, and his purpose here is to explain Americans to a primarily European audience. Even if we knew nothing about Auden, we would know this was his purpose because the American part of the comparison is developed in much more detail. He discusses European attitudes first to establish the audience's bearings in known territory before moving into the unknown territory that is his real subject.

3.   I think that all Auden's details would logically help develop his thesis if the audience considers them to be factually accurate. His attempt to dismiss the exploitation of Indians and

blacks is not an attempt to excuse it morally, which would have
nothing to do with his thesis, but rather, to show that Americans
do not see such exploitations as a source of wealth. I doubt
that this is factually accurate, at least for today's Americans,
who know that the Black Hills were full of gold and who have been
brought up on the myth of an antebellum South peopled exclusively
by spoiled whites and exploited blacks. Auden presents the
European rentier as a carefree enjoyer of his wealth and his
American counterpart (unless he is actively making more money) as
sad, alcoholic, and neurotic.

THE ALTERNATING PATTERN OF COMPARISON

Discussion Questions (p. 173)

1.   Hawkins tells us that the comparison between brain and
computer is popular in the "computer fraternity"--which probably
means that it has been discussed in print as well as orally and
that the terms of the discussion have been fairly technical. It
may also be that the discussion has tended to glorify the computer.
Whatever the tendency of this shop talk, Hawkins restricts it (or
converts it) to a defense of the superiority of the brain.

2.   Nontechnical readers might have trouble remembering five
rather technical features of the computer while they wait to
compare them with the brain's corresponding features. By using
the alternating pattern, Hawkins allows readers to make comparisons
immediately; they only need to keep one plate spinning at a time.

3.   Hawkins's purpose here is the third listed on p. 168. He
wants to show that though the computer and the brain are compar-
able, the brain is superior. By using the brain in the second
position, he allows it to trump the computer's aces. The final
position is naturally more emphatic.

CLASSIFICATION

Like comparison, classification is a common pattern of
development because it is a powerful intellectual tool, useful in
all disciplines. Like comparison, it is a pattern students too
often mistake for a purpose unto itself. A student who writes an
essay (in response to the exercise on p. 176) demonstrating that
people can be divided into three classes--those who use machines
frequently, those who use them occasionally, and those who almost
never use them--may have to confront the question, "So what?"
The system is consistent and complete, but is it significant?

Though significance is the major stumbling block in the
classification paper, don't underrate the difficulties that
consistency and completeness will pose for some of your students.
I have found pie diagrams useful in teaching these concepts. For

Baker's essay, a pie diagram of the classification scheme looks like this:

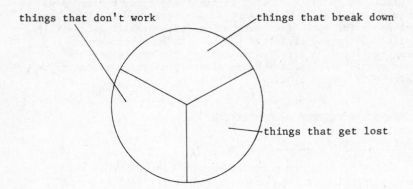

things that don't work

things that break down

things that get lost

In Baker's view, every object would fit into one slice of the pie or another, and no object would fit into more than one slice. Compare this to a situation I found myself confronted with in France, where I found a mailbox with the three openings marked "local," "overseas," and "airmail."

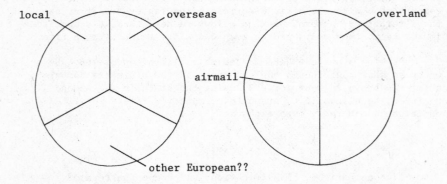

local

overseas

overland

airmail

other European??

Here I was attempting to airmail a letter overseas. Into which slot should I drop it? The scheme is not consistent, since two of its categories are based on destination and the third is based on mode of transport. It is as though Baker divided objects into those that don't work, those that break down, and those that are larger than a breadbox. What would we do with my car, which certainly belongs in two of these categories?

Discussion Questions (p. 176)

1.   Baker's title prepares us for both his subject and his tone. "Three Types of Inanimate Objects" would have prepared us for neither. His evidence is, of course, perfectly unscientific,

but notice how cunningly he imitates our habit of talking about science as a large, autonomous force rather than the opinions of fallible scientists: "Science has not yet solved the mystery . . ."; "Science is utterly baffled . . ."

2.   Baker assumes that his readers will be amused by this essay. He certainly makes no attempt to inform or persuade. He assumes that they have had a good deal of experience with the treachery of inanimate objects.

3.   I suspect that Baker shuffles his categories in the thesis to produce a funnier opening line. Had he said, "those that break down, those that get lost, and those that don't work," the last item would have seemed an anticlimax, too nearly repeating the first. The "get lost"" ends his sentence with a slight surprise. In the body of the essay, though, "don't work" must come last because the item that never works is the reductio ad absurdum, the ne plus ultra, the end of the line. Anything that follows would be an anticlimax.

PROCESS ANALYSIS

        Notice that the text discusses three types of process papers: how to do something, how something works, and how something is done. I've had somewhat better luck with how-something-is-done papers than with the other two categories. For some reason, the how-to-do assignment tends to produce papers on topics that almost everyone knows how to do, papers for which there is not a real audience. How something works tends to produce excursions into remote areas of automotive and technological knowledge that leave the uninitiated audience behind. Both of these problems can be forestalled, of course, by careful assignments and reminders of the importance of writing for an audience. Notice that both the Orwell essay and the writing exercise on p. 180 have the writers describing processes they have only recently learned about, thus keeping the relation of audience and writer fairly close.

Discussion Questions (p. 179)

1.   Orwell makes his subject interesting by stressing the larger-than-human scale of the mining operations and their violence. He makes it significant by showing the dangers the process creates for miners. Among the more interesting sentences are the following:

a.   The comparison of scooping coal from between rock layers and scooping out the middle layer of a Neapolitan ice (British term for ice-cream cone)—a comparison that both explains the process and sets it in comic juxtaposition to a process much smaller and more pleasant

b.   The description of the coal cutter, "an immensely tough and
      powerful hand-saw . . . with teeth a couple of inches long
      and half an inch or an inch thick"--more evidence of scale
      and violence

c.   The description of the cutter's awful noise and the clouds
      of coal dust that "make it impossible to see more than two
      or three feet and almost impossible to breathe"

d.   The observation that "of course" the explosive charge is
      sometimes too large and brings down the roof (presumably on
      the head of the blaster)--an indication of the casual
      danger of the process

e.   The description of the dirt-heaps, "like hideous grey
      mountains"--another indication of scale and ugliness

2.   Orwell assumes that his readers are not familiar with the
mining process, that their closest contact has been a view of the
"dirt-heaps." His second sentence tells them that he is not
going to confuse them with a technical explanation, but tell them
what they could see for themselves if they entered the mine.

3.   The Road to Wigan Pier is part reportage on the life of
miners northern England, part socialist tract (if the independent
Orwell can ever be said to have written a tract). Social criticism
is obviously one purpose of this passage, as Orwell tries to make
the educated English reader more sensitive to the ugliness and
danger of life in the mines.

CAUSAL ANALYSIS

      Causal analysis may be the most intellectually difficult of
the methods noted here because it requires the student to push a
thesis forward without stumbling into the pitfalls of post-hoc
reasoning or oversimplified causes. But the rewards can be worth
the dangers, since much of the lively debate that goes on around
us amounts to conflicting causal analyses. If you have students
who appear headed for the pitfalls, you might have them read the
discussion of causal reasoning in Chapter 10, pp. 357-360.

Discussion Questions (p. 183)

1.   Reading Goodman's title, the audience will naturally wonder
why being a secretary is a health hazard and will thus be prepared
for a discussion of causes. They will also wonder what the
health hazards could possibly be and so will be prepared for a
discussion of effects.

2.   My suspicion is that Goodman's primary audience is neither
cardiologists nor bosses nor secretaries, but feminists and (as
they used to say in the McCarthy years) their fellow travelers.
Goodman's Pulitzer prize-winning column often discusses women's

issues, and when she collected several of her pieces in At Large, she put "Being a Secretary Can Be Hazardous to Your Health" under the heading "Women in the Age of Transition." Notice the assumption from the outset that the secretary is a woman and the boss is a man--an assumption that might have been labeled sexist except that Goodman is chalking her cue for another shot at the oppressors of women. She finally addresses secretaries directly in the last paragraph, but only after a remarkable if clause that would narrow her audience far too much for a syndicated column. She doesn't really mean that she is addressing herself exclusively to women who do clerical work, have blue-collar husbands and three or more children, have a dead-end job, can't express anger, and have either a Type A male or a computer for a boss. What she really means is that working women in American today face all these threats.

3.   I think Goodman's larger purpose is to show the reader that "it is powerlessness and not power that corrupts women's hearts" (paragraph 4). She doesn't want us to read heart in the exclusively medical sense.

DEFINITION

Typically, a student model of definition is the short "scientific" definition they find in dictionaries. Because the apparent objectivity of such definitions obscures the dangers and opportunities of semantics, you may need to alert them to the functions of stipulative and extended definitions. For the stipulative definition, there is no better starting point than Humpty Dumpty's conversation with Alice in Through the Looking Glass:

"I don't know what you mean by 'glory'" Alice said.

Humpty Dumpty smiled contemptuously. "Of course you don't--till I tell you. I mean, 'there's a nice knock-down argument for you!'"

"But 'glory' doesn't mean 'there's a nice knock-down argument,'" Alice observed.

"When I use a word," Humpty Dumpty said, in a rather scornful tone, "it means exactly what I want it to mean--nothing more and nothing less."

"The question is," said Alice, "whether you can make a word mean so many different things."

"The question is," said Humpty Dumpty, "which is to be master--that's all."

In discussing Laurie Lee's essay, you may want to ask your class whether he uses the word charm Alice-fashion (in conformity to general usage) or Humpty-fashion (according to his own purpose). The truth lies, of course, somewhere between the extremes. You may also want to ask what the effect of Lee's accumulation of examples and comparisons is on a reader's understanding of the word. Surely his extended definition is not used to clarify the definition in the dictionary, but to impress upon the reader a new and somewhat different meaning.

Discussion Questions (p. 187)

1.   Charm seems such an innocuous word that Lee attempts from the outset to broaden its shoulders and show that it is a force in the world--hence the opening sentence.

2.   Lee doesn't assume that his audience has charm. He assumes that they want it: "You know who has it. But can you get it, too?" He first seduces his readers into helping him define charm by asserting that charm is "certainly . . . not a question of learning palpable tricks." The certainly tells readers that Lee believes them to be above this popular misconception. He then defines the word very indirectly, especially in paragraph 4, where the reader is entrusted with the business of translating into human terms his comments on the charm of inanimate things.

3.   Lee's purpose is to correct a debased understanding of what charm is, to show that it is not definable or attainable in the same sense that, say, a proper French accent is. He wants the reader to see it as an outgrowth of good character, a powerful weapon to be sure, but not one accessible to those who covet powerful weapons. Thus his opening assertion holds true, but in a paradoxical way.

Review Exercise (pp. 188-190)

It is possible, with some slight stretching, to find each of the strategies mentioned in the chapter exemplified in the Forster essay.

Narration is the dominant strategy of the fourth paragraph, where Forster tells of his encounter with "his" bird. Description makes a couple of modest appearances in the final paragraph--in the opening complaint about his exposed and rather trashy woods and the contrasting description of the walled-in footpath near Lyme Regis. There are several examples of illustration; the second paragraph gives us the rich man of the parable as one illustration of "heaviness," the householder with his furniture, servants, and insurance stamps as a second, and the fourteen-stone (approximately 200-pound) bishop in his pulpit as a third. The same paragraph gives us two brief examples of comparison (or contrast): the rich man to the camel and the bishop to the Son of Man. The contrast between Forster's exposed woods and the "able chap's" wall-protected woods in the final paragraph is another. In the fifth paragraph is a rather subtle classification

of the uses of the material world: creation, property, and
enjoyment. Twice Forster uses process analysis: first in
describing the steps from the publication of his book to the
purchase of the wood (first paragraph), and next in tracing the
links between furniture and insurance stamps (second paragraph).
Though Forster never sets about constructing a formal definition
of heavy in the second paragraph, he is clearly insisting on a
stipulative one that gives the terms a special meaning for human
psychology and behavior.

The whole essay is an example of causal analysis, demonstrating the effects of ownership. There is also a thread of process
analysis running through it as Forster imagines his decline from
a "light" unpropertied man to a "heavy" builder of stone walls.
Forster's thesis is that property has made him heavier and more
acquisitive, and has taken from him some capacity for enjoyment
and creativity. Though Forster's purpose is partly to amuse by
painting a comic portrait of himself, his larger purpose is to
warn the reader that there are dangers in ownership. As Thoreau,
whom Forster admired, put it, "A man is rich in proportion to the
number of things he can afford to do without."

QUIZ

Like the other quizzes in this manual, this one is intended
less as a way of evaluating students than as a way of helping
them review and consolidate their reading. This quiz could be
run on a half-sheet mimeo and given orally as a generator of
class discussion. Ask students to identify the pattern of
organization of the essay from which each quotation comes and
then discuss the significance of the quotation.

1. "If you've got it, you need almost nothing else, neither
   money, looks, nor pedigree." [Definition, from Laurie
   Lee's "Charm" (p. 185). The "it," of course, is charm, and
   Lee is here elaborating on his opening sentence that charm
   is a weapon.]

2. "Pliers, for example, and gloves and keys are almost
   totally incapable of breaking down." [Classification, from
   Russell Baker's "The Plot Against People" (p. 174). Since
   these objects can't break down, they get lost.]

3. "I want to have as much money as possible myself and others
   to have as little money as possible." [Comparison, from W.
   H. Auden's "The Almighty Dollar" (p. 169). The statement
   of a hypothetical European, showing his pragmatic and
   Machiavellian attitude toward money. An American might
   make the money "as a proof of his manhood" and then give it
   away.]

4. "My mother made tea and the women sat talking in low voices
   beside the kitchen table." [Description, from Louise
   Bogan's "The Neighborhood" (p. 164). The women are in the

kitchen because only it and the sitting room have heat.
Little Louise hears them from the sitting room.]

5.   "You're walking on the bottom!" he would shout. "Get your
legs up!" [Narration, from Garrison Keillor's "Drownings
1954" (p. 160). The shouter is the teacher of the unsuccessful swim class.]

6.   "This must be considered as an act of self-sacrifice on my
part, since even I cannot pretend to like the taste of
finely minced worms, generously mixed with jackdaw saliva."
[Illustration, from Konrad Lorenz's King Solomon's Ring (p.
166). The jackdaw in loave with Lorenz is the final illustration of the tendency of birds reared in isolation to
fixate on the wrong mate.]

7.   "To initiate free choice in a machine the operator would
have to insert into its program random numbers, which would
make the machine 'free' but uncoordinated--an idiot."
[Comparison, from Gerald Hawkins's Stonehenge Decoded (p.
172). This is the final sentence of the passage and a
clear indication of Hawkins's purpose of showing the
superiority of the brain.]

8.   "Incidentally it makes one of the most awful noises I have
ever heard, and sends forth clouds of coal dust which make
it impossible to see more than two or three feet and almost
impossible to breath." [Process analysis, from George
Orwell's The Road to Wigan Pier (p. 178). The "it" is a
coal-cutter, and the effect on the miners is not incidental
at all to Orwell's purpose, which is partly to show the
misery of mining.]

9.   "It is powerlessness and not power that corrupts women's
hearts." [Causal analysis, from Ellen Goodman's "Being a
Secretary Can Be Hazardous to Your Health" p. 181). The
sentence shows how Goodman connects the problems of
secretaries to concerns of women at large.]

In the summer of 1978, while I was flying over the Atlantic and reading the _Atlantic_, my eyes fell on the following passage in an excerpt from Theodore H. White's forthcoming book _In Search of History_. I'll number the sentences for ease of reference.

> (1) The Latin School taught the mechanics of learning with little pretense of culture, enrichment, or enlargement of horizons. (2) Mr. Russo, who taught English in the first year, had the face of a prizefighter—a bald head that gleamed, a pug nose, a jut jaw, hard and sinister eyes that smiled only when a pupil scored an absolute triumph in grammar. (3) He was less interested in the rhymes of _The Idylls of the King_ or "Evangeline," or the story in _Quentin Durward_, than in drubbing into us the structure of paragraph and sentence. (4) The paragraph began with the "topic sentence"—that was the cornerstone of all teaching in composition. (5) And sentences came with "subject," "predicates," "metaphors," "similes," "analogies." (6) He taught the English language as if he were teaching us to dismantle an automobile engine or a watch and the assemble it again correctly. (7) We learned clean English from him. (8) Mr. Graetsch taught German the same way, mechanically, so that one remembered all the rest of one's life that six German prepositions take the dative case—aus-bei-mit _nach-von-zu_, in alphabetical order. (9) French was taught by Mr. Scully. (10) Not only did we memorize passages (_D'un pas encore vaillant et ferme, un vieux pretre marche sur la route poudreuse_), but we memorized them so well that long after one had forgotten the title of the work, one remembered its phrases; all irregular French verbs were mastered by the end of the second year.

Perhaps because my Atlantic/_Atlantic_ situation had sharpened my eye for mirrory, this paragraph struck my fancy. Here was White, half a century after attending the Latin School, writing a paragraph that is partly about the man who taught him to write paragraphs. And what are the characteristics of the paragraph?

It begins with a topic sentence. It comes with subjects and predicates, of course, and also with a metaphor (the cornerstone in sentence 4, echoing the structure in sentence 3), a simile (sentence 6), and a close brush with analogy (the consistency of the diction making the school seem like a factory or workhouse). My curiosity was piqued, and I read the rest of the article as a collection of paragraphs. Sure enough, they were almost without exception in the Russo manner: sturdy, foursquare creatures with topic sentences and carefully controlled metaphors. You might expect that such paragraphs would become monotonous, but they certainly don't; through book after book White varies his sentence structure, finds wonderful detail to support his topic sentences, and continues to reap the rewards: Book-of-the Month Club selections, National Book Award, Pulitzer Prize.

I'm not trying to sell Russo's pattern for the paragraph, which many writers find rigid and somewhat Victorian, but I do want to argue that teaching your students an appreciation for the topical paragraph as a unit of composition will serve them over the long haul. The key, once again, is purpose. Encourage students to think of very paragraph's purpose and of how that purpose fits into the larger purpose of the essay. In the White paragraph above, for instance, the writer never drifts--every sentence hammers home the nuts-and-bolts nature of the Latin School. And the paragraph as a whole goes right to the point of White's chapter, the hardships (and concomitant opportunities) of his early life. If your students learn half as well as White did how to divide a subject into topics that can be treated in a paragraph, how to develop those topics fully and clearly, and how to give their development a sound and comprehensible structure, they may, fifty years from now, have reason to thank their composition instructor.

Most of Chapter 6 is devoted to the four characteristics of topical paragraphs--unity, completeness, order, and coherence. Learning these characteristics can help students master good paragraphing if they use them as guidelines when they critique their own papers or one anothers'. After my class has read this chapter, I routinely "drub in" the guidelines by making them the criteria by which all topical paragraphs are judged and commented on. The chapter also treats special paragraphs--introductions, conclusions, and transitions--which have very different characteristics.

Perhaps the best way of managing class discussion of the paragraph is to duplicate specimens from your students' writing and to examine them according to the chapter's principles. If you assign the exercises on completeness (p. 204) and coherence (p. 215), they will create sets of specimen paragraphs for discussion. The exercise at the chapter's end is also an excellent review of the chapter's concepts.

UNITY

Discussion Problem (pp. 198-199)

There is a point in the flight of a moon-bound spacecraft where it moves from one gravitational field to the next. One second it is a satellite of earth, and if its momentum stopped it would eventually fall back to earth. A second later it is caught up in the gravitational field of the moon and begins an inevitable fall to the lunar surface. I remind my students of this astronautical fact and tell them that the real question here is when the paragraph leaves the gravitational field of its purported subject, the itinerant street preacher of the first sentence, and gets caught up in the gravitational field of a second subject, the role of the bank in the town. Your students will very likely see that the shift occurs in the general area of sentence 4 or sentence 5, but there is a much more specific answer. See if they can find the two words that show us the author has drifted into the gravitational field of the bank: the almost certainly in sentence 4 that leads inevitably to an explanation.

Possible revisions will depend on the subject of the essay. If the essay is a general description of the town, the author could break for a new paragraph before sentence 5, but this would leave two rather underdeveloped paragraphs. The author could delete "almost certainly" from sentence 4 and return to the preacher for sentence 5: " . . . and a number sitting on the bank steps. For each of these groups he had his special messages. He recited the beatitudes to his little group of followers." The bank could then be discussed in a separate paragraph. If the essay concentrates on the preacher, the writer will have to sacrifice any bank material that can't be worked unobtrusively into sentences clearly related to the preacher.

COMPLETENESS

Exercise (p. 204)

The first paragraph could be developed as follows:

You cannot and should not try to remove all anger from your life. If you react mildly to everything, you will often be supressing your true feelings. But you must learn to recognize situations where expressing your anger may be counter-productive. Sometimes your anger is only partly connected with the person you are confronting, or not at all connected--and expressing it simply further complicates a difficult situation. For example, no one benefits when the lawyer, nauseated by an

oncoming flu and nervous over an upcoming
case, shouts at a secretary who has made a
typographical error. But even where your
anger is perfectly appropriate and
justifiable, your self-interest may demand
that you be cautious in expressing it. If
the secretary takes this opportunity to make
a few caustic comments on her boss's wardrobe
and work habits, she may join the ranks of
the witty unemployed. The moral is obvious:
learn to count to ten.

Here is one student's excellent revision of the second
paragraph:

To excel in any skill, it is not enough just
to be talented. My uncle, for instance, is a
very successful radio announcer. In a sense, he
always seemed a "natural" for show business: he
easily starred in high school plays and was a
disc jockey on his college's radio station. But
this was just apprentice work. When he decided
to become a professional, he began to develop
very special skills. He learned to drop his
voice to a deep bass or raise it to imitate the
high-pitched, cracking speech of an old man. He
took courses in linguistics and learned the
international phonetic alphabet so that he could
"read" the exact sound of French and German and
of all varieties of English. He can now do
commercials in which he presents himself as a
French-Canadian hockey player or a German wine-maker
or a black businessman from Chicago. To do one
commercial as a New England farmer, he spent
weeks listening to and imitating recordings of
Robert Frost. He once had to do a commercial as
an upper-class Bostonian, and he now has hours of
tapes of himself imitating the speeches of John
F. Kennedy. In announcing, as in every kind of
skilled activity, there are special techniques
that have to be learned by practice. You need a
combination of talent and technical proficiency.

ORDER

Notice that on p. 204, the text defines <u>order</u> as direction
of movement. Some student paragraphs are unruly, full of non
sequiturs, a problem that better fits under the topic of coherence.
The lack of order this section attempts to remedy is stagnation
rather than unruliness. The student may, for instance, assert in
the first sentence that when he came to college he had no friends.
In the second sentence he may declare that he knew no one. In
the third, he may reveal that he was lost in a sea of faces and

couldn't make contact with his peers. In his fourth, he may declare that he had left all his friends behind. In his fifth . . . but you get the idea. Such paragraphs have no direction of movement, no purpose: they do not move up to greater generality or down to greater specificity, or from the whole to the parts, or from effect to cause. The four orders listed in the text don't exhaust all possibilities: you will certainly find some excellent paragraphs that don't fall neatly into one class or another. But every good paragraph moves in some direction.

COHERENCE

The second paragraph on p. 209 deserves pointing out. Much of the incoherence in essays comes from students' tendency to compose laboriously, clause by clause. Ideally, a composition class should increase their range so that they make the paragraph the unit of composition and learn to do their pencil biting at more meaningful intervals. Meanwhile, however, students will have to revise their paragraphs into coherent form. The text gives them a clear model of revision in the treatment of the Jefferson paragraph and also points out some of the techniques by which coherence is achieved: pronoun reference, repetitive structure, contrasted elements, and transitional markers.

As a graphic illustration of coherence at work, you can give your students a paragraph that can be scrambled and put back into its inevitable order. I've used half a dozen different ones over the years, but my current favorite is from George Orwell's "Marrakech":

(1) When you walk through a town like this—two hundred thousand inhabitants, of whom at least twenty thousand own literally nothing except the rags they stand up in—when you see how the people live, and still more how easily they die, it is always difficult to believe that you are walking among human beings. (2) All colonial empires are in reality built upon that fact. (3) The people have brown faces—besides, there are so many of them! (4) Are they really the same flesh as yourself? (5) Do they even have names? (6) Or are they merely a kind of undifferentiated brown stuff, about as individual as bees or coral insects? (7) They rise out of the earth, they sweat and starve for a few years, and then they sink back into the nameless mounds of the graveyard and nobody notices that they are gone. (8) And even the graves themselves soon fade back into the soil. (9) Sometimes, out for a walk, as you break your way through the prickly pear, you notice that it is rather bumpy underfoot,

and only a certain regularity in the bumps tells
you that you are walking over skeletons.

Because I want my students to _hear_ the language at work, we do
this exercise orally. I make up nine sheets of paper, each with
one of the sentences typed on one side and the first and last
words of the sentence written in large letters on the other. I
shuffle the sheets and hand them to nine students who go to the
front of the room, arrange themselves in a line and read their
sentences aloud (the rest of the class seeing only the words in
large print). One the first reading, we listen for the opening
sentence--no very difficult task, though it is worth noting why
students reject other sentences as possibilities. Sentence 2,
for instance, is impossible because of an inexplicable demonstra-
tive adjective: "_that_ fact." Sentence 4 won't do because it
contains a pronoun without an antecedent. After we have settled
on a first sentence and moved it physically to the left of the
line, we start looking for the second, but if we can't find it
immediately we look for any other sentences that _must_ follow one
after another. Sentences 3, 4, 5, and 6 cluster together largely
because of repetitive structure (the short questions) and pronoun
references (_they_), but the transitional marker (_or_) tacks 5 and 6
together with absolute certainty. With much reading and
rereading and much discussion of the elements of the sentences
that make the paragraph coherent, we always put the paragraph
back together in fifteen or twenty minutes.

Discussion Problem (pp. 212-213)

Obviously, the paragraph on the right is the revision. It
makes the original more coherent in two ways:

1. The original is a collection of observations not held
    together by a consistent purpose. The first sentence
    appears to declare the writer's purpose to be a defense of
    opera from the charge of silliness, but by sentence 5 that
    purpose has faded. The writer is too amused by the rivalries
    of singers and by Voltaire's quip to remember the initial
    purpose of defending opera's dignity. In the revision, the
    writer reconciles humor and purpose by changing the initial
    assertion. In effect, he or she concedes that opera used
    to be silly, but asserts that all that is over now. This
    ploy keeps Voltaire's quip in the paragraph and even allows
    some expansion on the foibles of the singers, but uses both
    of these as contrasts to the improved operas of today.

2. The lack of coherence in the original paragraph comes
    partly from the lack of a consistent perspective. It
    dances nervously among the popular perspective (opera as
    silly art form--sentence 2), the author's presumably more
    informed perspective (sentences, 3, 4, and 5), and Voltaire's
    perspective (sentence 6). In the revised version, the
    writer's own perspective dominates because the other two
    are knocked in the head by careful transitions and comments.

Notice that the popular view in sentence 3 is hedged by an
introductory word (<u>traditionally</u>) that makes the statement
suspect, and that it is followed immediately by a
transition (<u>but</u>) to a sentence that tells us why we cannot
accept the traditional view. Voltaire is similarly
handled. The author includes his statement; it is too
amusing to omit. But the statement has both feet in
concrete and is headed for the bottom--it was made a couple
of centuries ago, we are told, by an eighteenth-century
gent whose testimony can be dismissed out of hand.

Exercise (p. 215)

A straightforward way to make the paragraph coherent would
be as follows:

(a) Heavy snows are rare when the weather is
very cold, because the ice particles are too dry.
(b) At warmer temperatures--just below 32°--ice
particles are incompletely frozen and are wet
enough to stick together and form large, heavy
flakes. (d) As the temperature drops further,
the ice particles are drier and the snow becomes
powdery rather than flaky. (e) When temperatures
drop below zero, moisture immediately freezes
into dry, glittering ice dust without adhesiveness.
(f) Usually the frigid air is too dry to produce
even a light snow.

Notice that sentences b, c, and d are a logical sequence arranged
by the drop in temperature. The last sentence echoes the initial
(topic) sentence.

Because I like to get my students into the habit of
finding everyday illustrations of scientific and technical
processes, I have them search for a common example of the bonding
between ice and moisture. What experience does everyone have
with this phenomenon? The following version incorporates the
obvious answer.

(a) Heavy snows are rare when the weather is
cold because the ice particles are too dry. (b)
As anyone who has put a wet finger on an ice-cube
tray can testify, water sticks to ice. (c) At
warmer temperatures--just below 32°--ice
particles are incompletely frozen and are wet
enough to stick together and form large, heavy
flakes. (d) As the temperature drops further,
the ice particles are drier and the snow becomes
powdery rather than flaky. (e) When
temperatures drop below zero, moisture
immediately freezes into dry, glittering ice dust
without adhesiveness. (f) Usually the frigid
air is too dry to produce even a light snow.

SPECIAL PARAGRAPHS

The section on introductory, transitional and concluding paragraphs is as clear an exposition as possible on a subject that remains a great mystery. I don't know where good introductions and conclusions come from, and have that the best method of provoking them from students is simply to praise them whenever possible. The text mentions Rod's introductory hook (from p. 141). His conclusion (p. 145) is almost as good. Wally's essay (pp. 29-31) has a delightful introduction and a conclusion that is slightly less successful. Mary's essay (pp. 148-152) has a fairly straightforward introduction and one of those marvelous conclusions that amount to ending on just the right note.

REVISING PARAGRAPHS

Exercise (p. 228)

The principal problems with the first paragraph are with its unity and coherence. The problem of unity is most obvious in the last sentence, which is comically irrelevant to the rest of the paragraph and should simply be omitted. The vague reference of the <u>they</u> that starts the third sentence makes both sentence three and sentence four difficult to interpret. Is it the parents or the makers of the documentary who talk about the milestones in Murrow's career? I've assumed that it is the parents.

> a) When CBS did a documentary recently on the late Edward R. Murrow, I was fascinated to see the respect my parents had for this radio and television commentator. b) Tears were almost in Mom's eyes when she spoke of the day it was announced that Murrow was dead of cancer. c) Dad spoke admiringly about his coverage of the bombing of London during World War II and about his service as head of the Voice of America in Europe after the war. d) They both recalled his famous confrontation with Senator Joseph McCarthy that helped to put an end to the political witchhunts of the 1950s. e) Though I had scarcely heard his name before, I began to understand how important he was to the people of his generation.

The second paragraph lacks unity and completeness. It contains a series of generalizations so crowded together that none of them can be adequately developed. In my revision, I've selected one idea--that immorality existed in former generations--and illustrated it. The fuzzy ideas that people are (or are not) less hypocritical today and that "young people today are pretty moral" belong elsewhere.

a) There is much talk today about "the new morality," by which people generally mean "the new immorality." b) But immorality is hardly new, and it would be hard to prove that it is increasing, since every generation has its libertines and its prudes. c) Even Queen Victoria, that bastion of the old morality, lived in a family whose behavior she sometimes found shocking. d) Her uncle and predecessor on the throne, for instance, fathered ten illegitimate children in a prolonged affair with an Irish comedienne. e) Her son, later Edward VII, was so notorious for his "indiscretions" that he was virtually banished from the palace for 30 years. f) The new morality may not be a worsening of our conduct, but an increasing frankness in talking about human behavior, which was never as spotless as some people like to imagine.

The third paragraph appears to be an introduction to a paper persuading young drivers to follow the 55 m.p.h. speed limit--a topic on which the author is not likely to have anything interesting to say. It may be worthwhile to point out the weakness of the subject before you roll up your sleeves and try to improve the paragraph. One weakness in the original is a lack of coherence caused partly by the choppiness of the sentences, which tend to treat one idea each and to show no connections. Another is the failure to put all four reasons for obeying the speed limit (mentioned in the last two sentences) into parallel constructions. The best advice I could give the writer would be to keep the introduction brief, avoid the extraneous comments about driver's education classes and 25 m.p.h. zones, and try for a modest hook:

The speedometer on almost any car made in the last decade runs to 120 m.p.h., and the manufacturers still give us models that cruise comfortably at speeds of 70 or 80 m.p.h. So why--unless there is a patrolman lurking behind some billboard--would anyone drive 55? There are a number of good reasons: to reduce wear on the car, to decrease the chance of an accident, to save gas, to make the United States less dependent on foreign oil.

Your students can probably invent more colorful hooks than this.

The fourth example appears to be a topical paragraph suffering from general fuzziness. It is, perhaps, acceptable in terms of completeness and order. But it lacks unity and coherence. As a first stop toward unity, we should give it a topic sentence that clarifies the subject, audience, and purpose--one that tells parents (or potential parents) that they should not overprotect their children. To improve coherence, we can sharpen the paragraph's focus by repeated pronoun references to the spoiled

children. We can also tighten up cause-and-effect statements and
tidy up the paragraph by removing some deadwood and repetition
(e.g., "hardships and difficulties," "pampered and spoiled".)

> While it is natural for parents to want the
> best for their children, they should not protect
> them from all hardships. When parents treat
> their children like delicate figurines that must
> be sheltered from the shocks of life, the children
> become spoiled. Their lives are deceptively easy
> because some adult intercepts all potential
> problems before they feel the effects. They
> never learn to make decisions, because there is
> always an adult to do this for them. Eventually
> they grow into frustrated men and women who
> cannot cope with adult problems because they had
> no experience mastering childhood difficulties.

The fifth paragraph is well developed but lacks unity and
has some peculiar problems with order and coherence. Notice that
it pursues two ideas: Oklahoma's unique position as a dry state,
and the questionable nature of its dryness. The writer needs to
decide which of these ideas is central to the purpose of the
essay in which the paragraph appears. (I have assumed that the
wet dryness is the central point.) The problem with order can be
seen most clearly in the first four sentences, each of which
includes a statement that Oklahoma is the only dry state. It is
as though the author forgets from one sentence to the next what
has been said. A problem with coherence appears in the second
half of the paragraph, where the author seems to get too entangled
in the details of getting names on bottles to remind the reader
that the consequence of mislabeling is complete circumvention of
the prohibition law. Here is a possible revision:

> (a) When South Carolinians allowed liquor
> into their state in 1977, Oklahoma became the
> last dry state. (b) But the dryness is awfully
> damp. (c) Although the original prohibition law
> of 1920 outlawed all liquor, today's law only
> attempts to forbid the sale of liquor-by-the-drink.
> (d) Even this modest law is often abused.
> Anyone over twenty-one can buy a bottle of
> liquor, take it to a private club, and be served
> by a bartender. (e) The theory is that the
> customer is drinking his own liquor, rather than
> buying a drink. (f) To sustain this theory, the
> law states that anyone who drinks from a bottle
> must have his name on it and that there should be
> only one name per bottle. (g) In practice,
> however, many bottles have several names on them,
> and many have no name at all. (h) It takes a
> good deal of imagination to call a state dry when
> its citizens can belly up to a bar, hand some
> cash to a bartender, and get drinks from a bottle
> marked only by a Jack Daniels label.

In this version, the clever statement about damp dryness is moved near the front of the paragraph and becomes the topic sentence (b). The discussion of name labels is given coherence by transitions contrasting theory with practice (e, f, g), and a final sentence is added to show how the abuse of the private bottle provision makes prohibition a mockery.

CHAPTER 7 SENTENCES: PATTERNS OF EXPRESSION

Some of my friends who teach composition are primitivists
when it comes to the sentence. They look at the garbled and
convoluted syntax in one paper and label it-- as Ken MacCrourie
did--"Engfish": the sort of thing students can write only by
forgetting all they know about the spoken language and attempting
to write in the contrived style they think teachers prefer. They
look at the simple, monotonous, undeveloped sentences of other
papers and declare that students write that way only when they
have been frightened by years of red-ink correction. If they
weren't frightened, the natural complexities and rhythms of the
spoken language would not be so suppressed. Carried to its
logical extreme, this philosophy (to which I partly subscribe)
would eliminate the need for Chapter 7. We could simply tell our
students to write naturally.

But I assign this chapter, and my students do every exercise
in it. Even if their speech were as lucid and fluent as my
friends want to believe it is, I don't think they could become
good writers by merely learning to record their spontaneous
utterances. The best writing culminates a process, largely a
process of revision. The sentence is not, thank goodness, a
butterfly to be captured, but a lump of clay to be molded and
remolded. The chapter emphasizes the plasticity of the sentence,
showing students how to expand it, combine it with another
sentence, or give it a standard, balanced, or periodic form. It
specifically instructs students on the great goals of revision:
clarity, emphasis, economy, and variety. It also reminds
students that the malleability of the sentence should make it an
instrument of their purpose.

If you intend to ask your students to do all the chapter's
exercises, give some though to the amount of work you are
imposing on them (and on yourself if you intend to grade the
results). In my own class, I divide the chapter into five parts
(breaks at pp. 238, 248, 257, and 263) so that the additional
burden of the exercises will be distributed over five class days
and will not interfere with the students' constant regimen of
journal writing and drafting. I collect the assignments as they
fall due and occasionally discuss an exercise for a few minutes
or ask a student to put a specimen answer on the board, but
generally I treat the chapter as self-teaching. Students who
find the exercises difficult know they can get my help during
office hours or they can go to the writing lab.

EXPANDING AND COMBINING SENTENCES

Exercises (p. 233)

This apparently simple exercise can be treacherous if you insist on great grammatical accuracy in identifying the boundaries of modifying words, phrases, and clauses, since modifiers are sometimes tucked one inside another, like Chinese boxes. In discussing the exercise, you might insist on an exact identification of the subject and verb, but allow some latitude in the grouping of modifiers. Your discussion needn't touch on such terms as adverb, subordinate clause, and partitive: the exercise invites the student to get an overview of the sentence without an intervening cloud of technicalities. In my answers, I have followed the text's convention of not treating a, and, and the as modifiers. I have set my parentheses more for convenience than for thoroughness.

1. I did the assignment (as well as I could.)

2. The kitten was meowing (plaintively) (under the porch).

3. (Whatever it costs), I want it.

4. (In the attic) we found an album (full of old family portraits). [Some students may mark full as a separate modifier.]

5. (On the walls) (of the stuccoed, crumbling villas), the paint peels, (unnoticed) (by human eyes). [Some students may mark stuccoed and crumbling as separate modifiers within the of phrase. Others may mark one long modifier from the sentence's beginning to the comma and another long modifier stretching from unnoticed through eyes. These are sensible answers.]

6. But (as I approached the bridge), the euphoria dissolved. [Being a conjunction, but is properly neither part of the basic sentence nor a modifier. Let the students do with it what they will.]

7. (With a crash (of gears) and a lurch) we were off, (bounding down the half-completed road), then (swooping and looping hairpins) (up the lower slopes) (of Mont San Angelo). [Students need not mark of gears as a modifier: it is a prepositional phrase within a prepositional phrase. They may mark bounding, half-completed, and lower as separate modifiers.]

8. (In May 1975), (during the spring music festival) (that opens every year) (with a performance) (of Smetana's "Ma Vlast") ("My Homeland"), I went (to Prague) (for the first time). [Students may mark spring, music, every, Smetana's, and first as separate modifiers. They may mark everything between the commas as one long modifier.]

EXPANDING SENTENCES BY MODIFICATION

Examples on p. 236

These are not the exercise examples, but the ones included
in the text. "Memories make me homesick" could be expanded to:

Whenever I see flowered wallpaper, memories of
that old farmhouse make me homesick for Missouri.

"Beauty contests exploit sex" could be expanded to:

Beauty contests like the Miss American Pageant
exploit sex more insidiously than any Playboy
gate-fold.

Exercise (p. 236)

Besides being amusing in itself, the picture has sufficient
detail to invite sentences with many modifiers. For example:

Standing before his easel on a winter's day, an
artist looks at a fully clothed model, but paints
her nude, lounging in the sun, isolated from the
surrounding city.

or

A man in an overcoat gazes curiously at the
painting and the model, his hands—neatly folded
behind has back—holding the chain of a dog who
gazes with equal curiosity at the photographer.

COMBINING SENTENCES BY COORDINATION

Exercise (p. 238)
By their nature, sentence-combining exercises allow a
number of different answers. In discussing them, you may want to
remind your students of the range of their options by soliciting
a variety of solutions.

1. Tuition and the expense of living away from home keep many
    young people from going to college. [The object of the
    first sentence and the subject of the second are combined
    to form a compound subject of a single predicate.]

2. Energy consumption and inflation are two major problems in
    this country. [The two subjects are fused into one compound
    subject of a shared predicate.]

3. Journalism, secondary school teaching, and the law are now
    overcrowded. [Series of subjects.]

4.   The camp director, our class sponsor, and a native of the
     area warned us of the danger of shooting the rapids.
     [Series of subjects.]

5.   The prisoner lost 65 pounds by fasting, escaped from his
     cell through a small skylight, and fled the state. [The
     three predicates are made into a series governed by the
     same subject.]

USING PARALLEL STRUCTURES

Exercise (pp. 241-242)

1.   a.   We hold these truths to be self-evident:
          ⎡ that all men are created equal
          ⎣ that they are endowed by their creator with certain inalienable rights

     b.   The book is full of stories
          ⎡ of sinking ships and burning towns
          ⎢ of killing cold and windlashed waves and
          ⎣ of reckless men engaged in dangerous pursuits.

2.   a.   Big cars are more powerful, more comfortable, more
          prestigious and saver in a crash than small cars, but small
          cars are less costly to repair, easier to park, less
          expensive to buy, and more fuel-efficient.

     b.   The football fan watching on TV sees close-ups of the
          action, hears expert commentators explaining fine points,
          is treated to replays of exciting plays, and sits in the
          comfort of his living room.

3.   Watching football in the stadium
     Panoramic view of the plays
     Comments of crowd
     Stadium atmosphere
     Sense excitement being in crowd

3.   cont. The football fan watching on TV sees close-ups of the
     action, hears expert commentators explaining fine points,
     is treated to replays of exciting plays, and sits in the
     comfort of his living room; but the fan in the stadium sees
     the panoramic sweep of plays developing on the field, hears
     the colorful and often humorously obscene comments of his
     neighbors in the stands, absorbs the atmosphere provided by
     bands and cheerleaders, and gets caught up in the shared

excitement that frequently brings the crowd roaring to its feet.

COMBINING SENTENCES THROUGH SUBORDINATION

Exercise (p. 244)

As I noted on a previous exercise, many answers are possible to these exercises, and it may be worth your while to explore several options in class. For four of the sentences, I have given two versions different enough in their effect to provoke some discussion of style and emphasis.

1. Since I had always wanted the rustic country life, we bought a sturdy old farmhouse a mile out of town.

2. State University won the Valley Tournament championship last night in a 98-84 overtime game in which all-conference player Karl Weiner scored 35 points.

   or

   All-conference star Karl Weiner led State University to the Valley Tournament championship last night, scoring 35 points in the 98-84 overtime win.

3. A faulty railroad signal caused an express to plow into the rear of a freight train last night, killing five and injuring fifty.

   or

   Fifty people were killed last night when a faulty railroad signal sent an express into the rear of a freight train.

4. Looking like the devil, the mean and snarly bull waits patiently on the outskirts of the arena for the ripe moment to attack his prey.

   or

   On the outskirts of the arena, the mean and snarly butt waits patiently, looking like the devil waiting for the ripe moment to attack his prey.

5. Though the rough and rugged exterior of the restaurant makes it resemble a New England fishing shack waiting on the coast of Maine for some old mariner to return to port, it is in Kansas.

   or

In Kansas is a restaurant with the rough and rugged
exterior of a coastal fishing shack waiting for one of
Maine's old mariners to return to port.

THE RELATION OF COMBINATION TO PURPOSE

As with most good sentence-combining exercises, this one
should produce a variety of answers that may be fruitfully
compared in class. One way of provoking a class discussion of
the relation of syntax and purpose is to duplicate some student
answers without telling what purposes they serve. Have the class
vote on which of the two purposes a given sentence seems to
serve, and then discuss the reasons for their votes.

Cluster A

Purpose 1 Since the color and style of clothes reveal an
individual's personality and attitudes, people should be free to
dress as they choose. They should not be forced to wear the
required "appropriate attire" of formal situations: a dress or a
suit and tie.

Purpose 2 Although clothes like blue jeans and a tee shirt
can reveal an individual's personality by their color and style,
they are not appropriate in professional situations where people
judge others by the appropriateness of their appearance.

Cluster B

Purpose 1 Frozen dinners once consisted of such dull items
as lima beans, gooey potatoes, and mystery meat, but to satisfy
the new American concern for healthy, interesting, and balanced
meals, today's frozen food companies have developed more sophisti-
cated fare: beef bourguignon with glazed carrots, asparagus
crepes with mornay sauce, vegetarian lasagna, even gourmet
dietetic dinners.

Purpose 2 Frozen dinners composed of such dull items as
lima beans, gooey potatoes, and mystery meat have long been a
part of the American way of life, but today's busy American can
enjoy a variety of healthy, interesting, and balanced frozen
meals: beef bourguignon with glazed carrots, asparagus crepes
with mornay sauce, vegetarian lasagna, even gourmet dietetic
dinners.

Cluster C

Purpose 1 Linda Ronstadt began her divergent career
singing country-tinged ballads, but moved through country rock to
rock, recording acclaimed versions of songs by such diverse
composers as James Taylor, the McGarrigles, and Elvis Costello.

Recently she has expanded her repertoire to include standards by such writers as Gershwins and Irving Berlin and has starred on Broadway in Gilbert and Sullivan's operetta <u>The Pirates of Penzance</u>. This season she is singing in Puccini's opera <u>La Boheme</u>.

[This cluster raises some interesting questions of audience that you may want to discuss in class. Can we omit most of the information about <u>Penzance</u> and <u>La Boheme</u>, assuming that the reader knows the composers and knows that comic opera is a cousin of our Broadway musicals? If we can, we could abbreviate our information and try to fit it into a single sentence.]

<u>Purpose 2</u> After beginning her career singing country-tinged ballads, Linda Ronstadt moved from country rock into rock, recording in a stylistic range that included the compositions of James Taylor, the McGarrigles, and Elvis Costello. But she has a vocal range that a number of classical music critics have called "operatic," and has recently changed her repertoire to include standards by such writers as Gershwins and Irving Berlin. After a Broadway appearance in the soprano role of Mabel in Gilbert and Sullivan's operetta <u>The Pirates of Penzance</u>, she is now singing a role in Puccini's opera <u>La Boheme</u>.

TYPES OF SENTENCES AND THEIR EFFECTS

THE BALANCED SENTENCE

<u>Exercise (p. 249)</u>

To save space and tedium, I will list only the combined sentence, from which the separate statements can be easily derived.

1. Milk chocolate is sweet and mild and, despite its empty calories, <u>seems</u> healthy; but dark chocolate is strong and bitter and seems "adult" in almost the same unwholesome sense that some movies are called adult.

2. A compact car gives you transportation reduced to its most functional and efficient level; the full-sized car gives you a traveling living room.

3. When you jog, you breathe in the fumes of passing cars, and when you swim, you bathe in the germs of a hundred strangers.

4. The rock singer often sounds like he is worked into a fever pitch, while the country singer sounds like he is hoping someone will happen along with the energy to pour him a drink.

5. You see a celebrity and your day is brightened; you find a hero and your life is enlarged.

6.   Education, for many students, is a sort of loitering
      between keggers, but unemployment, for most workers, means
      the unremitting labor of searching for jobs and bickering
      with social service agencies.

THE PERIODIC SENTENCE

Exercise (pp. 251-252)

      On the final examination, after we had spent weeks consider-
ing the nuances of the Bill of Rights, after we had read three
books on the Monroe administration, after we had dissected the
personal lives of Thaddeus Stevens and the other Radical Republi-
cans, the teacher asked a single question--"Please comment on an
event recently in the news."

REVISING SENTENCES

REVISION FOR CLARITY

Exercise (pp. 254-255)

1.   Minor revision: His sister formerly lived in Springfield,
      where she directed a local program that screened reports of
      child abuse and made referrals in case workers. She was so
      successful at the local level that she is now living in
      Washington, working for the Department of Health and Human
      Services.

      Major revision: Because of her success as director of a
      child-abuse program in Springfield, his sister now works
      for the Department of Health and Human Services in
      Washington.

2.   Minor revision: For several years controversy has centered
      on a commonly used herbicide called 2-4-5-T. Producers
      insist that it is not harmful to humans, but independent
      researchers say there is evidence that it can cause miscar-
      riages and cancer, among other problems. The controversy
      has been highly publicized recently because the herbicide
      is chemically similar to the defoliant used by the American
      military in Vietnam that is now suspected of causing cancer
      and other serious diseases.

      Major revision: The controversy about the harmfulness of a
      commonly used herbicide called 2-4-5-T has recently increased
      because of charges that a chemically similar defoliant used
      by the American military in Vietnam caused cancer and other
      serious diseases.

3.   Minor revision: My father has a friend who insists that he
      is dirt poor. I suppose that in a sense he is, because he
      invests all of his extra income in land. He says he can't

afford to put it in the bank where inflation decreases its
value more than interest increases it, he doesn't want to
bother with the problems that go along with rental property,
and he isn't interested in stocks and bonds. So he buys
land, on the theory that since no more is being made, its
value will keep rising.

Major revision: My father has a friend who insists he is
"dirt poor." Rather than put his extra income in the bank
or into rental property or stocks and bonds, he invests it
in land, on the theory that since no more land is being
made, its value is sure to rise.

REVISION FOR EMPHASIS

Exercise (pp. 256-257)

1. He said that although the UN had done much of which it
   could be proud and was still performing valuable services
   in many areas, it had failed in its chief function: to
   preserve peace.

2. I sometimes think that morality consists chiefly in the
   courage of making a choice.

   or

   Morality, I sometimes think, consists chiefly in the
   courage of making a choice.

3. The Supreme Court's decision about the legislative veto has
   caused much concern about foreign policy.

4. We have only recently begun to give attention to noise
   pollution, a problem important to our environment.

   or

   Despite its importance to our environment, we have only
   recently begun to give our attention to the problem of
   noise pollution.

5. The college's Disciplinary Committee expelled him yesterday
   afternoon on an accusation of cheating.

   or

   Accused of cheating, he was expelled from college yesterday
   afternoon by the Disciplinary Committee.

   or

He was accused of cheating and, at yesterday afternoon's meeting of the Disciplinary Committee, was expelled from college.

6. The governor said that, after he had considered the arguments for and against a stay of execution and had taken everything into account, he was in favor of mercy.

7. The doctor told me I could eat anything I pleased while I was on this diet, except animal fats.

8. Thomas Marshall, vice president under Woodrow Wilson, expressed our traditional neglect of the man in that office when he told visitors looking curiously through his doorway, "If you're not coming in, throw me a peanut."

9. Proposition 13, which was approved by the voters of California in 1978, stimulated nationwide concern about reducing taxes.

10. We can be sure that most candidates will promise a reduction in taxes.

    or

    Most candidates, we can be sure, will promise a reduction in taxes.

11. Pete Rose hit the ball to the right field wall, but after rounding first and second and diving into third in a head-first slide, he was called "Out!"

12. Because of a sudden airline strike, hundreds of American travelers stranded at the London Airport faced quite a serious situation.

Exercise (p. 259)

1. Once the danger was gone, we abandoned the safety precautions that we had observed so carefully.

2. John McEnroe played an almost perfect set.

3. The garage mechanic estimated that the repairs would cost $200.

4. Helen Caldicott spoke to a local women's club about the nuclear freeze movement.

5. Everyone in our group descended the path to the bottom of the canyon.

6. The National Rifle Association has persistently opposed gun control laws.

7. Each of our running backs scored a touchdown during the game.

8. He was not prepared for the test and so answered only half of the questions.

9. .The instructor said he would grade and return the papers within three days.

10. The American Hospital Association must surely recognize that many families cannot afford such costs.

REVISION FOR ECONOMY

Exercise (pp. 262-263)

1. Often ~~the~~ words ~~that-he-uses~~ do not convey ~~the~~ meaning ~~that-he-intends~~. [8 words for 14]
   (his ... his)

2. She looked ~~as-though-she-was-feeling-indisposed~~. [3 words for 8]
   (ill)

3. ~~As-far-as-the-average-citizen-is-concerned,-it-is-probable~~
   ~~that~~ (M) most people are (probably) not greatly concerned about
   the ∧ scandals ~~of-politicians~~. [11 words for 23]
   (political)

4. When we studied defense mechanisms, ~~which-we-did~~ in psychology class, I discovered that I used most of the ~~mechanisms~~ ~~that-are-discussed~~ in the textbook. [19 words for 26]
   (ones)

5. Just before ~~the-time-when~~ World War I ~~broke-out~~, Alsations ~~who-were~~ of French descent were outraged by ~~the-act-of~~ a German soldier's slapping a cobbler ~~who-was~~ (lame) across the face with a sword. [25 words for 37]

6. ~~Concerning-the-question-of~~ (W)hether men are stronger than women, ~~it-seems-to-me-that-the-answer-is-variable,~~ depending(s) on how one interprets the word stronger. [14 words for 27]

7. When, ~~after-much-careful-and-painstaking-study-of-the-many~~ ~~and-various-problems~~ ∧ involved (space flight), experts ~~in-charge-of-the~~

~~different-phases-of-our-space-flight-programs-make-the~~
decided
~~decision~~ to send a rescue ship to bring back the astronauts

~~who-were-in-space~~ in Skylab II, about a thousand ~~people-set~~
workers   readied it
~~to-work~~ at Cape Kennedy ~~each-with-his-or-her-own-duties-to~~

~~perform,-to-get-the-rescue-ship-ready-to-fly-into-space-and~~

~~bring-back-the-astronauts.~~ [27 words for 80, but perhaps a

little too lean]

REVISION FOR VARIETY

Exercise (pp. 265-266)

1. Shakespeare's chronicle history of <u>Henry the Fifth</u>, a drama
of kinghood and war, is essentially a play about a young
king's coming of age.

2. Henry V, who has been an irresponsible young price before
has accession to the throne, had to prove his worthiness as
king by leading his army in war.

3. and 4. After invading France and capturing Harfleur, he
tried to withdraw his troops to Calais; but he and his men
were confronted by a numerically superior French army at
Agincourt.

5. In a famous passage in Shakespeare's play, Henry urges his
soldiers on to an incredible victory, in which the superior
mobility and firepower of the English proves too much for
the heavily armored French.

6. See 1-5.

Review Exercises (pp. 266-267)

1. This exercise shows that a collection of short, simple
sentences not only lack variety, but also coherence. In the
revision below, I've noted the source sentences in the right-hand
column. Note that the last two sentences of the revised version
break away from the subject-first order of the source's
sentences.

     The most successful lobbyists working in state   1

     capitols are highly paid experts in legislative   2

     strategy available to almost any group that can pay for   5 their services. They are skillful, professional   4

workers who know more about the legislative process   3

than most state legislators do. Not likely to apply   6

old-fashioned direct pressure to politicians, they

generally try to persuade legislators' constituents to   7

apply the pressure. Then they can claim that what   8

their pressure group wants, the public also wants.   9

2. The problem with this exercise paragraph is wordiness. The original contains 166 words; the revision below contains 72.

misconceptions
One ~~of-the-conceptions-not-founded-in-fact-that~~

many people have about ~~the-nature-of~~ language is

that it ~~is-one-of-those-things-that~~ will "hold still"

~~and-refuse-to-change.~~ And many ~~of-those~~ who know

that ~~this~~ English ~~language-of-ours~~ has changed
continuously
ₐthrough the years, ~~and-continues-to-the-present-time~~
suspect
~~to-change,-have-the~~ suspicion that ~~there-is-some-~~

~~thing-that-is-not-good-about~~ this change ~~from-the~~
is decadent
~~status-quo.~~ You may have heard someone ~~express~~

~~his-or-her-regret-about-the-fact~~ that our language

is ~~in-this-day-and-age~~ no longer the "grand old

language of Shakespeare." ~~The-person-who-would~~
He
~~express-that-regret~~ would be surprised to ~~become~~
learn
~~cognizant-of-the-fact~~ that Shakespeare was ~~one-of~~

~~those-people-who-were~~ denounced for ~~corrupting-and~~
C
polluting the ~~English~~ language. ~~But~~ ¢hange in the
deplorable
language ~~that-we-speak-and-write~~ is not ~~to-be-de-~~

~~plored:~~ it is simply a fact ~~that-is-with-us-in~~

~~our-lives.~~

CHAPTER 8 DICTION: THE CHOICE OF WORDS

Obviously, students' diction will improve best as they
practice their own writing. No aspect of writing is harder to
comment on than the choice of words. Sometimes you can analyze a
large organizational problem in a couple of sentences, but you
can blither for half a page arguing that <u>enthusiasm</u> is preferable
to <u>passion</u> in a given context. In this chapter, <u>Writing with a
Purpose</u> provides general guidelines for diction (appropriateness,
specificity, and imagery) and gives the student practice with
revision to remove vagueness, jargon, triteness, and ineffective
imagery.

DENOTATION AND CONNOTATION

The distinction between denotation and connotation often
seems blurry to students, since every word has both and since the
explicit and implicit meanings intertwine. To make the distinction clearer, we sometimes oversimplify connotation, saying that
it is positive, negative, or neutral. But properly speaking,
connotation embraces all implicit meaning: we sometimes talk
about the sexual connotations of a word, for instance. To help
students understand the distinction between denotation and
connotation without oversimplifying it, a friend of mine sometimes
has them imagine themselves in the situation of a college student
who takes her steady boyfriend home for Christmas vacation. If
grandmother comes to visit, what are some of the words the
student could use to introduce him? Students may suggest some or
all of the following:

> gentleman friend, co-hab, suitor, young man,
> boyfriend, flame, steady, sweetheart, crush,
> heartthrob,fiancé, swain, lover, beau, dreamboat,
> admirer, live-in, truelove, guy I'm hanging
> around with.

Once these expressions are on the board, the class tries to group
them into those that differ in connotation only and those that
differ in denotation. There is no definitive grouping, but the
students may arrive at a consensus that <u>co-hab</u> (a useful but not
very common coinage), <u>live-in</u>, and probably <u>lover</u> belong in a
separate denotative group. <u>Fiancé</u> and <u>suitor</u> also have denotations that separate them from the bulk of the expressions. But
among those that are left, the student can choose largely on the

basis of connotation, since the denotations are very close. That
is, she can choose the term that _implies_ what she wishes about
the relationship. The class may enjoy discussing the connotative
difference between introducing the fellow as, for instance, "my
young man" and "my flame" or "the guy I'm hanging around with."
Will "young man" imply a more formal relationship with honorable
intentions? Will "hanging around" alarm grandma by its hint of
looseness, or will it reassure her by suggesting that nothing
serious is afoot?

Another way to make the distinction clearer is to examine a
passage from Mary's essay (p. 151), where religious connotation
is very important. You could, for instance, ask students to
select Mary's wording each time the following passage offers an
alternative:

> But the size of the pile is not the only
> status symbol among the Woodies. The (hierarchy,
> pecking order) within the group is based on an
> intricate balance between many variables. The
> obvious (symbolic, principal) object--the stove
> itself--is not nearly so important as evidence of
> an (awareness of, adherence to) Woodie (ideas,
> principles). . . . Woodie gatherings always
> involve the (revelation, disclosure) and/or
> (admission, confession) about last month's gas
> bill, and suggestions for how to improve stove
> efficiency.

Denotatively, one choice is roughly equivalent to another, but
because of Mary's purpose of gentle ridicule, she consistently
chooses the word with religious connotations.

THREE QUALITIES OF GOOD DICTION

APPROPRIATENESS

The purpose of this section is not, of course, to encourage
students to adopt a false formality when they write for college
classes ("A good party is characterized by a congenial atmosphere
which is conducive to intimate interpersonal relationships").
Instead, it encourages them to consider the range of diction the
language offers and to judge the level of formality appropriate
to their subject, audience, and purpose. I also like to remind
my students that appropriateness of diction is a matter of truth
to oneself. One of Rod's revisions in Chapter 4 illustrates this
point very well. He decided that "bummer," "lousy," and "stuff"
didn't belong in his essay because they made him sound like he
was "still in high school" (p.138). He realized that he had
chosen words that made him sound like a caricature of himself:
Rod as the Holden Caulfield of the 1980s. Students more often go
to the other extreme, choosing words that make them sound as if
they died some years ago in a subcommittee meeting. One way to
help students avoid such inappropriate diction is to have them

read their papers aloud in small groups. Another is to have them
evaluate each others' essays by answering the question, "If you
had to judge from word choice alone, what sort of person would
you imagine the author to be?"

Discussion Problem 1 (pp.275-276)

The speaker here seems to be speaking urgently, naturally,
and convincingly. His diction is colloquial, unlearned, and in
the context, very effective. If we attempt some superficial
corrections, we will produce a speech as zany as Eliza
Doolittle's:

> One time I perceived a fly that was trapped in
> a spider's gossamer and observed its suffering.
> These people that have been telling lies to frame
> me are going to suffer like that fly did. They
> are going to recline wakefully at night worrying
> about it and it is going to be with them at morn.
> Their quotidian experience is going to be wondering
> when they are going to be framed, or their
> progeny, or their friends and neighbors. On the
> Last Day they are going to face Him with it, and
> I'm going to have an immaculate heart, because I
> have done no malfeasance.

This exercise should help your thesaurus-wielding students see
the danger of adopting a diction too far from their natural
voice.

Discussion Problem 2 (p. 276)

In the revision below, I've crossed out excessively informal
words and replaced them with more appropriate ones. Not every
case is clear-cut, of course. I've underlined words that might
be eliminated by some writers and kept others. Discussions of
these marginal cases give you an opportunity to remind your
students that appropriate diction need not be perfectly predictable and toothless. Even the most impeccably tailored writer may
occasionally loosen a collar button and say that a politician has
been hoodwinked.

One serious ~~rap~~ charge that has been made against pressure

groups is that they wield power without corresponding responsi-

bility. Because they do not have to stand the test of power by

winning elections, they are able to make ~~beefed-up~~ exaggerated claims about

the ~~clout~~ influence the people they represent give them. If these claims

are made confidently, timid members of Congress are likely to

be impressed. Some people think that this susceptibility of
                                        deceived
politicians to being ~~hoodwinked~~ is increased by the failure of

great political parties to support their members against the

pressure groups. Others feel that Congress itself is too
lenient toward
~~wishy-washy-about~~ propagandists. Whatever the cause, the ir-
                                    abuses
responsibility of pressure groups has fostered ~~ripoffs~~ that dis-
                                        educate
tort their legitimate function to ~~tip-off~~ legislators concerning

public policy.

SPECIFICITY

     No advice is more commonly given to student writers than
that they should use definite, specific, concrete language. Of
course, no advice could be worded more vaguely, generally, and
abstractly than that. Writing With a Purpose makes the advice
more specific by a set of good exercises, and you can help your
students still more by praising as often as possible their own
use of specific language. At the same time, you should remind
them that specificity is good only when it serves a purpose. The
Laurie Lee passage cited in Exercise 1, pp. 280-281, for instance,
would not be better if Lee had stopped to tell us when the pump
was made, how many square feet of tile were laid in the scullery,
where the jug was bought, and what muscles are engaged when you
make a mouth like a fish. Lee's purpose is to show an encounter
with well water in its elemental purity. His account is specific,
but it is not cluttered with details irrelevant to his purpose.

Exercise (p. 278)

1.   athlete, football player, quarterback, Joe Montana

2.   animal, quadruped, dog, bird dog, Labrador retriever

3.   TV newsman, member of the CBS news staff, anchor man, Dan
     Rather

4.   politician, legislator, senator, Senator Edward Kennedy

5.   vacation spot, West Indies, U.S. Virgin Islands, St. John
     Island

6.   plant, bush, decorative bush, rosebush, Tropicana rosebush

7.   criminal, thief, pickpocket, the man who stole my wallet

DICTION: THE CHOICE OF WORDS

Exercise 1 (p. 280)

Your students will very likely pick out the following words
and phrases: <u>green crawling scum</u>, <u>blue gulps</u>, <u>sparkling like
liquid sky</u>, <u>quivering in a jug</u>, <u>work your mouth like a fish</u>.
They may be less likely to see some more subtle examples of
concrete diction. Lee's verbs are particularly good: he doesn't
work the pump handle, he <u>swings on</u> it; the water doesn't go onto
the floor, it <u>breaks and runs</u>; he doesn't cover the water with
soap, he <u>froths</u> it with soap; the sides of the bucket don't seem
distorted, they <u>buckle</u>; and his breath doesn't seem loud, it
<u>roars</u>. Clearly the writer observed before he wrote.

Exercise 2 (p. 281)

In the paragraphs about swimming, the right-hand version is
clearly more concrete. Compare the following expressions:

<u>in the past</u>	<u>forty years ago</u>
<u>girls in rural communities</u>	<u>farmer's daughters</u>
<u>some neighboring stream</u>	<u>the crick below the pasture</u>
<u>some discarded article of clothing</u>	<u>her brother's outgrown overalls</u>
<u>tailored to fit the occasion</u>	<u>trimmed with scissors as her discretion might suggest</u>

In the paragraphs about the snake, the left-hand version is
more concrete.

<u>the biceps of my right arm</u>	<u>my arm</u>
<u>(detailed description of the feel of the snake's movements</u>	<u>I felt the snake moving.</u> <u>I felt the contraction of its muscles.</u>
<u>a flat, V-shaped head, with two glistening, black protruding buttons</u>	<u>Its ugly head and evil-looking eyes</u>
<u>A thin, pointed, sickening yellow tongue slipped out, then in</u>	<u>its tongue kept moving in and out</u>
<u>a sound like that of escaping steam</u>	<u>a kind of hissing noise</u>

IMAGERY

Hardly anything strains the judgment of student writers more
than the use of figurative language. Many are tempted to use it
because they know it is somehow important to English teachers.
Others are aware of the spectacular effects good writers
sometimes get from metaphor, simile, and analogy. But as soon as
they begin to pursue figures of speech as ends in themselves,
their prose will suffer. They should be encouraged to look for
situations where a figure would be useful, but they should also
learn to be severe editors of their own imagery. Does the
metaphor (or simile, analogy, personification, or allusion)
clarify the subject? Does it suit the audience? Is it
consistent with the purpose? You might have your students
evaluate these figures of speech from student essays in Unit 1:

Before long, the book looked like a Disneyland mortuary.
(Wally, p. 30)

[Accurate and funny, consistent with Wally's purpose of
being simultaneously informative and amusing and with his
endearing habit of being amusing at his own expense.]

Resolved to compromise my pride for a buck, I began
gathering my paints, brushes and canvas with all the
enthusiasm of the only girl in the eighth grade not chosen
for the pompom squad. (p. 30)

[Not effective, I think. Wally's problem is not that he
has not been chosen, so his analogy to the eighth-grade
girl looks like a mere joke gotten off at someone else's
expense.]

Whenever I think of our trip, I think of that monument
standing in the middle of downtown Washington like a big
paperweight. (Rod, p. 131)

[A striking image, suggesting massiveness and serenity.]

The Washington momument, like the man it honors, is a
rugged individual. (Rod, p. 135)

[Not bad, but the comparison seems too simplistic when it
is so baldly stated.]

Woodies are a loosely organized, but highly principled and
dedicated cult whose members are not only stove owners,
but also true believers. (Mary, p. 148)

[An analogy Mary maintains effectively through her whole
paper.]

DICTION: THE CHOICE OF WORDS

Exercise 1 (pp. 287-288)

Obviously, different readers will be struck by different
images. Rather than attempt an exhaustive list, I'll try to
point out some qualities of the diction that can be clearly tied
to the author's purpose.

Saint Exupéry's purpose is simultaneously to explain a fact
of natural history and to express his sense of wonder about it.
He does this by building a contrast between two sets of images.
The wild ducks and geese are consistently linked with large,
primal forces of nature. They occasion a strange tide that
sweeps over vast territories. Their great triangular flight is
compared to a magnet that attracts the barnyard fowl so that they
leap a foot or two into the air and try to fly. This image of
the barnyard fowl is the first of several that shows the littleness
of their ordinary existence. Their hard little heads are filled
with images of pools and worms and barnyards. Excited by the
passing of the wild birds, the domestic duck can only totter to
the right and left in its wire enclosure. What makes the passage
memorable, of course, is the response of the domestic fowl
(humble fellows like ourselves) to the "sense of continental
expanse," the "sudden love whose object is a mystery." Notice
that in dealing with these exalted feelings, Saint Exupéry's
diction is not concrete, but the concreteness elsewhere in the
passage keeps the style from seeming spongy or vague.

The Rozin paragraph attempts considerably less. Its purpose
is to persuade us that strip mining is "terracide," murder on the
grand scale, and its images are accordingly harsh and nightmarish.
The dominant image is of the giant shovels like mythological
creatures, their girdered necks lifting massive steel mouths high
above the tallest trees. If I were discussing this paragraph in
class, I'd raise the issue of audience. By making the mining
equipment into a mythological monster operated by the mysterious
they who also "cut, blast, and rip apart mountains," is he being
too partisan to persuade a neutral audience? Is he preaching to
the converted?

Just as the Saint Exupéry passage presents a metaphor for
human aspiration, the Golding passage presents a metaphor for a
destructive passion in the boys' psyche. I don't think, though,
that you need import such literary ideas into your discussion.
Within Golding's large literary purpose is the subordinate one of
describing a fire's progress from a small, beautiful thing to
something large, destructive, and terrifying. Thus the fire
starts as a flash of fire at the root of one wisp [of smoke].
Flames stir and crawl away. Grown slightly larger and more
active, but not yet frightening, one flame scrambles up [a trunk]
like a bright squirrel. This image of the squirrel is sustained
brilliantly for several sentences, but soon gives way to more
frightening images as the fire begins to gnaw at the whole
forest. We see acres of black and yellow smoke, a particularly
striking phrase because it makes the smoke seem so solid, so
different from the earlier wisps. The flames now creep like a

<u>jaguar</u>. And so the imagery builds, growing larger and more sinister until the final sentence when the noises of the fires merge <u>into a drum-roll that seemed to shake the mountain</u>.

Exercise 2 (p. 288)

The version on the left obviously gives the clearer picture of the tavern. The difference in quality shows most clearly in the different descriptions of the lighting. In the right-hand version, we don't learn that the electric bulbs are suspended, and so we don't know why the shadows move when the door is opened. In the left-hand version this mystery is solved, and we learn that the lighting is uneven and that the shadows <u>swing eerily</u> in the draft. The verb is precise and the adverb contributes to the effect.

Additional bits of concrete detail in the left-hand version are the type of stove (potbellied, woodburning) and the type of drink (beer). We also learn that the talk is local gossip and that the people around the stove are regular customers.

REVISING DICTION

ELIMINATING VAGUENESS

Exercise (pp. 290-291)

1. He is a doctor, but I don't know what his <u>specialty</u> is.

2. Our <u>sorority</u> is opposed to Brenda Ames for student president.

3. It was a <u>successful</u> party--<u>congenial</u> people, <u>exotic</u> food, and <u>hilarious</u> conversation.

4. What a <u>pleasant</u> surprise to meet so many <u>natural food enthusiasts</u> at the same <u>ham supper</u>.

5. The actors gave a <u>gripping</u> performance.

6. The judge said that the <u>argument</u> was <u>murky and convoluted</u> but that she would take it under advisement.

7. Mother is <u>complaining</u> about Jean's moving into her own apartment; she is really <u>angry</u> about it.

8. One <u>disadvantage</u> of the <u>merger plan</u> is its effect on prices.

9. I thought that the new TV series was <u>witty</u> but it got <u>very low</u> ratings.

10. The price they are charging for steak is <u>the highest in town</u>.

DICTION: THE CHOICE OF WORDS

Exercise (p. 291-292)

The more specific choices are underlined in the following
version of the paragraph:

> The whole surface of the ice was <u>a chaos</u> of
> movement. It looked like an enormous <u>jigsaw</u>
> <u>puzzle</u> stretching away to infinity and being
> <u>crunched</u> together by some invisible but irresis-
> tible force. The impression of its <u>titanic</u> power
> was heightened by the unhurried deliberateness of
> the motion. Whenever two thick <u>floes</u> came
> together, their edges <u>butted</u> and <u>ground</u> against
> one another for a time. Then, when neither of
> them showed signs of yielding, they rose <u>quiver-</u>
> <u>ingly</u>, driven by the <u>implacable</u> power behind
> them. Sometimes they would stop <u>abruptly</u> as the
> unseen forces affecting the ice appeared mysteri-
> ously to lose interest. More frequently, though,
> the two floes--often ten feet thick or more--
> would continue to rise, <u>tenting up</u> until one or
> both of them toppled over, creating a pressure
> ridge.

ELIMINATING JARGON

Exercise (p. 295)

The essential information in this jargon-laden passage
amounts to this:

> Sentence 1: One evening at work a fellow interested in
> weightlifting showed me a book called <u>Big Arms</u>, by Bob
> Hoffman.

> Sentence 2: I wasn't much interested in athletics, but I
> found the book surprisingly interesting.

> Sentence 3: It took me a while to realize how interesting
> it was.

> Sentence 4: The book got me so interested in weightlifting
> that I bought a weightlifting set. I work long hours,
> with little sleep and irregular meals. But I exercise in
> my free moments.

By combining sentences, we can produce this simplified revision:

> One evening at work a fellow interested in
> weightlifting showed me a book called <u>Big Arms</u>,
> by Bob Hoffman. I wasn't very interested in
> athletics, but after I'd read the book for a
> while, I found it surprisingly interesting--so

interesting, in fact, that I bought myself a
weightlifting set. Now, despite my working
hours, little sleep, and irregular meals, I work
out in my free moments.

ELIMINATING TRITENESS

I suppose that when computer editing programs like "Writer's
Workbench" become widespread, everyone writing on a word processor
will be able to push a button and have all the clichés appear on
the screen, flashing and begging for removal. Some students and,
I'm afraid, some teachers take the computer's view that every
cliché is a plain error. But good writers occasionally use
clichés to add a colloquial touch. I notice that Garrison
Keillor rounds a corner, that Louise Bogan's house is cold as a
tomb, that Lorenz's goose falls head over heels in love, that
Auden is concerned about poor Mother Earth, that Baker's scientists are struck by the fact, and Ellen Goodman discusses various
and sundry statistics. Writers on style will consistently object
that clichés are "stale," "threadbare," "shopworn," "flyblown,"
or "hackneyed"--thus attacking cliche with cliché. If you tell
your students that clichés must always be voiced, you will be
setting an impossible standard and a useless one. As Writing
With a Purpose points out, triteness comes from a writer's
insensitivity to the overused phrase. Your job is really to make
your students more sensitive to the cliché and more wary of it.

Discussion Problem (p. 297)

The football passage is as trite in its content as it is in
its expression. Since it provides no new insight, it cannot be
made fresh by a trick of rephrasing. The following revision is
merely less offensive:

Wherever American men play football--on a
sandlot, on a high school field, or in a college
or professional stadium, they learn that they can
win only through cooperation. They remember this
lesson when they leave the field. In society,
former players are not renegades, but responsible
citizens, reliable husbands, and loyal employees.

This version is 53 words long, the original 244.

DICTION: THE CHOICE OF WORDS

ELIMINATING INEFFECTIVE IMAGERY

Exercise (p. 299)

1.   Students surged into the corridor.

      or

      Students crowded the corridor.

2.   You have been selected for this program so that we can make
      our best people still better.

3.   The defense attorney said she thought the truth would emerge
      during the trial.

4.   The president's ill-advised action has derailed national
      policy, and unless Republicans and Democrats in Congress
      work together, it may take months to get it back on the
      tracks.

      or

      The president's ill-advised action has damaged national
      policy, and unless the members of Congress ignore party
      lines and work together, it may take months to repair the
      damage.

5.   Some of the things those people say just make my hair stand
      on end. (A cliché, of course.)

      or

      . . . make my flesh crawl. (Another cliché.)

      or

      . . . frighten me.

CHAPTER 9 TONE AND STYLE

Style is partly a question of technical proficiency, but mostly it is a question of judgment. One problem I encounter in teaching style is that very bright students sometimes become so intrigued with the technical aspect that their judgment is overwhelmed. I remember one year, for instance, when my class analyzed the technical virtuosity that underlies some very moving passages from Martin Luther King's "Letter from a Birmingham Jail." We talked about the network of classical and biblical allusions that elevates the essay, the frequently metaphorical language, the antitheses and alliterations, the uses of parallelism and repetition to heighten emotional impact. We examined the very long periodic sentence that accumulates shocking examples of the abuse blacks have suffered at the hands of their white neighbors and ends, ". . . then you will understand why we find it difficult to wait." Some of my best students were entranced and moved by the essay. King had made them feel the grandeur and pathos that underlies human affairs, and they wanted to express that feeling of grandeur by emulating his style. In a sense, they did well, but I hardly knew how to comment on sentences like these:

> When the grave is dug, when its sides are smoothed
> and its corners precisely chiseled with a sharpened
> spade, when the dog's body is carefully laid in
> the walnut coffin, arranged in a comfortable
> sleeping position, groomed for eternity, then my
> work is done.

> Just as the ancient Greeks strove for arếtế,
> which we may translate as excellence in all
> things, so the campus police strive for ideal
> order in campus parking policy.

I now try to anticipate the problem of star-struck students by prefacing every discussion of style with warnings about excess. No one has delivered such a warning more clearly than E. B. White in The Elements of Style:

> Write in a way that draws the reader's attention
> to the sense and substance of the writing rather
> than to the mood and temper of the author. If
> the writing is solid and good, the mood and
> temper of the writer will eventually be revealed,

and not at the expense of the work. Therefore,
the first piece of advice is this: to achieve
style, begin by affecting none--that is, place
yourself in the background. A careful and honest
writer does not need to worry about style. As he
becomes proficient in the use of language, his
style will emerge, because he himself will
emerge, and when this happens he will find it
increasingly easy to break through the barriers
that separate him from other minds, other hearts--
which is, of course, the purpose of writing, as
well as its principal reward.

George Orwell is even more severe in "Why I Write": " . . .it is
also true that one can write nothing readable unless one constantly struggles to efface one's own personality. Good prose is like
a windowpane."

If we took the White/Orwell position to its logical extreme, we would abandon the teaching of style altogether and
would simply wait for it to emerge. But we all know that styles
don't grow entirely of internal necessity, like bones. They are
reached out for, admired, analyzed, imitated, altered, and
finally so digested that they don't seem affected. Orwell admits
that his style was formed on literary models before it was
sharpened by political purpose, and White's "A Slight Sound at
Evening" begins with his middle-aged reflection on how powerfully
Walden affects young people with sensitivities like young E. B.
White's.

I suppose that the best advice a writing teacher can give
to students is to learn to read for style. They should develop a
conscious appreciation of the good stylist and practice imitating
styles they particularly admire until they are internalized and
transformed into something that seems natural. But they should
not imagine that good writers think obsessively about style, any
more than good tennis players think obsessively about the position
of their feet. Both of them are alert to the game that is being
played. The writer's question is not so much whether the style
is good in itself, as whether it is consistent with the subject,
audience, and purpose.

TONE

Mastering the vocabulary of style and tone is a step toward
developing a fully conscious appreciation of them. This section
is devoted largely to familiarizing students with the labels that
can help them analyze a writer's attitude toward subject and
audience. Most of your students will have encountered tone in
literature classes and may remember talking about ironic tones,
amused tones, tones of awe, and so on. By starting with the
distinction between affective and informative tone, the chapter
reminds such students that the writer needn't plunge into one
emotional state or another,but will make an initial decision

about how objective or subjective to be. Some students find the
concept of distance is elusive, but it is a useful analytic tool
and is clearly explained in the text.

INFORMATIVENESS AND AFFECTIVENESS

Exercise (pp. 305-307)

The passages presented in this exercise are not purely
informative or affective. Had the authors wanted to present
extreme cases, they might have chosen an encyclopedia entry to
represent one extreme and a curse to represent the other. The
chosen passages lie somewhere in the broad middle of the spectrum,
as will most of the writing students will be asked to do. In
your discussion, you'll want to emphasize the mixture of informative and affective language in each passage, but do point out
that they can be ranked relative to one another with tolerable
accuracy.

The White passage (#2) is the middle case. Your students
can see how thoroughly mixed the tone is if they will compare the
second sentence ("Every time the residents brush their teeth,
millions of gallons of water must be drawn from the Catskills and
the hills of Westchester ") with the last, with its nightmarish
picture of New Yorkers in their "cells" enveloped by a "fearful
pall" of fog that leaves men "groping and depressed, and the
sense of the world's end." The first of these sentences presents
a fact that is impressive enough in itself and is consistent with
the author's purpose of portraying the city as a megalopolis of
inhuman proportions, but the language is objective. He doesn't
choose his words or construct his sentence to heighten the
emotional impact of the fact. In the final sentence, on the
other hand, he arranges his images to prepare for a powerful
conclusion ("the sense of the world's end") and consistently
chooses words with strong connotations of gloom and unhappiness.
Throughout the passage, White balances information and affect,
but on close examination, we can see that the passage starts out
a bit more informational and ends up a bit more affective.

The Hansberry passage (#3) shows no such gradation: it is
more affective than informational throughout. Some of its
emotional impact comes from its syntax, a piling up of tribula-
tions stated in parallel clauses (I have . . . ., I have been . . . .,
I have worked . . . ., I see daily . . . ., etc.).
Largely, though, it comes from highly connotative diction:
lynching, victim of physical attack, racial and political
hysteria, ravages of congenital diseases, afflicted, greed and
malice, indifference to human misery, ignorance, feeling heart,
miseries which afflict the world.

The Conner passage (#1) is particularly interesting and
may provoke the most discussion. On the one hand, it appears to
be objective, reporting almost clinically the details of the
church's construction ("thirty inches from the ground") and the

behavior of hogs and fleas. But there is no doubt that Conner
finds the scene he is painting amusing and that he expects his
readers to see the humor of it. A few word choices give his
attitude away: "an <u>argument</u> among the members of the hog <u>family</u>,"
"a <u>prim</u> young lady . . . could not reach handily under many
layers of long skirts to <u>get at</u> the flea." Conner dignifies his
hogs and deflates the pretensions of his humans in these passages,
but fundamentally he lets the situation speak for itself. He
<u>assumes</u> an objective tone; he keeps a poker face.

DISTANCE

The text's discussion of distance is very clear, but you
might want an extra example to illustrate this rather abstract
concept. You can find an excellent one in Chapter 4. Rod,
you'll remember, found his third draft <u>too distant:</u> "One of my
problems is that I sound like a tour guide—a dull one." In the
fourth draft, he strives for familiarity and achieves it. In
fact, in his revision agenda he wonders if he has gone a bit too
far in one respect: "I am still not sure about the way I talk
about 'Old George.' It may offend some of my readers." You
might have your students compare the parallel passages below and
say why one seems more affective and close, the other more
informational and distant. I have underlined some words.

> In 1783, the Continental Congress voted to erect
> a bronze equestrian statue <u>depicting the father</u>
> <u>of our country</u> in Roman garb. This idea was not
> mentioned again until 1799, when Congress decided
> that a <u>pyramid-type mausoleum might be more</u>
> <u>appropriate.</u> . . .Senator Henry Clay of Kentucky
> <u>revived</u> the notion in 1832 and <u>managed to allocate</u>
> money for a twenty-ton statue of a toga-clad
> Washington, but this half-naked sculpture did not
> satisfy <u>a group of local citizens.</u> (pp. 137-138)

> <u>It all began</u> in 1783 when the Continental Con-
> gress voted to erect a bronze equestrian statue
> of <u>George</u> dressed in Roman garb, wielding a
> spear. Sixteen years later, Congress decided
> <u>George</u> might <u>look better as a pyramid.</u> Three
> decades later <u>somebody</u> thought <u>George looked best</u>
> dressed in a toga. This last idea was actually
> turned into a twenty-ton statue. But <u>George</u>
> <u>looked a little cold</u> in his toga. Not satisfied
> with a half-naked George, the <u>good people</u> of
> Washington . . . (pp.141-142)

CHAPTER 9

STYLE

STYLE DEFINED

On problems with the definition of style, see the comments at the beginning of the chapter. The Twain passage is funnier, of course, if you read it in conjunction with Emmeline Grangerford's poem, which is a wonderful example of _affecting_ a style rather than writing from conviction.

Ode to Stephen Dowling Bots, Dec'd

And did young Stephen sicken,
    And did young Stephen die?
And did the sad hearts thicken,
    And did the mourners cry?

No; such was not the fate of
    Young Stephen Dowling Bots;
Though sad hearts round him thickened,
    'Twas not from sickness' shots.

No whooping-cough did rack his frame,
    Nor measles drear with spots;
Not these impaired the sacred name
    Of Stephen Dowling Bots.

Despised love struck not with woe
    That head of curly knots,
Nor stomach trouble laid him low,
    Young Stephen Dowling Bots.

Oh no. Then list with tearful eye,
    Whilst I his fate do tell
His soul did from this cold world fly
    By falling down a well.

They got him out and emptied him;
    Alas it was too late;
His spirit was gone for to sport aloft
    In the realm of the good and the great.

LANGUAGE AND RANGE OF STYLES

At first glance the text's analysis of formal, moderate, and colloquial styles may appear unnecessarily complex, but I have found it very useful in improving students' ability to judge wisely in forming a style. The problems my students encountered after reading Martin Luther King, for instance, amounted to the failure to distinguish between a formal style appropriate only to grand subjects and a moderate style appropriate to their own subjects.

Most students are simply unaware that there is a moderate style. Their teachers have too often suggested that styles divide into the formal and colloquial, and have urged one or the other. "Do not use contractions; they are unacceptable in formal writing," one of my teachers used to say. I never had her liberal counterpart, but I know he exists because he has urged several of my students to "loosen up, man, and just write like you talk." The text carefully delineates the three styles and points out that although none is inherently superior to another, the moderate style is best for most situations. The chart on p. 317 makes the tripartite division very clear.

One way to reinforce the distinction between the colloquial and formal styles and at the same time discourage inappropriate formality is to have your students translate the Mark Twain passage on p. 310 into a ludicrously formal style and then read out a few examples in class. Here is an example written in a voice too familiar to those who read scholarly journals:

> Since Miss Grangerford could produce such admirable work at the tender age of fourteen, she certainly seemed destined to take her place among our poetic immortals. Mr. Buck Grangerford has pointed out the remarkable fluidity of her composition, which seemed to spring to her pen unbidden by the conscious mind. He tells us that she would rapidly compose a line, and if she could discover no corresponding rhyme, just as quickly expunge it, draft another, and reenter the torrent of her verse. She was remarkably versatile; she could compose on almost any subject within the province of the mournful muse. On the death of any man, woman, or child she would compose an extempore "tribute" (for so she named these funerary verses) before the blood had cooled in the lifeless veins. It was said by her neighbors that she had her natural place in the last act of the human drama, seconding the physician and anticipating the mortician. Only once did the funeral director have to do his office without her having prepared the way: when she reached an impasse trying to find a true rhyme for a departed neighbor named Whistler. From this failure she never fully recovered, and though she never complained, her strength flagged, and she sank into her grave.

Exercise (pp. 316-318)

If you look carefully at the scale on p. 316, you'll see that point #3 is about midway between the formal and the colloquial, and that the other points are toward the formal end. I'd begin my discussion by asking which passage corresponds to point

#3--which is most colloquial, though not nearly as colloquial as the passage from Huckleberry Finn.

Most students will correctly choose the second example--by Greenbaum and Schmerl. It is clearly the least distant passage, and the diction is sometimes very colloquial: kids, lowdown, jocks, john. Six of the eight sentences are fragments. But it is not a strictly colloquial passage. The diction is sometimes more learned and abstract: aversion, assimilate, entrusted. And the last sentence is twenty-nine words long and fairly complex in its structure.

Point #2 belongs to the first example--by Boulding. There are no fragments here and no colloquial words. But the sentences are fairly short, an average of fifteen words each, and the diction is rarely learned (only "implication of validity" stands out). As in the Greenbaum and Schmerl example, the reader is addressed as "you," but here the distance between reader and writer is somewhat greater.

The Churchill passage, from a speech delivered to Parliament while Europe was falling to the Nazis, is obviously the most formal. Its nine sentences average thirty-four words each. The sixth sentence ("Even though large tracts . . .") is clearly periodic, but is not the most spectacular in the passage. The first sentence is periodic in its effect, though it is so grammatically complex that we would have to call it loosely periodic. It is full of parallel structures: the opening if clauses and the infinitives (to defend, to ride out, to outlive) being the most conspicuous. The long last sentence begins with one of the most famous parallel constructions in the language ("We shall fight on the beaches, we shall fight on the landing grounds . . .") The language is not learned, but is dignified, and though the passage is very affective, there is a great distance between speaker and listener. This is not a friend talking to friends, but a leader addressing a nation.

SOME PRACTICAL ADVICE ABOUT STYLE

This section doesn't add new information to the chapter, but distills what has gone before into six precepts, each with its brief explanation. Precepts about style are odd things. In one way, they seem perfectly useless. If students have inconsistent styles, after all, it isn't because they are unacquainted with the precept, "Keep your style consistent." It is because they don't notice the inconsistencies they create. But my experience tells me that precepts reinforced often enough gain force and begin to form a writer's judgment. I have spent the last decade chewing over E. B. White's advice to "Put yourself in the background" and "Prefer the standard to the offbeat," and now I am beginning to see what he means and to benefit by his advice. I would, therefore, direct my students' attention to these six precepts as often as possible in commenting on their own essays or professional examples. I would also urge them to consult the

Guidelines for Revising Your Style when they are preparing final drafts of papers. The six categories in the guidelines offer a capsule version of much of the instruction in preceding chapters.

Review Exercise (pp. 324-327)

1.   Baker's essay raises two objections against restorationism. The easier one to see is its impracticality, mentioned late in the essay: "It is a magnificent street to photograph but, because of the cobblestones, a terrible street to walk or drive on." Your students can hardly miss this point. His second objection is aesthetic and more implicit than explicit--that restoration is phony. Baker never calls a restorationist street lamp a replica or even an imitation, it is an "electrified fake gas street lamp." He never acknowledges the possibility that restoration may be the product of genuine historical interest. It is a money-making scheme plotted by local merchants who are willing to stand "in public places stirring boiling vats of candle wax for tourist snapshots" if only it will boost their sales of "wassail cups" and "yule logs." The tourists who support the restoration are not seekers after their roots, but novelty hunters for whom chic and nostalgic are flip sides of the same coin.

In effect, Baker is raising the same objections to the style of the restoration boom that Twain (as opposed to Huck) raised against poetry in the Emmeline Grangerford manner. Just as her "tribute" is phony mourning for a boy Emmeline didn't even know, restorationism is nostalgia for an era no one actually remembers or cares about. Like her stylized, stilted, deliberately antiquated diction ("No whooping cough did rack his frame/Nor measles drear with spots"), it is froth posing as substance.

Of course, there are things to be said in defense of the restoration boom. We are a nation in constant danger of forgetting its past, a nation in which the Gettysburg battlefield can barely be defended against encroaching shopping malls. It's worth pointing out the other side of the issue, if only to show your students how personal and controversial Baker's stand is.

2.   Analyses according to guidelines:

Guideline 1: What is the general impression of Baker's writing?

Baker's writing is uncluttered and about as clear as Orwell's windowpane. You can help your students see these virtues by drawing their attention to the first sentence, which says in eighteen words all the following things:

I visit Nantucket occasionally.

I was not surprised on my last visit to find that the restorationists were cobblestoning the streets.

I wasn't very happy about it, though.

I regard all this restoration business as a sort of disease.

I'm about to write an amusing essay about the situation.

The student who has learned to read for style should recognize such a sentence as the stylistic equivalent of the professional basketball player's effortless and astonishing fade-away jump shot.

Guideline 2: What tone has he established in his writing?

Clearly Baker's tone is affective: no one could mistake his attitude of amused disapproval. The distance between reader and writer is, I think, middling. It is certainly less than that in the Churchill passage (p. 318), and I think it is less than that in the Boulding passage (p. 316). Baker is not writing as a leader or a teacher, but as a fellow citizen who assumes that he and his readers have similar experiences and sensibilities. On the other hand, the tone is clearly more distant than that of the Paul Roberts passage (p. 308), which practically sticks its elbow in the reader's ribs. No one could be offended by its familiarity.

Guideline 3: How can we characterize the overall style of his writing?

Here is an essay in the moderate style. Look at the sentences that should logically be most colloquial--those in the conversation with Crowley--and you'll find that they don't sound very much like unedited speech, even the unedited speech of the very literate. On the other hand, the nonconversational parts of the essay are not formal. Very few words could be called learned--rampant, perhaps, or megalopolis, or precursor. Most are popular.

Guideline 4: Do his paragraphs work together to convey a sense of order and substance?

Some of your students will think that Baker fails to develop his paragraphs into large enough blocks of meaning to guide the reader along. Remind them that the essay originally appeared in the narrow columns of a newspaper, where paragraphs must be short to appeal to the eye. If we eliminate merely cosmetic paragraph breaks after "smoke of nostalgia" (paragraph 9), "handsome houses" (paragraph 11), "the tourists" (12), "with them" (14), "a reservation" (15), "isn't underwear" (16), and "for good reason" (18), we can re-form the essay into its natural topical paragraphs. Now the order of the paper is apparent. We have

an introductory hook (or two) in the engaging first paragraph and supposed conversation,

information about the location of Nantucket and its touristy nature (our first re-formed paragraph),

analysis of the Nantucketers' public-relations reasoning for
renovation (second re-formed paragraph),

analysis of the actual desires of tourists (third re-formed
paragraph),

a concluding paragraph that returns us to Crowley and his knee
britches.

Guideline 5: Are his sentences well constructed and easy to
read?

Baker has that easy range of sentence types and lengths one
expects from a professional. We get a few very short sentences:
"I cautioned my friend Crowley" and "I had seen these plagues
before." Occasionally we get a longer and more complex sentence
like the thirty-six worder that begins "Heavily dependent on
tourism . . .." An occasional sentence is highly wrought: "a
magnificent street . . ., a terrible street. . ., an agonizing
street. . .." is an impressive bit of parallelism. But most of
the sentences are standard, and all are easy to read.

Guideline 6: Have I used words as effectively as possible?

In one way, Baker's diction here is much like Mary's in
"Burn Again" (pp. 148-152). Early in her essay, Mary establishes
a parallel between the Woodie and the religious convert, and she
chooses words throughout her essay for their religious connotations. Here Baker establishes a comparison between restorationism
and disease and chooses his words accordingly. There is an
"outbreak of cobblestones," a "telltale rash" of street lamps, a
"raging epidemic" of quaintness. The "onset" of lamps is a "bad
sign." "In the worst cases," the inhabitants find themselves in
knee britches. Sometimes this medical connotation is more
subtle. Your students may not notice "the fever for chic" or
Baker's "diagnosis" of Nantucket's "ailment." Lest the gag
become tiresome, he drops the metaphor in the last parts of the
body of the essay, but he returns to it in the conclusion. Less
skilled writers paying such elaborate attention to connotation
will wander into denotative difficulties. Baker is very
sure-footed.

CHAPTER 10 PERSUASION

Persuasion papers can be frustrating for both students and teachers because they demand all the skills discussed in the previous chapters--especially those elusive ones presented in the chapter on tone and style--plus new skills of reasoning and emotional appeal. And even the most skillful persuasive writing is rarely an unqualified success. The paper that strives for seamless logic is too slow-moving and dull for some readers. The paper that persuades John by its emotional appeal strikes Jonathan as maudlin. Working in such murky waters discourages students who think of the persuasive paper as a logical or emotional steamroller that can flatten the resistance of any reader. Writing With a Purpose clarifies the situation by defining persuasion as "changing the reader's image" of the thing discussed. This flexible definition can give students a realistic gauge of success. S. I. Hayakawa has "changed the image" of readers who say, after reading his statement on pp. 363-365, "I still don't buy Hayakawa's general attitude toward welfare, but I can see that excessive welfare would create the same difficulties as an all-A grading system."

The teaching of persuasion inevitably involves the class in discussions of manipulation, which is persuasion's shirt-tail relative, never quite disowned. The liberally educated person, as Cardinal Newman noted long ago, should be able to disentangle the skein of a specious argument and examine it thread by thread. Teaching students to detect the defective threads of an argument and the hidden manipulations of an ad serves a larger purpose than helping them improve their performance on the next essay.

CHANGING THE READER'S IMAGE

The discussion of shallow and deep-rooted images can help sensitize your students to the limits of the persuader's powers and the futility of trying to take a deeply hostile audience by storm. Students should certainly reread it before they commit themselves to a topic like abortion or prayer in school.

FITTING PERSUASION TO THE AUDIENCE

I like to spend a few minutes in class pointing out what
the text does _not_ say about analyzing the audience. It doesn't
encourage students to view their audience with the cheap cynicism
of some advertisers. It doesn't encourage them to form erroneous
and degrading theories about the audience: "You can always
persuade blue-collar workers by wrapping yourself in the flag";
"Tell a woman she's not liberated unless she accepts your view
and you'll win every time." In fact, the text warns students
that such tactics won't work. I would particularly point out
guideline 2, with its statement that "identification with the
reader is not a trick," and guideline 3, with its warning that
you can't talk down to your audience.

MEANS OF PERSUASION

Exercise (pp. 337-338)

The rigidly correct answer is, of course, that Mencken is
so preoccupied with his name calling that his reader will dismiss
the description of Bryan as unfair. Such terms as charlatan,
mountebank, zany, poor clod, childish, and pathological slung at
Bryan do damage Mencken's credibility. Even more damaging, I
think, is his tendency to use such terms as peasant and common
man almost synonymously with ignoramuses and half-wits. Many
people who would not be offended by unfairness to Bryan must be
offended by the undemocratic tone of these comments. Still, I
can't let the passage go by without saying a word in its behalf.
Although it is too slanted to be a model of persuasion, it has
such vigor and interest that it may well "change the reader's
image" of Bryan. Students who are introduced to Bryan by this
passage will certainly form an image of him that only more solid,
careful persuasion can change.

Discussion Problem (pp 339-343)

One good way to encourage thoughtful discussion of this
article is to ask your students how it would affect the image of
the housewife held by four readers:

1. A dedicated feminist

2. A married woman interested in women's rights and roles, but
    without fixed views.

3. A "male chauvinist"

4. A man who divides the housework evenly with his wife and is
    supporting her while she goes through graduate school

Reader 1 will perhaps approve of the article and believe that it
portrays an all too typical husband/wife relationship, but the

article will not change her image; it will only confirm it.
Reader 2 may react in any number of ways to the article. She may
feel that the portrayal of the husband/wife relationship is a
grotesque exaggeration and dismiss the article from her mind, or
she may begin to see her marriage in terms of the sort of subjuga-
tion the article describes. It could change her image. Reader
3, if he is at all bright, will see what the article is driving
at, but will dismiss the charges as unfair. Reader 4 will very
likely be offended by the article, thinking that it unfairly
gives husbands a black eye and may begin to wonder if he should
withdraw his support of the feminist who is running for city
council. Discussing the article in such terms can reinforce the
text's discussion of fitting the persuasion to the audience. It
was, of course, first published in Ms., which reader 3 was not
likely to see.

Exercise (p. 345)

The first set of sentences about final examinations is not an
argument. The second presents a premise followed by a
conclusion.

The first set of sentences about John Jones is a conclusion
followed by a premise. The second set is not an argument.

The first set of sentences about "no woman" is not an argument.
The second is a conclusion followed by a premise.

The first set of sentences about students is a conclusion followed
by a premise. The second set is not an argument.

Discussion Problem (p. 348)

Conclusion   The Volkswagen is better than a mule because

Premise 1   the VW better withstands extreme cold

Premise 2   fuel for the VW is cheaper than feed for the
                mule

Premise 3   the VW is less likely to get stuck in the mud

Premise 4   the VW doesn't need shelter

Premise 5   the VW is easier to repair than the mule

Exercise (p. 349)

1.

Conclusion   In practice we are not able to define heredity
                or environment with precision.

Main premise	We are not able to define <u>heredity</u> except in terms of characteristics that may have been influenced by environment.
Subpremise	Some inherited characteristics of fruit flies appear only when the environment encourages their appearance.
Subpremise	An acorn will never grow into anything but an oak tree, but whether it becomes an oak tree depends on environmental conditions.
Main premise	The environment of individuals in a society is so complex that we cannot define it precisely.

2.

Conclusion	We cannot study heredity or environment apart from each other.
Main premise	We cannot do this with newborn babies.
Subpremise	Newborn babies have had nine months of prenatal environment.
Main premise	We cannot do it with fraternal twins.
Subpremise	A boy twin has a different environment from that of a girl twin.
Main premise	We cannot do it with identical twins.
Subpremise	Identical twins come from the same egg and thus have the same inheritance, but we cannot be sure that they have had the same environment while growing up.

3.

Thesis: It is not possible to define or study heredity or environment apart from each other (combination of conclusions from 1 and 2).

I. In practice we are not able to define <u>heredity</u> or <u>environment</u> with precision (first main premise for thesis, but also a conclusion from A and B below).

   A. We are not able to define <u>heredity</u> except as influenced by environment (first premise for I above, but also a conclusion for 1 and 2 below).

      1. Some inherited characteristics of fruit flies appear only when the environment encourages their appearance.

2. An acorn will never grow into anything but an oak
   tree, but whether it becomes an oak tree depends on
   environmental conditions.

B. The environment of individuals in a society is so
   complex that we cannot define it precisely.

II. We cannot study heredity and environment apart from each
other (second main premise for thesis, but also a conclusion
from A, B, and C below).

A. We cannot do this with newborn babies (first premise
   for II, but also a conclusion from 1 below).

    1. Newborn babies have had nine months of prenatal
       environment.

B. We cannot do it with fraternal twins (second premise
   for II, but also a conclusion from 1 below).

    1. A boy twin has a different environment from that
       of a girl twin.

C. We cannot do it with identical twins (third premise
   for II, but also a conclusion from 1 below).

    1. Identical twins come from the same egg and thus
       have the same inheritance, but we cannot be sure
       that they have had the same environment while
       growing up.

A few of your more rigid students may be alarmed that there
is only one subheading under the last three lettered entries. If
you think the point worth discussing, you can tell them that the
outline above violates the conventions in order to make the lines
of the argument clearer. The irregularity can be easily rectified
by reducing the offending arabic number entries to because
clauses attached to the lettered entries.

More productive for our present purposes than a quibble
about the conventions would be a discussion of the merits of the
argument. The subpremises at A-1 and A-2 in section I are both
weak: since only some of the fruit fly's inherited characteristics
require environmental encouragement, some must manifest
themselves without such encouragement; and the fact that an oak
can only grow to be an oak could be said to give us a definition
of heredity as the factor that sets the limits on environmental
influence. The whole of section II ignores the possibility of
studying newborn identical twins. II-B cannot be validly inferred
from II-B-1, since fraternal twins can be of the same sex. One
reason for outlining an argument is that it makes such weaknesses
apparent.

COMMON TYPES OF ARGUMENTS

Exercise (pp. 351-352)

1. Premise: The sound of <u>a</u> in <u>ale</u> may be spelled <u>ae</u> in <u>maelstrom</u>, <u>ai</u> in <u>bait</u>, <u>ay</u> in <u>day</u>, <u>e</u> and <u>ee</u> in <u>melee</u>, <u>ea</u> in <u>break</u>, <u>eigh</u> in <u>weigh</u>, <u>et</u> in <u>beret</u>.

   Conclusion: There is a tremendous lack of agreement between pronunciation and spelling in English.

   The premise is a statement of fact, the more forceful because every reader can verify it from personal experience. Some might object that <u>tremendous</u> is an incautious word, but we shouldn't become so wrapped up in the rigors of logical argument that we disallow all affective language.

2. Premise: The letter <u>a</u> has different pronunciations in <u>sane</u>, <u>chaotic</u>, <u>care</u>, <u>add</u>, <u>account</u>, <u>arm</u>, <u>ask</u>, and <u>sofa</u>.

   Conclusion: The same letter may be used for different sounds.

   The premise is a statement of fact and leads inevitably to the conclusion.

3. Premise: It is estimated that two-thirds of all the words in the Merriam-Webster unabridged dictionary have at least one silent letter.

   Conclusion: English is full of silent letters.

   The premise is a judgment. Because it is stated in passive voice, the reader doesn't know who made the judgment and ought to be suspicious of it. The writer should either identify the authority, assuming it is a valid one, or else produce some first-hand evidence: "On a random opening of the Merriam-Webster unabridged dictionary, I examined 100 words and discovered that 68 contained silent letters."

4. Premise: George Bernard Shaw, who in addition to being a great playwright was a powerful advocate of simplified spelling, repeatedly stated his opinion in the London <u>Times</u> that by adopting simplified spelling Britain could have saved enough money to pay the costs of World War II.

   Conclusion: The cost of typing, printing, and proofreading illogical spellings is high.

   The premise is based on testimony. Point out to your students how dubious Shaw's authority is here. Being a playwright certainly gives him no credentials as an economist or office efficiency expert. That he published the letter in the <u>Times</u> doesn't mean that the <u>Times</u> researched his claim and supported his view. In addition, Shaw was fond

of making provocative statements. Since the authority is
no authority, the reader is forced to speculate on the
economic effects of spelling reform and may begin to
wonder, for example, how much it would cost to re-educate
an entire nation of unsimplified spellers. If Shaw gave
some credible evidence and statistics, the writer should
cite them.

Exercises (pp. 354-357)

1. Some answers here are self-evident, others are disputable.
    A class discussion may help students discover how relatively
    cautious or bold they are in making generalizations.

2. This exercise deserves detailed discussion as a profession-
    ally written example of specious argument. A liberally
    educated person should be able to see its faults.

The Testimony of Authority

Dr, Egeberg's position in government makes him a formidable
authority, but we should look closely at what he actually says.
Although the writer is invoking his authority to strengthen an
argument about malpractice and maladministration, the Egeberg
quotation doesn't touch on these issues. It merely says that our
nation is "second-rate" in the distribution of health care.
Quite possibly Egeberg was talking about the need for more
research or more public funding of health care for the poor. The
writer may have quoted him out of context.

Statements of Fact

The most striking "facts" cited in the article are got at
secondhand from the nurse, whose credibility as a witness is
never established. We never hear, for instance, that she has
been cited for excellence in the performance of her duties or
that she is a head nurse with twenty years of experience, or even
that she is an RN. What we do know about her hardly adds weight
to her testimony. She is, as one of my students pointed out, an
untidy nurse who--probably despite regulations--risks her patients'
health by going to work with a cough. She is apparently low-paid
enough to want to sit in her little apartment getting back at
rich doctors by telling malicious stories to a writer, but
apparently not dutiful enough to report abuses to medical authorities. The student put the case rather strongly, but her argument
made the rest of the class read the article more carefully.

The writer's firsthand evidence is harder to discredit.
All the abuses listed on p. 356 are shocking. But Rapoport
doesn't tell us in which hospitals they occurred or when. Is
this to protect the identity of sources or to make public rebuttal
impossible? And several items on the list appear to be open to
different interpretations. For instance, The Merck Manual, a
standard medical reference book, warns physicians that in cases

of drug intoxication a live patient may stop breathing for up to
twelve hours, lose all reflex responses, not respond to noxious
stimulants like smelling salts, and have a flat EEG. My friends
in nursing tell me that the pulse is sometimes very hard to
detect in such cases. That Rapoport managed in his investigation
of dozens of hospitals to find "nurses who can't discriminate
between live and dead patients" may mean nothing.

The Typicality of the Cases Cited

Even given the most generous interpretations of the nurse's
motives, we can't imagine that she picked an average doctor to
talk about. She wanted to produce examples of outrageous behavior
and so naturally chose the most extreme case. Rapoport gives us
no reason to think that he visited his dozens of hospitals to
look objectively at the typical standard of treatment. In all
probability, he went looking for scandal and managed to find
some.

Orientals and Alcohol (pp. 360-361)

Though no discussion questions follow this passage, it is
worth examining critically. The central question is whether the
North Carolina investigators have created an experiment that
isolates genetic from environmental—particularly cultural—
factors. If one group is made up of <u>Americans</u> of European
extraction and another is made up of <u>Orientals</u> who are not native
Americans, but are, for instance, visiting students, then the
validity of the study is surely questionable. Wouldn't it be
likely in such circumstances that the Oriental subjects are
merely showing the effects of their cultural training about
alcohol? If the Orientals are second- or third-generation
Americans, the article should have noted this fact in reporting
the study.

Exercise (pp. 363-364)

Passage 1

This example certainly reinforces the text's warnings about
the difficulty of evaluating analogical argument. The alleged
similarities between impeachment and surgery are:

1.   They are both done to restore health rather than to punish
      (paragraph 1).

2.   They are both slow processes (paragraph 2).

3.   They both involve grave consequences if they are performed
      unnecessarily or omitted improperly (paragraph 3).

From these similarities, the writer shapes an argument for considering the impeachment deliberately and dispassionately.

The first similarity is, however, questionable, since impeachment is to some degree a punishment for "high crimes and misdemeanors." The second is irrelevant, since an argument that we should impeach slowly because impeachment is a slow process would be circular if it had any shape at all. The third similarity is persuasive.

That two-thirds of the analogy won't hold up under critical examination doesn't mean it is finally ineffective, of course. As the text points out early in the chapter, the purpose of persuasion is to change the reader's image, and this passage might cause a reader who has been inclined to see impeachment as a sort of vigilante justice to adopt a new "medical" image.

It might be useful at this point to remind your students that they have read two earlier essays that attempted to "change the reader's image" by analogy. The first was Mary's extended comparison of wood-stove owners to religious zealots (p. 154). The second was Russell Baker's comparison of the restoration fad to a disease (p. 324). Both essays are examples of humorous but effective persuasion.

Passage 2

If you need something to stir up class discussion, the Hayakawa passage should be (in Dashiell Hammett's words) a swell spoon. Hayakawa, who as president of San Francisco State College earned a reputation as an opponent of the student radicals of the late sixties and early seventies, will be known to many of your students as an outspoken conservative senator. He is, of course, a very good writer and has an aura of integrity--in person or in print--that lends force to his arguments. He means what he says. Because of the conservative philosophy that underlies this passage, some of your students will be disposed to see it as a valid argument and more (I suspect) to see it as invalid. The trick is to get both groups to overcome their predispositions and judge the argument's strengths and weaknesses. Here are some questions worth discussing in class.

1.   What is the critical similarity Hayakawa sees between giving As to all students for just being enrolled and giving rich material rewards to citizens for just being alive?

     Students should understand that Hayakawa's argument doesn't hinge directly on fairness. He is not primarily saying that it would be unfair to give everyone a Cadillac just as it would be unfair to give everyone an A. The heart of the analogy is motivation. An overly generous welfare system, he says, diminishes people's desire to excel and accomplish things, just as the automatic A diminishes students' desire to study.

2. Does the analogy hold up at the simplest level? Do you
    believe that the desire to excel in school would be
    diminished by an all-A policy? Do you think that there
    would be an analogous decrease in the desire of people to
    do productive work if everyone automatically got the
    material equivalent of all As?

    I'd call for a vote on this, as well as encouraging
    discussion and debate. My guess is that most students will
    agree with Hayakawa thus far.

3. Does the analogy hold up in detail? Are welfare programs
    the material equivalent of all As? Does it seem likely
    that the most gifted and brilliant citizens will drop out
    of society and go on welfare?

    Once again, I'd encourage both discussion and a division of
    the house. My guess is that most students will not approve
    of the analogy in detail. My class was inclined to think
    that welfare was pretty much a D- proposition, though some
    gave it a C. One student very cleverly pointed out that
    the bright students who were leaving college in the 60's
    were getting <u>off</u> what they perceived to be an academic
    welfare roll and fleeing to the real world where they could
    test themselves. If the analogy held, a generous welfare
    system would drive people back to the workplace.

4. Is the base of the analogy factually firm? Did universities
    in the sixties and seventies really give As "to every
    student"? Were "most of the dropouts" the most brilliant
    and gifted students?

    Hayakawa deserves some deference because of his ringside
    seat, of course. But my students felt he was exaggerating
    enough here to lose credibility with any but the most
    sympathetic audience. Even if the best students were
    dropping out, we might wonder if high grades were the
    cause. There were reasons for disaffection among college
    students in that period.

    After examining the argument in detail, students can make
their own decisions about its effectiveness. Once again, you
should point out that persuasion involves changing an image and
that the real question is not whether Hayakawa's analogy holds up
in every detail but whether it is strong enough to persuade his
audience to see welfare programs in the image of the all-A
university (fictional or real) that he presents.

REFUTING FALLACIES

    The first time I taught a composition class, using a very
different edition of <u>Writing With a Purpose</u>, I lost my head
teaching this section and began to teach a plethora of fallacies
with their Latin names: <u>ad baculum</u>, <u>ad misericordiam</u>, etc. I
had a great deal of fun preparing the lesson, which included an

original and fallacy-ridden dialogue between the grasshopper and
the ant. It was, however, a terrible waste of my students' time,
since they had no need to learn such an extensive list of fallacies
and certainly didn't need to expend the bulk of their energy on
learning names. As the text says, "The skill you are trying to
develop is not identification, but analysis." The eleven fallacies
presented are the most important ones, and even among them, naming
the name is not so important as being sensitized to the fault.

Exercise (pp. 372-374)

1. Both legally and logically, this is a shifting of the
   burden of proof.

2. This is a tangle of illogic. It begs the question by
   assuming the father will be alive four years from now, in
   which case it is <u>of course</u> true that he needn't buy insurance
   until then. There is also a sort of stereotyping--or at
   least a feeble understanding of statistics--in the assumption
   that since an average man of forty-four will live twenty-
   five more years, the father will necessarily do so.

3. There is an oversimplifying of causal relations here.
   Isn't the effect of intelligence a more likely explanation
   of large vocabulary and success coinciding so often? If
   so, vocabulary and success are not related as cause to
   effect, but are common effects of the same cause. At best,
   vocabulary is a contributing cause of success, not a
   sufficient one.

4. This argument begs the question. It tries to prove that
   teen-agers are too immature for marriage by using the
   unproven premise that their high divorce rate is caused by
   their being too immature for marriage. There may be other
   causes for the high divorce rate: parental interference,
   say, or a clear-headedness that encourages them to get out
   of a bad situation quickly.

5. Here is a clear case of the either-or fallacy. Your
   students should be able to propose half a dozen middle
   courses.

6. An obviously faulty analogy, but one I've heard English
   teachers use.

7. Hasty generalization. Two students are taken as representative of the entire population.

8. The argument assumes a single (and questionable) cause for
   a complex of causes. Our "poor defenseless human being"
   can build shelters against the weather, plant crops, build
   fires, and make weapons that will kill either the impala or
   the predator that hunts it.

9. Extension. A never attacked Faulkner, O'Connor, or Mc-
    Cullers, never showed a prejudice against the South. He
    even admitted that Wolfe was sometimes very good.

10. A particularly gross example of argumentum ad hominem, and
    probably of extension. The speaker attacks the appearance
    of the women rather than their arguments, and it is unlikely
    that anyone at the meeting actually said she hated men.

11. The either-or fallacy again. Surely the expenses and the
    personnel can be divided between the United States and its
    NATO allies.

12. This can be viewed as an oversimplification of causes or,
    more narrowly, as an after-this-therefore-because-of-this
    (post hoc) fallacy. We can't assume, just because the
    Spock era preceded the violent demonstrations, that his
    child-rearing methods were the cause of them. We certainly
    can't assume that they were the <u>sufficient</u> cause.

13. An obvious hasty generalization.

14. A faulty analogy that may fool some of your students.
    Football players are not comparable to the general population
    because none of them is elderly or an infant, none suffers
    from an obviously debilitating disease, none is morbidly
    obese. Football could be quite deadly and still not
    outscore old age, disease, and obesity in the slaughter
    game. The argument is also somethings of a red herring,
    since it distracts us from the obvious danger of injury and
    concentrates our attention on death.

15. Again the fallacy of assuming that since A precedes B it
    must cause B (post hoc.)

16. The obvious fault here is a bad analogy. If pornography
    were like typhoid, we could wipe it out by attacking a
    nonhuman causative agent. But a scheme to destroy pornog-
    raphy by destroying pornographic books is doomed because
    more books will be made to fill the void, unless of course
    pornographers and their customers are locked up or executed
    or otherwise stopped. Then too, if pornography were like
    typhoid, it wouldn't be a matter of taste. But one
    person's pornography is another person's art, vague appeals
    to "the moral standards of the community" notwithstanding.

17. Hasty generalization, of course, though my own opinion is
    that further sampling would only strengthen the impression.

18. The argument ignores the burden of proof. What grounds
    does it give for the assumption that educated people make
    wiser choices? What evidence does it give that generous
    state support will improve the educational system? What
    evidence does it give that the wise are better citizens
    than the foolish?

CHAPTER 11   THE ESSAY EXAMINATION

The essential skills of examsmanship are today just what they were when T. H. White learned them in the Boston Public Latin School in the 1920s: "One must grasp the question quickly; answer hard, with minimum verbiage; and do it all against a speeding clock."[1] But surprisingly little attention has been paid to exactly how these skills differ from the skills of ordinary essay writing.

In the first place, since the question is often a surprise, the ordinary methods of planning—brainstorming, journal writing, and so forth—seem inapplicable. Unless the question is given out in advance, there is no opportunity for drafting, and revision is impossible. Much of what we ordinarily say about choosing a subject is beside the point when the subject is as rigidly prescribed as in the essay exam, and audience and purpose take on special meaning.

I usually begin my discussion of the essay exam by presenting my students with this bleak picture of its anomalous nature and then have them think about how their knowledge of other types of writing can be modified to help them with the in-class essay.

PLANNING AND DRAFTING

By the time you discuss the essay exam, your students should be aware that planning ordinarily means thinking-in-writing and that such thinking is often only indirectly related to the essay they will eventually produce. In Chapter 2, for example, Jenny began with an observation of "crosswalks and intersections," which set her to thinking about social interactions (or their absence) on the streets and sidewalks and in such places as the dormitory laundry room. This thinking about the curious impersonality of many places where people's lives cross prepared her to find something to say about the Varsity Barbershop.

-----

1. In Search of History (New York: Warner Books, 1978), p. 34.

Friends who are trained in study skills tell me that an analogous indirect preparation takes place when students keep journals or in some other way reflect in writing on the things they study in class. They may never write precisely on the upcoming exam question, but they have written in the area of it and find it much easier to engage the question when they are finally confronted with it. The same friends tell me that one standard bit of advice they give students about preparing for essay exams is to form the habit of going over lecture notes every week or two and looking for likely essay questions--looking, in effect, for hypotheses embedded in the lectures. They encourage students to draft answers to these questions as a way of preparing for upcoming exams. As with every other assignment, the best preparation for writing is to write.

SUBJECT, AUDIENCE, AND PURPOSE

At first glance, the choice of subject appears to be entirely the teacher's consideration, and many students fail to take a second look at the situation: they study their notes and read their books dutifully and wait for the blow to fall. Better students think actively about essay subjects all the time, trying to see what is significant, interesting and manageable from the teacher's perspective. Their training as writers helps them understand the way the teacher organizes the course according to a purpose. In a survey history course where the lecturer has repeatedly emphasized the effect of the industrial revolution on women, farmers, and laborers, they learn to read the textbook in the light of those themes and to organize their notes around them. They know roughly where the blow will fall and will be prepared to meet it.

The problem of purpose and audience is particularly difficult in the essay exam. Rarely are students asked to amuse or persuade their teachers, and they can hardly presume to inform them. I once met with a student who had been sent to the writing lab because her answers on history exams were pitifully underdeveloped. When I asked her whether she knew any specific information that would support the generalizations she had made in her paragraphs, she began to pour out one excellent detail after another. Why hadn't she included these details? "Because he already knows all that stuff, anyway."

So who is the audience for the essay exam? I often advise students to keep a dual audience in mind. The bulk of their imaginary audience will be made up of themselves and their classmates knowing what they knew the day before the class began, but somewhere in that crowd will be the professor, capable of detecting any errors or omissions in what they have to say. In effect, the student's job is to write a lecture for the class, to write simply and directly for an audience that is intelligent, but uninformed. Ideally, at the end of the lecture, the professor will rise from a seat in the back of the room, burst into applause, and say, "Bravo! Couldn't have done better myself!"

READ THE QUESTION CAREFULLY

The text's warning about key words merits pointing out. One of the most common complaints I hear from professors is that their students answer every essay question as if it asked them to summarize. One professor says that his students interpret every question to mean "GO!" and will fill their bluebook with anything remotely connected with the topic.

Reading the question carefully means reading it in a way that discloses the teacher's purpose, of course. Unfortunately, some teachers ask questions that seemed designed to jam the student's radar:

> Using Le Corbusier's Savoye House and Frank Lloyd Wright's Kaufmann House as typical examples, contrast the architectural styles of these two men as expressions of their beliefs of what a house should be. How do these beliefs affect the allocation of space? To what different ends do the men use line and material? How can their works be said to show different attitudes toward technology?

For some reason, this sort of question is very popular on our campus. Its intent is, I'm sure, to guide the student's response to the central issue. But how does the student decide what the real question is? Which one discloses the professor's purpose so that the student can adopt that purpose in framing an answer? Position often helps: the real question ordinarily precedes its lesser branches. Sometimes, however, the purpose can only be inferred by reading the question against the backdrop of the whole course. Take the following example from an American history exam:

> Write a well-argued essay discussing some of the arguments and techniques used by Americans to prevent the implementation of British policies which seemed detrimental to American interests. Your essay should include a substantial discussion of the way in which environmental factors aided or hampered the Americans in their struggles against England.

My guess is that the second sentence is not an additional assignment, but a hint. The whole question amounts to this: "Write an essay showing how Americans used environmental factors to argue against and resist British policies." The second sentence tells the student, "Don't be stupid. Remember that my purpose in the first several lectures of the course was to show the way environmental factors affected American resistance to British Rule."

Let's examine a more impenetrable example from political science.

By referring to Mannheim, Watson, Madison, and any
theorist discussed by Professor C-----, develop a
conception of the "democratic personality" (include
democratic values in your discussion). What
evidence is there in the Constitution of 1789 that
the Founders were committed to a democracy? Is
there any evidence that the amended Constitution
is more democratic today when compared to the
original document?

I suspect that the real assignment here is to write an essay
showing that "the democratic personality" was (or, more likely,
was not) better embodied in the Constitution of 1789 than in the
Constitution of today. Since students are to show their knowledge
by assuming an uninformed audience, they must begin with a
definition of the democratic personality. But their ultimate
purpose is to evaluate changes in the Constitution in light of
the definition. My speculation may be far afield, of course;
students who have taken the course should be able to make a
better guess because they have seen the purpose behind the
lectures. Is the professor primarily interested in "the democratic personality" in its own right? Or does the professor view
this construct as a tool for evaluating the Constitution, which
is the real focus of his course?

The above examples are from a collection of actual exam
questions which our writing lab routinely uses in helping students
master test-taking skills. One effective way to help your
students read questions wisely is to have them bring copies of
old essay questions to class for discussion.

THINK OUT YOUR ANSWER BEFORE WRITING

The text's discussion here is clear and really needs no
further comment, but I'll add a bit of advice given me by a
professor when I faced comprehensive exams: "Assume that you are
going to faint dead away after the first or second sentence."
The logical corollary of this advice is that you should make the
first sentence or two a direct, self-contained answer to the
question, so that the examiners will assume you'd have done
beautifully if only you'd had smelling salts. The practical
consequence of following this advice is that the first couple of
sentences outline the entire answer and set its direction. Just
as Hemingway, when he found himself in writing trouble, looked
back to the last true sentence he had written, the student mired
in an examination answer can look back to the essay's beginning
and recover his purpose.

Notice how perfectly all the good examples in the text follow (or anticipate) this advice.

WRITE A COMPLETE ANSWER but DO NOT PAD YOUR ANSWER

Students might take the advice in these sections more to heart if they considered the psychology of exam grading. Except in very high-level courses, instructors don't ask a question without having a fairly clear idea of the answer they are looking for. By their lectures and their reading assignments, they have tried very hard to prime students with the information and the perspective needed to frame a good answer. Inevitably, when a student fails to write a complete answer, the teacher feels a sense of failure, too. Failure begets frustration and frustration can beget anger, especially when a student pads an answer. From the teacher's perspective, the padded answer looks like an insult: "Not only did I not pay attention to what you were trying to teach us, but I don't think you're gonna pay much attention to what I have to say in this answer. It'll blow right past you. This whole course is a sham."

Discussion Problem (pp. 393-399)

Question 1

Answer 1 misses the purpose of the question so widely that it takes us entirely out of the scope of a course in library science. Rather than showing Morris's contribution to book design, it scatters some information willy-nilly--including tidbits abouts Morris's medievalism, his poetry, his chair design, and his wallpaper patterns. It ends with the observation that Morris started the arts and craft movement, a wildly irrelevant observation that must have stunned the teacher who had framed a question intended to highlight Morris's raising of book design to a higher and more "professional" art.

Answer 2 says more that is to the purpose in the first sentence than Answer 1 does in nine. It is a direct, self-contained answer to the question, and it serves as a controlling topic sentence for the paragraph. Notice that both answers mention the large initial letters, the "medieval" typeface, and the decorative borders. In the first answer, though, these details are presented against the backdrop of Morris's interest in the Middle Ages--a perfectly correct observation, but not at all to the point. In the second answer, they are presented against the backdrop of Morris's desire to produce a unified work of art in which the printing matches the subject matter--an equally correct observation that is precisely to the point.

Question 2

About this question I must make a confession of using quasi-unorthodox means to dramatize a point to my students. To

prepare a writing lab presentation on the essay exam, I copied
both answers on transparencies. After discussing the question
for a minute, I asked students to choose the better answer to it,
switched on the overhead projector, and put up each answer <u>with
the image so out of focus that the words were illegible</u>. When I
switched off the projector and asked for a vote, the students
unanimously chose answer 1 because it <u>looked like</u> a contrast
answer--an introduction, two body paragraphs of equal length, and
a conclusion. Answer 2 <u>looked</u> too unbalanced to be a good
contrast essay.

Answer 1, in addition to being a clear model of the divided
pattern of comparison discussed on pp. 168-171 of the text, gives
the very clear contrasting examples of the red-head-dreading
woman and the delusional Moses.

The writer of the second answer must have had a good set of
notes from the lecture on defense mechanisms, a subject he finds
irrestistible although it is only tangentially related to the
question. We could form the start of a sensible answer by
combining information from the second sentences of each paragraph:
"The chief differences between neurosis and psychosis are the
extent to which a person is aware of his psychological processes
and the extent to which he is out of touch with the outside
world." I don't know enough about psychology to now how accurate
this answer would be, but I have the impression that the writer
has the necessary information if he would only keep his wits
about him and address himself to the question.

Question 3

Answer 1 is, once again, a good example of the divided
pattern of comparison. It is also a fine example of ascertaining
the purpose of the question and adopting that purpose in framing
an answer. Clearly, the teacher wants the students to understand
how both paintings figure into the general historical development
of Renaissance painting. The student wisely discusses the
paintings against precisely that backdrop. Notice particularly
the first and last sentences of each paragraph, where the writer
holds the painter in one hand and the period in the other and
ties them together in a sturdy knot.

Answer 2 is probably the strongest of our weak answers. It
shows a good deal of knowledge about the particular paintings,
but it misses the purpose of the question. There is no attempt
to "illustrate the difference between early and late Renaissance
painting."

SOME ADVICE FOR NEW INSTRUCTORS WHO ARE WRITING ESSAY QUESTIONS

1.   Remember that the essay examination ordinarily tests substance
     rather than style, and quite properly so, since style is
     usually the product of revision. In other classes, students
     will not be asked to write an in-class essay on such general

topics as "an event that changed my life." They will be
asked to write on topics they have been trying to master for
some weeks and have been studying with ferocious concentration
for a few days. The great trick is to bring that knowledge
to bear, "to answer hard, with minimum verbiage." In
composition classes, I often give questions that ask students
to evaluate essays in terms of what they have learned in
class. If, for instance, we had just studied Chapter 9, I
might ask them to compare the tone and style of Rod's second
and third drafts from Chapter 4. Their grade will depend on
whether they can produce a substantial and well-organized
essay that is fundamentally correct. I tell them not to
worry about their style.

2. Consider your test format carefully. If you don't give your
   students some advance notion of what the question will be,
   the single-question exam may be unfair, since it may catch
   some students off-guard who were generally well prepared.
   You can, of course, ask two or three short essay questions,
   though you must be very sure that the questions can be
   satisfactorily answered in the time allowed. Very often, I
   announce three questions well in advance of the test and
   tell my class that I will throw one out on the day of the
   exam, letting them choose which of the survivors they want
   to write on. I know then that they will spend some productive
   time preparing for at least two questions and will not bark
   their shins on an unexpected question. Giving them only one
   of the three questions on the day of the exam is a bit more
   rigorous and may be the best course to follow if your
   college has a tradition of difficult essay exams.

3. Word your question very carefully. A half hour spent
   drafting the question, chasing down colleagues to critique
   it, and redrafting if necessary will be well spent. It may
   save you a few hours of writing explanatory comments on the
   tests and a few more lying in bed with your teeth clenched.
   If you are trying to test your students' understanding of
   the techniques of persuasion by getting them to analyze
   Martin Luther King's "Letter from a Birmingham Jail," don't
   ask them, "Why is the essay persuasive?" Someone will quite
   sensibly answer that it is persuasive because it was
   perfectly pitched to the historical moment and will begin to
   talk about the progress of civil rights in the early 1960s.
   Instead, ask your students to "show how King's essay employs
   the means of persuasion discussed in Chapter 10." In
   framing your question, decide what pattern of organization
   you want the essay to follow, and word your question in a
   way that indicates the pattern clearly.

4. Write an A answer under the same constraints that you are
   placing on your students. Whenever I try this, I learn
   something. Ocassionally, it is that I have written a
   question that can't be answered in the time frame and under
   the circumstances. If, for instance, I had written the King
   question above for a closed-book, closed-note exam, I would

probably discover I was demanding too much of the students'
memories. More often, I decide that the question will do in
the circumstances, but I discover how far from ideal an A
answer will have to be. When I finally grade the paper, I
am alert to student responses that are in some ways superior
to my own.

5. Consider your proctoring duties and keep them inconspicuous.
    If you give out the questions in advance and make the exam
    open book and open note, you may have committed yourself to
    the wretched task of keeping an eagle eye out for cheaters.
    Students won't be insulted if you tell them that they may
    bring in a note card containing no more than 50 words,
    written on one side only, to be turned in with the exam. If
    you don't decide in advance what to do about people who want
    to continue writing after the period has ended, you may find
    yourself in the awkward position of balancing politeness and
    fairness in dealing with those fortunate enough not to have
    a class the next hour. Everyone will understand if you
    announce that all papers must be turned in by the hour's
    end.

6. Before you start to grade the exams, spend some time browsing
    through strong and weak answers. The tendency is to start
    with unrealistically high standards, and so, in effect, to
    penalize people for being at the top of the stack.

CHAPTER 12 THE CRITICAL ESSAY

Students who have mastered the material in the previous
chapters should have little trouble writing critical essays, but
some of them will have great difficulty reading literary works
intelligently. Let's drop our roles as writing teachers for a
few minutes, then, and consider the problem from the perspective
of a college-level reading teacher.

With a few alarming exceptions, college students have basic
reading skills mastered, of course. They can all turn the
printed text into words and the words into sentences; they have
adequate vocabularies for most of what they read. What they
often don't have is adequate experience reading different types
of material effectively. Some, for instance, are good readers of
newspapers and magazines and have acquired the unconscious habit
of reading the lead of an article with great attention, browsing
through the remainder halfheartedly to see if there are any
interesting tidbits in it, and thinking of the pictures as
window-dressing--fun to look at, but rarely integral to the
article. Such reading habits can cause real trouble when students
must read science textbooks, where the middle passages of a
chapter section are just as important as the lead and where a
chart or graph in the upper right-hand corner of p. 256 may be a
key for understanding the whole chapter. The freshman going into
Chemistry 1 may have to learn a new kind of reading, with new
expectations of what to look for and where to look for it.

Reading literature is, of course, different from reading
either the newspaper or the chemistry book, and part of your job
is to ensure that your students know how to go about reading a
story or poem. The text helps greatly by discussing ten elements
of a literary work that good readers are especially alert to:
character, plot, dramatic conflict, theme, structure, symbol,
irony, point of view, and voice. Students who are going to read
literature well enough to write good papers must be thoroughly
familiar with all these terms, but my own experience tells me
that for fiction, students should learn first to think of situation, character, conflict, and (always after the other three)
theme. Having laid these cornerstones, students can fit the
other six properly into the edifice. But if they start with
symbol, for instance, without attention to situation, their
interpretations tend to be unsound. For many poems--including
those in this chapter--a sensible base might be situation, theme,
structure, and (last) symbol. The worst interpretations of

poetry I have seen have been those that jumped to the symbolic level without pausing first to consider the situation. Once, for instance, I had a student interpret Henry Reed's "Naming of Parts" as a symbolic account of an attempted rape: he was so distracted by all the talk about breeches and bolts and cocking pieces and bees "assaulting and fumbling the flowers" that he would not see the literal situation in which a recruit is being given a weaponry lesson.

Perhaps that student's interpretation tells us more about the good condition of his glands and the poor condition of his psyche than about anything else, but it also introduces the other great problem of teaching students to read literature well: a good deal must be unlearned. Somewhere in their secondary education, too many students learn that literatures is "deep stuff"--too deep for them to understand with their common sense mental equipment, and perhaps too deep for their teachers as well. They have heard interpretations of literature that struck them as being terribly strained and have concluded that to interpret is to strain, to defy common sense. I often feel that my biggest challenge in dealing with nonliterary students is to convince them that creative writers aren't Martians and that they are really trying to communicate with the reader on the basis of common experience. The best tool I have found for impressing that point on them is a technique roughly based on the clairvoyant-reading strategy of reading specialist Anthony Manzo. This technique encourages students to think about a poem or story before they read it and it make some intelligent guesses about what is to come. Whether their guesses are right or wrong, students will discover that they are doing the same kind of thinking the author must have done in the process of writing. This discovery discourages them from treating a work of literature like a hieroglyphic inscription they are incompetent to translate.

Prewriting exercises for "King of the Bingo Game," "Snake," and "Hunting Song" are included below. You might want to do one in class and assign one or two others as journal writings to be done before students read the chapter.

PLANNING THE CRITICAL ESSAY

"KING OF THE BINGO GAME"--A PREREADING EXERCISE

To reinforce the point that writers think in the same ways as ordinary people and at the same time to sharpen student's eyes for the elements of a literary work, read them the title, author, and first paragraph only of "King of the Bingo Game." Then tell them that you are going to ask them to anticipate roughly what directions the rest of the story will take. Ask them the following questions, and encourage them to make notes on the answers so that they can see how successfully they have read Ellison's mind.

1. What kind of man will our main character turn out to be?

Students have abundant evidence that he is unlikely king
material. He is so poor that he can't afford peanuts, let
alone doctors' bills for Laura. Both his speech and his
failure to have a birth certificate announce his low social
status. He has fairly recently arrived from the rural
South (which may explain the absence of a birth certificate)
and appears to have no friends other than Laura. Students
who know Ellison or have read about the migration of
southern blacks to Harlem and other northern ghettos may be
sure after the first paragraph that the main character is
black; others may suspect that he is. All in all, he is a
man with no advantages and tremendous liabilities, and your
students will probably guess that the story is more likely
to be about his helplessness than about his hidden strengths.

2.   Will we discover that he plays bingo frequently or infrequent-
     ly? Why does he play bingo?

Your class may be confused about the relation of the movie
to the bingo game--the combination is probably outside
their experience, but is explained later in the story.
Most will agree that bingo must be more than a pastime with
the protagonist and that he gambles on bingo in a desperate
attempt to win the money he needs to survive and to keep
Laura alive.

3.   Assuming that the author has an interest in psychology,
     what psychological conflicts is he likely to develop in the
     story?

You may need to reread the paragraph if you don't get good
responses to this question immediately. If your students
listen with psychologists' ears, they should hear the
protagonist's doubts about his own sanity and expect that
one conflict will be his attempt to keep himself sane.
They may also hear an emerging conflict between his image
of himself as a poor, helpless soul who would beg a few
peanuts if he dared and an image of himself as a hero who
might at any moment find the trapdoor, pass through the
wall, and rescue the girl.

4.   Assuming that the author has an interest in sociology, what
     societal conflicts is he likely to develop in the story?

Even a fairly dull reader should sense an incipient conflict
between the haves and the have-nots, between the outcast
and society. Those who have guessed that the protagonist
is black will anticipate a racial dimension to this conflict.

5.   Assuming that the author has an interest in philosophy and
     given the means by which the protagonist intends to improve
     his situation, which of the philosophical issues below is
     likely to be developed in the story?

A. Appearance vs. reality
B. Free will vs. determinism
C. Mind vs. matter

Gambling naturally raises the issue of determinism. Also, some of your students may have actually pointed out in discussing the first question that the protagonist has several cards dealt against him.

6. Will the man win the bingo game? Will the story have a happy ending?

Discussing this questions will help your students think about the relation of character, situation, and theme to plot. If they have decided that the protagonist is a natural loser and the story is going to be about his inevitable destruction, then they will say that he surely can't win the game. On the other hand, some will point out the title, which suggests that he will. In fact, he both wins and loses in Ellison's story.

"SNAKE"--A PREREADING EXERCISE

Students can think about these questions after they have heard the author and title of the story and the first paragraph.

1. Why do most people fear snakes?

This question is only loosely related to the story but might fetch some responses that will make students more receptive to the story.

2. What is the most famous encounter between humans and a snake?
There should by no trouble here. Below is the Revised Standard Version of Genesis, Chapter 3, verses 1-7:

Now the serpent was more subtle than any other wild creatures that the Lord God had made. He said to the woman, "Did God say 'You shall not eat of any tree in the garden'?" And the woman said to the serpent, "We may eat of the fruit of the trees of the garden; but God said, "You shall not eat of the fruit of the tree which is in the midst of the garden, neither shall you touch it, lest you die.'" But the serpent said to the woman, "You will not die. For God knows that when you eat of it you will be like God, knowing good and evil." So when the woman saw that the tree was good for food, and that it was a delight to the eyes, and that the tree was to be desired to make one wise, she took of its fruit and after she also gave some to her husband, and he ate. Then the eyes of both were opened, and they knew

that they were naked; and they sewed fig leaves
together and made themselves aprons.

3.   What was the effect on humanity of this encounter?

There were, of course, several effects: the advent of
death, pain in childbearing, the need for people to earn a
living by the sweat of their brows. The most important for
Saroyan's story is "the knowledge of good and evil," which
ended the innocence of Adam and Eve, necessitated clothing,
and generally took us from simplicity to sophistication.

4.   What is the snake a symbol of in Freudian psychology?

The phallus, surely.

5.   What is the evolutionary relationship between humans and
snakes?

Some of your students will know that all mammals, including
humans, presumably evolved from reptiles.

6.   From a biblical scholar's point of view, what conflict is
likely to arise in an encounter between snakes and humans?

Some students will surely suggest the conflict between sin
and innocence. Others might suggest the conflict between
knowledge and innocence.

7.   From a psycholanalyst's perspective, what conflict is
suggested by an encounter between a snake and a person?

It would be very nice to hear your students say "The
conflict between human beings' sexual and nonsexual nature."
My guess is that you'll hear something enough like that to
be confident that your students are ready to read Saroyan's
story.

Exercise (pp. 425-426)

1.   This question gives the student a good opportunity to think
about the ambiguity of the snake as a symbol. It is clearly
associated with the woman: just as the man finds it
"beautiful" and "amazingly clever" but a "symbol of evil,"
so he finds her "lovely but evil." On the other hand, the
snake is associated with the man himself: "To touch a
snake was to touch something secret in the mind of man,
something one ought never to bring out into the light.
That sleek gliding, and that awful silence was once man."
If the man killed the snake in the first scene, symmetry
would certainly demand an adjustment in the second scene,
but probably not the killing of the woman. Perhaps the
killing of the snake in the first scene would amount to a

killing of the man's desire for the woman, and so the second scene would simply vanish.

2. This is such a good question that it deserves two answers. The first and more obvious is that giving the man and woman any identity would decrease their power as symbols. Like Adam and Eve, they are to represent all men and all women. The second answer is that the man can't be a used-car salesman and the woman a typist if they are to represent Saroyan's vision of man and woman in 1931--many millennia after the Fall. The characters are embodiments of sophistication and indirection: they are distinctly "unnaked . . . in the year 1931." The man whistles Schubert, Verdi, and Brahms, and the woman plays the piano and laughs "softly, intelligently." They don't discuss their feelings openly; the "never intrude." They are the most subtle creatures in the Garden.

3. This is a terribly difficult question. The woman seems more intelligent than the man and deeper. She may mean that the man seems--by her standards--callow in his curiosity about this symbol of his sexual nature. What is "splendid" may be his naivete, which--again by her standards--looks almost like prelapsarian innocence. Whatever she means, she doesn't mean to offend the man or to be very distinctly understood by him.

4. Almost every sentence in this story adds additional evidence to this interpretation. It's best, of course, to let your students discover the evidence rather than take the bloom off it by pointing it out too quickly.

TYPES OF EMPHASIS

"HUNTING SONG"--A PREREADING EXERCISE

Students can think about these questions after they have heard the author and title and the first line of the poem.

1. Who is hunting and what is being hunted?

    The first line gives us the fox, and the hunter inevitably follows.

2. Besides the fox and the hunter, what creatures will we probably see on the hunt?

    The hounds will likely come first to your students' minds and then the horse. The inevitability of this little cast should prepare them to appreciate on aspect of Finkel's poem--the simplicity and completeness of its structure. It should also prime them for the surprise appearance of the sentient log in the fourth stanza.

3.   How does a fox hunt end?

       If it is successful, in the death of the fox, of course.
       The inevitability of this answer should show your students
       how naturally the theme of the poem evolves from the
       situation.

4.   What color do we associate with a fox hunt?

       Red, surely, because of the hunter's traditional red coat
       and because of the redness of the fox.

5.   What other associations do we have with this color?

       Blood will inevitably come to mind, but some students may
       remark that red often has cheerful associations--it is
       always the first crayon a child wears to a nub. Both
       associations are useful in the poem.

6.   What, besides fox hunting, is this poem going to be about?

       "Death," they will say, and so without having read the
       poem, will have arrived at a more likely interpretation
       than the unfortunate student who wrote the essay on pp.
       432-433. You certainly won't want your students to
       conclude that the best way to understand a poem is to avoid
       reading it. What you will want them to see is that poems
       are less puzzling and more enjoyable if readers keep their
       wits about them and use the knowledge and experience they
       have.

Discussion Problem (pp. 431-432)

       If your students have done the prereading exercise above,
and discussed the study questions on p. 429 and the essay that
follows them, not many will think that "Symbolism in 'Hunting
Song'" is a good essay. I would nonetheless try to get them to
evaluate the essay and discuss their evaluation. One good way to
do this is to ask first for those who feel the essay is of A or B
quality to raise their hands and then call on them to explain
their grades. Follow the same procedure for those who think the
paper merits a C and for those who would give it a D or an F. Be
particularly alert in guiding the discussion for any echoes of
the "anything goes" school of interpretation. Except for correc-
ting this fallacy, you will probably want to let the students
arrive at their own conclusions, which will probably be the
correct ones.

       They may properly praise the writer for noticing that the
last stanza forces the reader to look for a "deeper meaning than
a mere fox hunt." They should, however point out at least the
following major faults:

THE CRITICAL ESSAY

1. The student comes to the poem so determined to force his interpretation on it that he misreads the connotation of one word and the denotation of another. For most readers, <u>song</u> simply does not have the religious connotation that the student assumes it to have: <u>Song of the South</u>, <u>Song of Hiawatha</u>, and <u>Song of Myself</u> come to mind as quickly as <u>Song of Solomon</u>. And <u>to lollop</u> does not mean "to loll," but "to proceed with a bounding or bobbing motion" (<u>Webster's Third International Dictionary</u>).

2. The student draws elaborate parallels between the hunt and the betrayal of Jesus, but fails to keep the analogy consistent at the most elementary level. In discussing the first stanza, he tells us that Judas is the fox, but in discussing the second stanza, he tells us that the hounds are like the crowd that cried, "Crucify Him!" Now it appears that the fox is Jesus. This new alignment holds in the discussion of the third stanza, where Pilate is the hunter, but shifts once more in the interpretation of the fourth stanza, which associates Jesus with the log.

3. The student finds disproportionate symbolic significance in details so natural that they need no symbolic meaning. That a fox going through a hollow log should go "in one side/And out the other" should hardly send intelligent readers far afield in search of symbolic meanings, nor should a hunter's wearing the traditional red coat. I would not have my symbolic interpretation of a poem rely too heavily on the greenness of the grass or the blueness of the sky.

WRITING THE PAPER

All the advice in this section is valuable, but I would especially emphasize items 3 and 4. Oversummarizing and over-quoting are probably the most common mistakes students make in critical essays.

Exercise (pp. 438-443)

"Bears"

1. The diction tells us that the speaker is an adult.

2. One thinks, of course, of teddy bears. But this child must have had other experiences: her bears are large enough to climb the stairs and heavy enough to impress her with their "thick nocturnal pacing." She may have seen live bears at the zoo, of course, or heard about them in stories. She did not, by the way, see them on television, since she was born in 1929.

3.   Here we come to a question to which there may be many
     legitimate answers. Some interpreters will say that the
     bears in the poem are stuffed animals and that they have
     literally gone to other children. My own impression is
     that, whether the poet owned stuffed bears or not, the
     important bears are the ones her childlike imagination
     could conjure. They have vanished because the imagination
     has dwindled as she grew.

4.   Who doesn't wish to regain the imaginative powers of
     childhood? But see #6.

5.   Other children, presumably, own the bears now, though
     perhaps in other forms. Not every child will imagine
     bears, but I hope that every child imagines.

6.   The source of pride is ownership, but not primarily ownership
     of literal bears. It is the pride of a child who has
     created a private world. The fear is testimony to the
     power of the creation: no child's world is a cloudless
     day, and the bears are embodiments of this child's inevitable
     fears. They are fearsome, as bears should be: they are
     not the toothless bears of the Disney vision. There may be
     a second fear, as well: the well-adjusted one that the
     bears will vanish.

"The Going Away of Young People"

Stanza 1

1.   Perhaps the household routine has been shattered by the
     departure of the young person. Perhaps the mother is left
     so listless by the departure that she can't interest
     herself in the housework. The structure of the poem may
     give us another reason: the opening image becomes a
     metaphor for the mother's past joy in her child and her
     present inability to reorder her life without the child.

2.   It is darkened emotionally by the absence of the child.
     The "late sleeper" is a complex phrase. Clearly it refers
     to the child, and it may say two things simultaneously:
     first, that the child ordinarily sleeps late (in which case
     the mother might have expected the room to be literally
     darkened by curtains): second, that the child sleeps there
     no longer--she is a late sleeper in the same sense that
     Richard Nixon is a late president or John Glenn is a late
     astronaut. Of course, Late in the second sense is most
     frequently used in referring to persons recently deceased,
     and the phrase gains force by this somber connotation.

3.   Once again, there is a level of verbal complexity in the
     talk of forgotten love that may partly elude your students.
     Forgot many mean "failed to remember" or "left behind" or
     both simultaneously. "You forgot your love" could, then,
     mean "you failed to remember your love (for me?)" or "you

left behind my love for you." The poet blends both meanings
for a moment and entertains the possibility of mailing
forgotten love (sense 1--unremembered) as though it were a
thing left behind (sense 2). All this is fairly fine-spun
and may not be worth making an issue of.

4.   The "chore of strings/And paper" is a wry comment on the
     impossible task of wrapping up love in a bundle acceptable
     at the post office. The "stuff I'm used/To stumbling over"
     is this same curiously bulky love, here associated with the
     odds and ends (such as the hi-fi) that young people inevitab-
     ly leave in their parents' houses. The mother will rid
     herself neither of the odds and ends nor of the love.

5.   "The timbre of hi-fi turned off/Strings the psyche." Your
     students may have a hard time interpreting these lines
     because of the unusual use of the verb strings. Given the
     musical context, it might mean "tunes": we can say, for
     instance, that a violinist strings his or her instrument.
     If so, the silence of the hi-fi, which presumably would
     have been playing loudly if the child were home, brings the
     mother's psyche up to a certain emotional pitch. My
     intuition (certainly not my dictionary) tells me that
     another meaning is possible. A note sounded on another
     instrument (the trumpet, say) will sometimes set up a
     sympathetic vibration on the corresponding string of a
     piano or harp. The poet may be using this metaphor to
     describe the mysterious and unexpected effect the silent
     hi-fi has on the mother's soul. Whatever the exact import
     of the second of these lines, the first is clearly an
     oxymoron--and improved version of the "deafening silence"
     we have all heard too much about. The silent hi-fi saddens
     the speaker by reminding her of the departed young person.

6.   Undoubtedly she is sad and depressed. Some of your students
     may talk about "the empty-nest syndrome," an expression
     that does only partial justice to the complexity of the
     speaker's feelings.

Stanza 2

1.   The sailers-away are primarily the young people, who "hang
     full sail" in the window, like ships not quite over the
     horizon. Webb Salmon, my predecessor in writing this
     manual, correctly pointed out that the "sailers-away" in
     the window might also evoke the image of curtains billowing
     in the autumn wind.

2.   The obvious signs are the untended lawn and the empty
     garage, open like a screaming mouth. On the one hand,
     these signs suggest the simple absence of the young people
     who might mow the lawn and keep their cars running in and
     out of the garage. On the other hand, they suggest a
     lassitude that has struck the homeowners who no longer see
     any reason to keep the lawn trimmed and the garage door

closed. They are becalmed--their house is a ship in a windless sea. The <u>windows</u> may be becalmed because they are closed: no wind stirs the curtains. They may be becalmed because no one looks out of them, trying to see a young person.

3. The first house is not yet becalmed because the memories of the young person are still fresh and the young person's return is still anticipated. Notice the opening of the window in the last stanza.

4. Oh, yes!

5. It appears that the speaker is the same, but the voice and the implied audience change. In the middle stanzas, the speaker doesn't address the departed young person ("you"), but seems to address her fellow sufferers ("we" and "our").

6. Students should be able to see the common theme of "The Going Away of Young People."

Stanza 3

1. The italics suggest that these are the remembered words of another speaker--perhaps the words of the young person who has just gone away. But the commonness of the expression links the generations. Perhaps she said the same thing to her mother. The words are, at any rate, consistent with the attitude of the speaker, who resists viewing the parting as permanent.

2. See #1. Though it is no answer to the question posed, let me add that this stanza opens the poem up and makes it appeal deeper and more universal. Not just a mother's parting with a child, but "all leave-taking is permanent." A woman who has given birth to a child may find special meaning in "We can't be sewed back up," but every human will feel the sorrow and the fear of finding that he is now a generation nearer the grave.

3. The September is faded because it is a generation old--the September when the mother herself left home.

Stanza 4

1. We can only guess at the occasion for the sympathy, guess that this woman, too, is becalmed by the going away of her offspring.

2. Again, we can only guess why the woman says she has failed, but the context gives us some indication. She has lived in her house long enough to see the woods razed to make room for other houses. She has seen time and streets and traffic encroach on the home she made (probably) for the children who are now gone. Her dream has collapsed. <u>Too</u>

is an alarming word. Whatever the speaker may mean by it, in the context of the poem it seems to encompass our principal speaker, her mother, and perhaps humankind—all who inevitably lose their dreams and purposes.

3.   Despondency, loss, an inability to clear the table, close the garage door, and go on as if nothing had happened.

Stanza 5

1.   The windows, which have appeared in every stanza, have till now been connectors to the outside world. They admit the sunlight in stanza 1, provide a view of the departing children and of the neighbor's house in stanza 2, reveal another generation looking out in stanza 3.

2.   In this stanza, the windows close the speaker in. They are muffled, fogged over. They are mirrors in which she can see only herself.

3.   The opening of the window in the last three lines seems like an escape from her isolation. Structurally, of course, these lines return us to the opening stanza and the hope that the young person will return for the love (or even the hi-fi?) left behind.

In a previous edition of this manual, Webb Salmon commented so sensitively on a practical problem in teaching this poem that I will quote him at length:

> Since the experiences being recorded in the poem
> are those of a mother rather than a young person,
> college freshmen are likely to be less sensitive
> to these experiences than their parents, and for
> that reason some students may judge the poem sen-
> timental, which in a sense it is. They may object
> to the absence of a father in the poem or to the
> barrenness of a life that has no existence outside
> of the parent-child relationship. It may be difficult
> for them to understand that such objections have no
> pertinence in the reading of this poem. The poem
> is what it is and it is not about the young person's
> view of leaving home or about father-mother
> relationships, nor is it about how to adjust to
> the going away of young people by plunging
> oneself
> into social or community activities. In this poem
> there are no other children and no father, and
> why does not matter; in this poem there is not,
> and cannot be, any activity for the mother that
> will keep her mind off the departure of the
> child. Perhaps there will be opportunities in
> the discussion to suggest to students that a
> poem has to be true only to itself. It should be
> judged by how well it does what it attempts to
> do, not by standards that exist outside the poem.

CHAPTER 13 PLANNING THE RESEARCH PAPER

The research paper is treated in two chapters in this
edition of Writing With a Purpose so that the authors can offer a
comprehensive treatment of planning and researching this major
project. You may want to have your class discuss Chapter 13
before they embark on their research, delaying your discussion of
Chapter 14 until they begin their actual drafting. If I were
doing this, I'd have them read Ken's research paper (end of
Chapter 14) as part of their preparation to discuss Chapter 13.
Some of them will have had very little experience with the
research paper. Seeing Ken's finished project will give them an
idea of what they are setting out to accomplish.

UNDERSTANDING THE ASSIGNMENT

The text's distinction between the survey and the argument
can save you and your class a great deal of misunderstanding.
Most of my students, without having thought very hard about the
issue, assume that a research paper is a pastiche, closer to the
survey than to the argument, but not really one or the other.
Both their past experience with research papers and their humility
in the face of written sources compel them to become passive
conveyors of information rather than writers. Their papers are
too often lumps of xerography in a thin broth of false transitions.

The true survey is, of course, a much more noble enterprise.
Its uses are, however, fairly specialized and academic. In
underclass courses generally, and certainly in most composition
courses, the argument is the more common and useful assignment.
Students may be intimidated by the challenge of constructing "a
convincing, original argument" from printed sources. Reassure
them that the word argument doesn't imply a toe-to-toe battle
with one or more of their sources. They needn't show that Samuel
Eliot Morrison is wrong on some point of American naval history
or that Woodward and Bernstein misunderstood the relationship
between Haldeman and Nixon. What they need to do they have been
doing for the whole semester: finding a personal perspective on
a subject of some public importance and seeing their subject
against a larger backdrop of meaning (see pp. 21-22 of this
manual).

MAKING A SCHEDULE

The general schedule laid out on pp. 449-450 takes into account two realities of the research paper: the surprising amount of time it takes to "work a subject up," especially if the researcher is inexperienced; and, more importantly, the long gestation period it takes most writers to feel comfortable with a subject outside their immediate experience. Once again, your students will need to be reminded that steady work--even apparent drudgery--is the surest invitation to inspiration. Since your students are taking four or five courses concurrently, they will not have the luxury of immersing themselves in their subject for whole days--the preferred regimen of most researchers I know and the one that makes them most receptive to sudden insights. But a long preparation schedule can help them make up in duration what they lose in intensity.

As a practical matter, you may find eight to ten weeks too large a block of the semester to give exclusively to the research paper. My own practice is to give out the assignment very early and to encourage students to start thinking about it and doing light research while other papers are in progress. I may, for instance, ask them to write a journal entry on a potential topic ten weeks before the paper is due, even though one or two less weighty papers fall due in the time between. Sometimes a student's thoughts in the intervening weeks will begin to crystallize around this journal entry, so that upon turning to the research paper in earnest, the student discovers a good deal of material waiting.

Once you enter the block of the semester reserved for the research paper, you should probably help your students stay on schedule by requiring them to turn in portions of their planning materials (journal, note cards, hypotheses, outline, draft) at reasonable intervals. Otherwise the pressure of other classes may encourage them to procrastinate on an assignment where procrastination is very dangerous. I sometimes have students bring in such prewriting for discussion in their groups. This procedure keeps an audience constantly before the writer and also educates the audience so that they can become useful advisers on the paper's progress.

SELECTING A SUBJECT

The guidelines for selecting a research subject are one of the passages in the text that look commonplace and prove very useful. You might have your students practice using them by evaluating the following topics:

Women's Rights in America (needs restriction)

Growing Up in Oklahoma City (too autobiographical?)

This Year in Popular Music (too current)

No-Fault Automobile Insurance (too dry to live with?, not
interesting to readers)

The Origin and Diffusion of Races (too broad and abstruse for the
writer to prove anything?)

Reactions of German-American Pacifists to the Great Sioux Massacre
of 1864 (too specialized for library resources)

The Case for Censorship of Violence in Films (too subjective?)

Offset Printing (too restricted to require multiple sources?)

Some of these topics might be developed in surprising ways, of
course, and produce good papers. A student who decided to talk
about the social impact of offset printing technology might make
good use of several fascinating sources, but a student who merely
describes the process will probably produce an inferior encyclopedia article. Try to discuss both the weakness of potential
topics and ways those weaknesses can be avoided.

Ultimately, the most important class discussion of topics
will center on ones your students are considering for their own
papers. Long before I expect my students to produce substantial
work on the term paper, I have them write their prospective
topics on the board and spend the bulk of a class period evaluating
them one at a time. This discussion can be very informal, but
should hit on all five of the criteria mentioned in the text and
should be thorough and frank. If, for instance, you have a
student who wants to write on no-fault automobile insurance, you
can ask the class in their role as audience how interesting they
are likely to find the paper and what the writer might do to make
it more interesting. If a student chooses abortion as a topic,
try to involve both the writer and the class in a discussion of
what can be _proved_ about the topic. Someone should have the
sense to see that you can't _prove_ abortion is murder or _prove_
that it is simply an assertion of a woman's right to control her
own body: both these positions are too subjective to be bases
for a research paper.

The selection of a term paper topic is an exception to my
general rule of leaving students increasingly to their own
devices as the semester progresses. Very few undergraduates have
enough experience with research papers to know at the outset that
a given topic is likely to be becalmed by a lack of sources or
swamped by abstruse definitions and scholarly literature. No one
benefits when a student wastes six or eight weeks struggling with
a topic that leads nowhere, so I often advise students to drop
topics that they will eventually regret choosing. At the same
time I make it clear that wise selection of a topic is part of
the assignment and is ultimately their responsibility. My
estimate of a topic's fruitfulness may be dead wrong.

For several years I assigned my students carefully restricted
subjects that I had already researched, a procedure with four

obvious advantages. First, it keeps them from selecting topics
that turn out to be unresearchable. Second, it ensures that the
teacher knows the topic well enough to guide the research.
Third, it makes it more difficult for students to buy or borrow
someone else's paper. Fourth, it produces a set of papers alike
enough that they can easily be compared for grading purposes.
Eventually I dropped this procedure because it forced students to
work in isolation. If everyone in the class is writing a
research paper on the historical significance of Martin Luther
King's "I Have a Dream" speech, no one who comes up with an
unusual source or a brilliant insight will want to share it and
so give away a competitive edge. My present practice is to open
up a broad area for research and let students stake their claims
where they will. I might, for instance, tell them that they can
find any subject that interests them so long as their paper gives
the reader information on how that subject has changed in the
last twenty-five years. The twenty-five year stipulation serves
several purposes. It limits the number of prewritten papers
available to unscrupulous students, it allows me to prepare
myself as a research adviser by spending a few pleasant
afternoons browsing through twenty-five-year-old newspapers and
magazines, and it gives the class some sense of common direction
and cooperation. A student doing a paper on the demise of the
New York Yankees might notice an ad in Newsweek that could be
useful to a classmate researching the changing roles of women. A
student writing about Harry Golden should surely have something
to say to a student writing about race relations. Such exchanges
are natural opportunities for collaborative learning.

Discussion Problem (p. 453)

Most of the text's considerations on selecting a subject
are echoed in Ken's journal entry. He can't live with radio
because the topic is too familiar. This is worth pausing to
discuss. The tendency of students to play it safe in choosing a
research topic often leads to boredom that envelops both writer
and reader. Most people write better when they write with a
sense of discovery. Ken doesn't abandon his fixed interests
entirely, though, in a search for the exotic. He stays in the
general area of technology where he has already developed a
personal perspective ("Most people think technology is a dull
subject, but it is really fascinating"). He considers the need
to restrict his general topic of the telephone to something he
can "Cover . . . in ten pages." He notes that what interests
him most about his subject—its engineering—would not appeal to
his readers, and we might add that it is in some ways too restricted, since one source might give all the necessary information.
When he begins to consider topics that might interest his readers,
he has some curious things to say. Why is it a damning objection
to "How to cut costs of phone bills" that such a topic sounds
"too much like a magazine article"? Probably because Ken knows
his research should produce something more thought-provoking and
unexpected than the typical Sunday supplement feature. The next
potential topic, "How phone bills are figured," throws him to the

opposite extreme, a topic so <u>specialized</u> that his research might
produce no significant information. As the finished product will
prove, Ken's choice of advertising turns out to be very productive.
Though it has a special contemporary interest, it is not <u>too</u>
<u>current</u> to find published information. Though it clearly needs
restriction, it is eminently <u>restrictable</u>, since it can be
narrowed chronologically or by medium (say, magazine advertisements) or by purpose of the ads. It is a comfortable compromise
between his special knowledge and the knowledge and interests of
the general public, and it turns out to be a subject about which
Ken can prove something, though he cannot anticipate just what at
this point.

FINDING SOURCES

This section provides the essential information about
research that ought to be common knowledge among college students
and never is. Good and clear as the presentation is, it can't
replace an actual visit to the library to see the physical layout
of the resources. Like most university libraries, ours offers
orientation tours every semester, conducted by trained librarians
who can amplify the information given in this section. I always
take advantage of this service if I am assigning a research
paper.

Some instructors get their students into the swing of
research by setting them some small research tasks that require
them to make use of the library's resources. For instance, you
could ask your class to answer the following questions and make
notes on the resources they use:

1. Who was Benjamin Sonnenberg? (New York advertising execu-
    tive)

2. How may delegates voted for and against the execution of
    Louis XVI in the French National Convention? (387 for, 334
    against; surprisingly close)

3. How many pages are there in the Oxford University Press's
    1970 edition of Boswell's <u>Life of Johnson</u>? (1492)

4. In what year were the Moors expelled from Granada? (1492
    A.D.)

5. Charles "Pretty Boy" Floyd kidnapped the sheriff of a small
    midwestern town in June 1933. What was the name of the
    town, and after whom was it probably named? (Bolívar,
    Missouri; Simón Bolívar, South American liberator)

The first of these questions will lead inevitably to biographical
indexes, the second to an encyclopedia, the third to the card
catalog, the fourth to an encyclopedia, the fifth to a newspaper
or periodical index (such as the <u>New York Times Index</u>). Such
questions are easily invented and can give students some useful

practice, but I wouldn't overburden them with a long assignment of this sort.

Discussion Problem (pp. 457-458)

Dorothy Canfield Fisher's remark that writing a draft is like "skiing down a steep slope she wasn't quite sure she was clever enough to manage" (p. 95) could apply equally well to the early stages of research. At this point, neither Ken nor we can predict confidently what bits of information will be useful in the final paper, since research, like drafting, is partly a question of discovering a specific subject and purpose. Nonetheless, we can make some educated guesses. The biographical information on Bell doesn't seem very fruitful: it fits neither with Ken's proposed subject of advertising nor with his strong interest in the effect of technology on people. The patent battle, though interesting in its own right, seems beside the point for the same reasons; but Britannica follows its articles with brief bibliographies, and the bibliography following an article that discusses the phone company's history is likely to include a source of information on the company's advertising policies. In his last paragraph, Ken finds some information of great potential interest. The history of telephone technology is likely to be related to the history of advertising, and both will have their effect on ordinary people. We can see Ken warming to the historical perspective in his inquiry about the quality of life before the telephone and in his speculation about modern "connectedness."

Rather discouraging at this point is Ken's difficulty in finding encyclopedia references about advertising for telephone services. He needs to find some material directly on this subject.

Browsing through the McGraw-Hill Encyclopedia of Science and Technology probably didn't uncover a reference to McLuhan's "global village," but it made Ken remember McLuhan, a potentially productive source. Here is an example of systematic work paying off in an unexpected way.

EVALUATING SOURCES

An accomplished researcher once told me that the great trick is knowing what not to read. This section is filled with practical skimming and scanning strategies to speed the research process.

Exercise (pp. 472-473)

Having your students compare their rankings and comments is a good in-class exercise. Here is the list I would bring to class if I were one of your students:

1. Brooks, <u>The Telephone: The First Hundred Years</u>: The title
   suggests comprehensiveness and historical perspective. I'd
   hope, among other things, to find a useful and reasonably
   current bibliography here. Within ten seconds of getting
   the book in my hands, I'd be checking the index for "advertising."

2. Atwan, McQuade, and Wright, <u>Edsels, Luckies, and Frigidaires</u>:
   There's a good chance that this book will contain nothing
   on phone advertising, but it could be a gold mine. It will
   take only a moment to find out. Even if it doesn't contain
   directly useful information, it is fairly current and may
   contain a good bibliography.

3. McLuhan, <u>Understanding Media</u>: Though I am not personally
   fond of McLuhan, his book might be pertinent to the theme
   of the phone's effect on our way of life. Worth a look.

4. Mumford, <u>Technics and Civilization</u>: Though less current
   than Brooks' book, Mumford's will be scholarly (even those
   who don't know of the author might guess so from the title)
   and might contain useful historical insight and a good
   bibliography. Also sounds likely to discuss the phone's
   effect on society.

5. Weiner, <u>Technology and the Telephone</u>: Current and perhaps
   relevant to the historical view of the phone's development.

6. Danielian, <u>A.T. & T: The Story of Industrial Conquest</u>:
   Though the book's usefulness will obviously be limited to
   the period before 1940, it may contain information on
   Bell's early advertising techniques. Not likely to lead to
   other useful sources, given its early date of publication.

7. Mubon, <u>Mission Communication: The Story of Bell Laborato-
   ries</u>: Since this is a house publication from Bell
   Laboratories, it isn't likely to contain a substantial
   bibliography or any revelations about advertising strategy,
   but it sounds like a form of advertisement itself and may
   give an idea of the image the company wants to project.
   Also fairly current, and so useful in fleshing out the
   technical side to the present day.

8. Clarke, "Communication in the Second Century of the
   Telephone": May contain information on the present state
   of technology as well as a preview of future technology,
   but it seems by now that we have all the technological
   information we are likely to need.

9. Field, <u>The History of Bell's Telephone</u>: With a date of
   publication this early, most of the history Ken is interested
   in won't appear. There is a chance that the book will give
   some information on what life was like before the phone,
   and so give us a sense of audience for early phone ads.

10. McKenzie, <u>ALexander Graham Bell</u>. Very likely this will be too biographical to be relevant to Ken's subject.

11. Federal Communications Commission, <u>Investigation of the Telephone Industry in the United States</u>: In all probability, the investigation will concentrate on issues of monopoly or trade practices, which are not relevant to Ken's present focus. With a 1939 date of publication, the report would, at any rate, only cover a part of Ken's historical range.

12. American Telephone and Telegraph Company, <u>The Yellow Pages as an Advertising Medium</u>: Yellow pages advertising is not relevant to Ken's present purpose of studying how the phone company sells <u>itself</u>.

TAKING NOTES

Many students who have not done research will feel imposed upon if you ask them to use bibliography cards and note cards made up in the form the text describes. They need to be told that the system presented here has evolved and won almost universal acceptance simply because it saves time. The student who doesn't make proper bibliography cards discovers while typing the paper that he doesn't know the date of publication of some source and must waste a half hour on a needless trip to the library. The student who puts more than one note to a card wastes fifteen minutes trying to remember what happened to the other note she <u>knows</u> she made for such-and-such a topic.

Notice that the text consistently emphasizes the selectivity necessary to good notetaking. Some students see this stage of research as merely mechanical. They go to the library to copy, by hand or by Xerox, page after page of undigested material. Better researchers see note taking as a more intellectual process and leave the library with a smaller quantity of material that they are more likely to find useful. They also leave with a better sense of their purpose and their focus, which they have been considering critically while they evaluated the usefulness of source material.

CHAPTER 13

Exercise (pp. 479-480)

1.   Quotation card:

Subject heading   Author and page #   Source card #

Diversification of Market   Toffler, p. 232   ①

"The mass market has split into ever-multiplying, ever-
changing sets of mini-markets that demand a continually
expanding range of options, models, types, sizes, colors,
and customizations. Bell Telephone, which once hoped to
put the black telephone in every American home — and
very nearly succeeded — now manufactures some one
thousand combinations... of telephone equipment from
pink, green, or white phones to phones for the blind, phones
for people who have lost the use of their larynx, and
explosion-proof phones for construction sites."

Shows how Bell's attempts to appeal to a diverse market
fit into the general "de-massification" of American
business.

Comment

2.   Summary card:

Subject heading   Author and page #   Source card #

Diversification of Market   Toffler, p. 248   ①

Toffler argues that in the "third wave" society begins to
"de-massify," creating a maze of small markets to
which business must adjust. He gives as examples Bell's
increasing range of models and colors and the department
store's breakdown into "boutiques." He acknowledges
that some see such changes as mere manipulation of
consumers, but argues that they also reflect a real
diversification of society and its needs.

Puts Bell's attempts to market into historical perspective.

Comment

3.   Paraphrase card:

Subject heading   Author and page #   Source card #

Diversification of Market   *Toffler, p. 248*

①

Though Toffler admits that the tendency of companies like Bell to multiply colors and models beyond necessity may be partly a money-making ploy, he also argues that it is a necessary response to his "Third Wave" (information age) society. The population today is more differentiated than in previous eras, divided into small groups with special needs and wants.

Possible explanation of Bell's recent tendency to stress the diversity of its product.

Comment

CHAPTER 14 WRITING THE RESEARCH PAPER

The chapter on writing the research paper is as practical
and direct as the one on planning the research paper and is
neatly tied to it by continuing to trace the progress of Ken's
paper on telephone advertising. His completed paper, usefully
annotated on facing pages, ends the chapter.

ORGANIZING A PRELIMINARY OUTLINE

I usually collect the preliminary outline (with hypothesis)
because it gives me a good chance to check on my students'
progress. For students who have researched intelligently,
constantly thinking of and rejecting hypotheses and collecting
only material that is pertinent to the paper's emerging purpose,
composing the preliminary outline should be simple. But students
who see research as a mechanical task of amassing material
usually run aground at this point. Their notes, taken almost at
random, cannot be organized sensibly, but they attempt to include
them all anyway because they represent so much work. Individual
conferences with such students can be very useful. One thing I
try to do in such conferences is to encourage them to step away
from their immediate difficulty and remember the whole process.
They must eventually produce "a convincing, original argument"
about their subject: if they don't do that the game is lost no
matter how cleverly they deploy their stacks of note cards. I
then set them to work considering hypotheses and setting aside
note cards that they can't connect with them. They may end up
tossing two-thirds of their note cards overboard, but they begin
to pull themselves off the rocks.

Ken's preliminary outline represents a midpoint between the
shipwrecked outline and the outline organized by a strong sense
of purpose. As the text points out, it organizes the notes into
a survey, but not an argument. If we look closely at the
subheadings, though, we see the embryo of an original
argument--that the theme of telephone ads is an echo of some
large social changes. A good conference would help Ken see that
this interesting hypothesis is in the outline but is smothered by
the merely chronological main headings.

DEVELOPING A THESIS

A good way to demonstrate the importance of the thesis in organizing research material is to discuss the exercise on p. 489 at length, actually producing outlines appropriate to each thesis. I sometimes have good luck on such projects if I divide the labor, assigning one-fourth of the class to each outline as a homework assignment or in-class group activity. Then I have one student put each outline on the board and explain the rationale behind it. The important thing to emphasize in discussion is the very <u>different</u> papers each thesis will produce. Even in a research paper, the facts don't speak for themselves; they are made articulate by the intelligence and purpose of the writer.

Exercise (p. 489)

In each outline, added information is put in parentheses and significant relabeling is indicated by underlines. The main headings are all significantly altered.

Hypothesis 1 : The advertisements for one product, the telephone, reveal how Americans have changed their attitudes toward technology.

I. Early ads have to sell Americans on benefits of basic technology.

    A. (Plain, common sense people using phone)
    B. (Instruction on how easy it is to use)

II. By mid-fifties, ads assume that Americans are ready to associate advanced technology with the good life.

    A. Direct appeal to "good life" theme
    B. <u>Convenience</u> of installing total phone system
    C. <u>Advantages</u> of increasing technology available

III. Ads in the sixties show that Americans are awakening to technology as a tool of great power.

    A. Concentrate on the improving technological capacity of AT&T
    B. Focus on phones as <u>the</u> business tool
    C. <u>Even emphasize power of domestic user</u>--Direct Dial Long Distance

IV. Contemporary ads emphasize the "friendliness" of increasingly exotic technology.

    A. Fusion of phones with computers

    B. Show increasing level of human interaction with
       machines--information transmission and information
       processing become one process
    C. More emphasis on service than equipment

Hypothesis 2: The advertisements for the telephone illustrate
how AT&T prepared Americans for the introduction of new
technology.

  I. The earliest phone ads teach consumers how to use the
     telephone.

     A. (Many ads literally "how to")
     B. (Users in ads generally plain people with no
       technological glitter)

 II. Ads in the mid-to-late fifties show consumers how to use
     a total phone system.

     A. Explain the process of getting equipment in place
       for total phone system
     B. Associate expanded systems with the "good life"

III. Ads in the sixties emphasize the phone owner as
     "liberated" user of the phone system.

     A. The autonomous domestic user--Direct Dial Long
       Distance
     B. Focus on phones as the tool with which
       businesspersons could conquer space and time.

 IV. Contemporary advertising emphasizes the integration of
     computers into the telephone system.

     A. Fusion of phones and computers
     B. Shows increasing level of human interaction with
       machines--information transmission and information
       processing become one process

Hypothesis 3: The advertisements for the telephone document
America's growth from an agricultural to an industrial to an
information-based society.

  I. Early ads sold the phone as a link connecting the
     isolated farms of an essentially rural America.

     A. (People in ads usually farmers and farm wives)
     B. (Emphasis on phone as link between isolated farms)

 II. Advertising after World War II often emphasized the
     telephone as a business tool.

     A. Focus on phone as the business tool

    B. Concentrated on <u>aspects of new technology most</u>
       <u>useful to business</u>

III. Contemporary advertising presents the phone as part of an
    integrated information network that includes computer
    technology.

    A. Fusion of phone with computer
    B. Show increasing level of human interaction with
       machine--information transmission and information
       processing one process

Hypothesis 4: AT&T's advertisements helped change Americans'
perception of the telephone from a novelty to a convenience to an
essential tool.

  I. In the earliest ads, the phone is presented as an almost
    miraculous invention, a sort of magic carpet.

    A. (Many "first encounter" ads)
    B. (Phone calls treated as special events)

 II. After World War II, ads consistently link the phone with
    ease and efficiency.

    A. Focus on phone as <u>the</u> business tool
    B. Explain <u>advantages</u> of total phone system
    C. Begin to focus on variety of domestic
       services--Direct Dial Long Distance
    D. Appeal to "good life" theme

III. Contemporary ads encourage the consumer to keep up with
    the new telephonic technology.

    A. Fusion of phone with computer
    B. Show increasing level of human interaction with
       machine--information transmission and information
       processing one process·

Of course, none of these outlines is as full and rich as Ken's
own formal outline, pp. 519-521.

WRITING THE FIRST DRAFT

    If it helps in times of crisis to know that our problems
are not unique, the two short paragraphs that head this section
could console a great many students. They exactly identify the
problems that 90 percent of my students have with their term
papers. The problem of "composing a simple, straightforward
introduction" is not the disease itself, of course, but a symptom
of an underlying malady. Ordinarily, I am an introduction-last
man: my standard advice to students writing short papers is to
write the body while the introduction simmers on the back burner.

But for longer projects like research papers, writing an
introduction first may be the better idea. Organizing the body
is a large and sometimes disorienting task, perhaps better
undertaken after the writer has charted a course by thinking
through the introduction—or an introduction. Usually the first
introduction will be substantially rewritten to make it fit the
whole paper more perfectly.

Exercise (p. 494)

The relationships among Ken's introductions are more
interesting than he realizes, I suspect. If we remember that a
true essay shows specifics against a backdrop of generalities
(see pp. 21-22 of this manual), we can see the first draft as an
intelligent and successful attempt to define the layers of his
paper: the most general backdrop is subtle historical/
technological change, defined in the first paragraph; the nearer
and narrower backdrop is AT&T as a company adjusting to that
history; the specifics are AT&T ads. Ken's purpose is to inform
his audience by holding ads up for examination against these
layered and related backdrops. He has defined his situation as
an essayist admirably, but he is essentially talking to himself,
thinking-in-writing about his method. His revision agenda shows
that he is aware of this fault: "Spend too much time explaining
the reasons for my choice. I think I sound defensive. Maybe I
should simply present my argument." His solution is essentially
to stop washing his hands and get down to the job that the
audience expects him to do: "get to stuff on telephone quicker,"
moving swiftly "from technology to advertising to telephone so
that I can end with a clear thesis."

Note that at this point, he still clings to the McLuhan
quote, arguing that it "helps readers see the importance of
advertising to historical research." In the revision agenda
following the second draft, he realizes that the quote is not
important to the reader ("gets in the way—too obvious"). I
suspect the McLuhan statement is pyschologically important to Ken
because it legitimizes the method he will follow, but he realizes
that he is doing his readers no favor by weighting down the paper
with his psychological and intellectual armor, so in a small act
of courage, he relegates it to an endnote. The favor he can do
for the reader is to provide a clear thesis, which he does in the
paper itself by asserting that AT&T "has used advertising to
create and exploit our need for a personal relationship with an
impersonal system."

Notice, by the way, that this thesis adds depth to the
paper by adding a backdrop still larger than the historical/tech-
nological backdrop of the first introduction. He now intends to
display specific ads against three widening backdrops.

universal human preference of personal to impersonal

rapid social/technological changes

AT&T advertising policy

specific ads

the reader

QUOTING SOURCES

Experienced teachers will certainly applaud the inclusion of this discussion. It clearly delineates all the problems my students have with quotation. Particularly useful are the criteria for quotation on p. 495. Students who include only those quotations that are substantive, memorable, and authoritative will not produce the scrapbooks that often pose as term papers.

When you teach the section on plagiarism, you will probably remind your students of your institution's policies concerning academic dishonesty.

DOCUMENTING SOURCES, LISTING SOURCES, TYPING THE FINAL DRAFT, GENERAL FORMAT

These sections are self-explanatory and are essentially for the student's reference. I would point them out, but not spend much time discussing them in class.

KEN'S RESEARCH PAPER

Given the difficulties the research paper poses, Ken obviously does a good job here. He would certainly get an A in my class. But his paper is not above criticism, and I think your class can benefit by a discussion of its strengths and weaknesses.

The major problem in a research paper, of course, is the organization of a great deal of material into one coherent essay. You can sharpen your class's awareness of the essay's success by asking them to relate the following quotations to the thesis (or better yet, to all four backdrops noted above). In effect, you are asking them to tell you the _purpose_ behind each expression.

1. "personable mail carriers . . . friendly telegraph operators (p. 525)

[Pre-telephone conveyors of information: fits broad conflict mentioned in thesis by pointing to conflict between personal association and technology; obviously related to changing technology theme; fits into AT&T policy as competition to be overcome.]

2. "most rural phones were on the party line" (p. 527)

[Fact introduced in paragraph on increasing number of phones around 1900: shows a successful reconciliation of the personal and the technological; describes a specific state of phone technology; anticipates AT&T public relations problem to come]

3. "Intelligent and vigilant, she could always be counted on to supply information, gossip, or emergency warnings." (p. 529)

[Description of central operator in small communities: helps personalize technology; represents a certain stage of phone technology; a public relations windfall for AT&T]

4. "The art work in many of AT&T's ads still celebrated the leisurely, predictable routines of rural life, but the copy announced a new technology that could assist city go-getters . . . to do business efficiently and effectively." (pp. 531, 533)

[Characterization of 1920s ads: shows conflict between personal world and world of efficiency with roots in technology; marks shift from rural to urban America; shows AT&T advertisers "creating and exploiting" need for a "personal relationship with an impersonal system"]

5. ". . . the copy concludes with the reassuring news that although the conversion to direct dial is inevitable it will be gradual." (p. 535)

[From 1930s ad: shows consumers' reluctance to sacrifice personal central operator as part of technological change; represents a technological change consistent with the social change to city life with its need for privacy; whole ad shows variety of AT&T techniques for making shift to impersonal go down smoothly.]

6. "Reach Out and Touch" (p. 545)

[Ad campaign theme: quintessential attempt to reconcile the personal and the technological; fits the technological advance of direct dial long distance and the social change of postwar mobility; AT&T creating and exploiting needs]

7.   ". . . your simple, basic, everyday telephone" (p. 553)

[The mechanism of "dramatic and exciting changes" from copy of
"Gateway to Tomorrow" ad: reconciles technological and personal
by making phone seem like old friend; ad shows transition from
traditional phone technology to computer age; obvious attempt by
AT&T to convince consumers that they have a continuing "personal"
relationship with Bell system]

8.   "'Let's Talk' number" (p. 555)

[Toll-free number at bottom of recent "Gateway to Tomorrow" ad:
disjointed juxtaposition of personal and technological; related
to computer revolution that is theme of ad; part of AT&T's
attempt to combine progressive and personal images]

The success of Ken's paper can be measured partly by the meaning
that accumulates around details such as these. Clearly, he has
not merely collected information; he has given it new meaning.

But not every paragraph is a success. The full paragraph
on p. 535, for instance, tells us something about AT&T's
advertising strategy during World War II, but has no relevance to
the personal-versus-technological theme announced by the paper's
thesis. The paragraph that follows it shows that AT&T's sales
boomed after the war, but has nothing to do with advertising or
personalized technology. The paragraph in the middle of p. 541
fails to relate the appeal to status to the paper's thesis. In a
sense, these paragraphs are transitions that smooth the paper's
chronological flow. But they are such longish transitions that
they become digressions. Ken could shorten them or rewrite them
to tighten their connection with the thesis.

These considerations of purpose and organization aside, Ken
manages his paper splendidly, as the notes on the pages facing it
point out. Encourage your students to read the notes as well as
the text so that they can learn some of Ken's techniques. I
would be especially careful to point out the following notes:

#6, which clarifies the issue of "common knowledge" in
acknowledging sources

#9, which explains the function of discursive (or explanatory)
notes

#10, which tells students how to acknowledge a source quoted in
another source

#11, which shows the use and acknowledgment of paraphrased
material

#12, which shows the effectiveness of a very short quotation
worked into Ken's own syntax

#14, which points out Ken's careful introduction to a quotation from a major source

#18, which shows how Ken establishes a source's authority before quoting

#25, which points out the effectiveness with which Ken blends sources

#31, which shows how Ken's conclusion effectively clinches the paper without seeming mechanical or imposed

CHAPTER 15 BUSINESS WRITING

Chapter 15, like several previous chapters, has human interest because it follows the progress of a particular student in particular writing situations. Maria Galvao finds herself, the summer after her sophomore year (when she is still very much a student), in an intriguing set of situations that are all created by that maelstrom of nonacademic circumstances we call the real world.

The best instruction in business writing always has this real-world flavor. Many instructors use a casebook method in creating assignments, presenting students with a situation and a bundle of information to be organized into memos, letters, and so forth. Later in this chapter I'll include one such case that might be useful to you in creating assignments for letters of complaint, inquiry, and response, and a memo.

LETTER OF COMPLAINT

Maria manages her complaint so deftly that you may have to draw your students' attention to the pitfalls she avoids. The best way to do this would be to have them write bad letters of complaint, ones that plead or threaten. Such an assignment could lead to class or group discussion that is amusing and educational. If time doesn't permit this sort of assignment, you could ditto a bad letter and submit it to the class for criticism. On the next page is an example with errors of form and tone.

no return address or date line

↓

Mr. Oliver Pendragon
Owner, Devon Apartments
72 North Skyway Drive
Mesquite, TX 75150

Dear Mr. Pendragon,

vague pronoun

↓

harsh, scolding tone

I won't beat around the bush, we are angry about the pool closing. Your supervisor, Billy Ray Burford, showed us the pool when we looked at the apartment and made a big deal about how it would keep us cool this summer, which is supposed to be one of the hottest in years. Not only that, but the swimming pool is mentioned in all the ads. That's false advertising, and some of us are thinking about suing. Or we might just move out.

in-appropriate diction

threatening tone

Billy Ray has left town, possibly because he didn't want to face us. We're having another meeting in a couple of weeks and would like to hear from you by then.

departure from paragraph format

vague time reference

inappropriate closing

Cordially,

Maria Galvao

Maria Galvao

RÉSUMÉ

One aspect of the résumé that I find students to be surprisingly naive about is the tailoring of it to fit the particular job they are applying for. A useful exercise to sharpen their sense of audience for the résumé is to have them look at Maria's planning inventory (pp. 576-577) and compose a résumé that would be appropriate if she were applying for a summer job as a counselor at a summer camp for children, ages eight to twelve.

Exercise (pp. 577-578)

Maria's important inclusions are the ones that show (directly or indirectly) her skills as a writer and meeter-of-the-public. Notice especially the detailing of her duties as editor of The Expositor, freelance writer for the Evening Globe, and campaign volunteer. Obviously, she has thought about how these experiences have prepared her for the internship and has presented them in a way that should appeal to the Campus Update editor.

She omits items that are unrelated to the type of job she is applying for: babysitting, waitressing, serving as Santa's elf. She also omits items that are from her childhood and "Personal Skills and Characteristics," which might appear in a letter of application, but are too subjective for the résumé.

LETTER OF APPLICATION

Either of the techniques mentioned in the two sections above might help your students see the effect of audience and purpose on the letter of application. You could have them write a letter of application for the camp counselor job, based on Maria's inventory (pp. 576-577). You could have them write inferior versions of her letter to Rae Morrow and come to class prepared to discuss their weaknesses. The next page shows one bad version of the letter to Rae Morrow that you could duplicate and discuss in class.

3200 Devon Road
Apartment 1B
Muncie, IN 47035
April 3, 1983

— omission of title

Rae Morrow
Editor, Campus Update
Ball State University
Muncie, IN 47306

semicolon for colon

Dear Ms. Morrow;

vagueness about position

I have heard that there may be some summer work available at Campus Update, and since I am putting myself through college, I thought I'd apply.

usage error

mistaken emphasis in presenting credentials

I have had alot of work experience, including working as a campaign worker on Phil Nightingale's Congressional campaign, doing research for Dr. Maureen Duffy, freelance writing for The Indianapolis Evening Star, and editing for The Expositor. I am a good writer, a hard worker, and a good listener. I have a wide variety of interests, including music, theater, jogging and politics.

I'm sure I could do a good job for you. If you have questions, please feel free to call.

no phone number given; no mention of interview

Sincerely yours,

Maria Galvao

format errors

Maria Galvao

P.S. I've enclosed a résumé.

The weaknesses of this version should help your students appreciate the strengths of Maria's actual letter.

LETTERS OF INQUIRY AND RESPONSE

Dr. Harvey's letter of inquiry is a fairly good model: it
is addressed to an appropriate person, comes directly to the
point, and gives the reader enough information to frame a sensible
answer. A couple of weaknesses might come out in class discussion.
Does the letter insist so much on the quality of the magazine and
Dr. Harvey's desire to subscribe that it seems sycophantic? Does
the second paragraph give unnecessary detail about his study of
brewery closings, given that the beer can collection is the
proposed subject of the article? I'm not sure of the answers to
these questions, but think they are worth discussing.

Once again, a good tactic for helping your students appreciate the quality of Maria's response letter would be to have them
produce a deliberately faulty one. The following page shows an
example:

July 13, 1983

Dr. Donald Harvey
P.O. Box 5732
Modoc, IN 47358

abrupt rejection

Dear Dr. Harvey:

I'm sorry to inform you that we aren't interested
in doing a story about your beer can collection.
In the first place, you are not a member of the
Ball State faculty, and our policy is to publish
articles about our faculty's research. Secondly,
a beer can collection is not research, and so
lies outside our scope.

*rigid
"policy"
stance*

I can't give you any better news about your
request to subscribe. The magazine is circulated
free to University faculty and staff only.

Thanks for your interest, though.

*barest courtesy:
no sympathy
or helpful
suggestion*

Sincerely yours,

Rae Morrow

Rae Morrow, Editor
Campus Update

Exercise (p. 586)

By contrast to the bad example above, Maria's letter is a
model of courtesy. She opens by thanking Dr. Harvey for his

letter and then delivers some information about Campus Update that explains indirectly why he cannot subscribe and prepares him for her statement, tactfully delayed and delivered, that the magazine is not interested in the story. Particularly well done is the third paragraph, which indirectly tells Dr. Harvey that the story is interesting and directly gives him useful information about where he might find someone interested in covering it.

She has managed to write a letter that delicately clarifies Dr. Harvey's misconceptions about the magazine and its purpose and at the same time makes Ms. Morrow seem like a helpful person rather than an impersonal instrument of policy.

MEMORANDUMS

Exercise (p. 591)

A. The subject of the memo has, of course, been dictated by Ms. Morrow, who is businesslike and pragmatic ("hardly earth-shattering news"). Maria's purpose is to propose the Chemical Dependency Project as a suitable subject for a cover story, and she sticks to that purpose admirably, keeping her memo brief by resisting the temptation to impress (or more likely oppress) Ms. Morrow with the details of the other stories she has researched. She presents her case very clearly, numbering her points for easy reference and dividing the advantages of the story from its disadvantages. The introduction of disadvantages has two good effects: it shows her balance and good judgment and invites Ms. Morrow to concur or disagree so that no one goes into the story blindly. Surely Ms. Morrow will be able to digest the memo at a glance and decide whether to proceed with the story, block it, or call Maria in for more information. Surely, too, she will be favorably impressed.

B. The subject, Maria says, is significant, since the program promises to have a positive impact on alcohol and drug users; it is interesting because it touches on both alcohol and physical fitness; despite some difficulties noted at the end of the memo, it is manageable. It is particularly suited to the university audience of joggers, drinkers, and researchers, and precisely fits Ms. Morrow's purpose of accentuating the positive aspects of research into alcohol problems.

POSSIBLE WRITING ASSIGNMENTS

Job seeking is in every college student's near future, so you needn't look for exotic ways of framing an assignment for the résumé or the letter of application. You can simply have your students target a potential employer and compose a suitable application.

For on-the-job writing, you could propose the following case. Have the student assume the role of Carol Johnson, who has decided to pay college expenses by opening a typing service: Accutype. Knowing that there is a big thesis/dissertation typing market and that these projects involve repeated typing of drafts, Carol decides to buy word processing equipment that will make the process of minor revision and retyping very fast and easy. She scrapes together $1,200 to order by mail the lowest priced computer, software, and printer from Cheapside Computer Corporation. By the time the equipment arrives, the fledgling business already has a customer: John Q. Telleman, who must start on his master's thesis immediately. It's a big job that Carol figures might net $200 by the time it goes through several drafts. But a few pages into the project, she discovers that there is a fault in the disk drive on the machine: the door won't shut when the disk is out of the machine. But this seems to be a merely cosmetic problem since the machine always has a disk in it when it is operating. Harmless as the problem is in itself, Carol fears that it might be a symptom of something more serious. Ordinarily, she would return the machine for repair or replacement during its ninety-day warranty period, but that option is not open since stopping work on Telleman's thesis would be too great a blow to her enterprise's good will.

> Assignment: Write a letter to the computer
> company to try to salvage the situation. Use
> your imagination in proposing solutions and
> supplying such details as the company's address.

This initial crisis past, Carol completes the first draft of Telleman's thesis and takes on several other jobs. One day, the note shown on the next page comes in the mail.

Dear Ms. Johnson,

   I just came from a meeting with my adviser,
and I am hoping mad. He said that draft you you
typed was so full of mispelled words that he
could hardly read it and it made him onder if I
was fit to be a graduate student in his departmint!
I think you should give me my mony back, and if
you dont, you can be sure that I'll let all my
friends know never to do busness with you in the
future.

                    Sincerely,

                    John Q. Telleman

                    John Q. Telleman

     Carol is shocked by the letter primarily because she never
dreamed that the shoddy piece of work Telleman had brought in
scrawled haphazardly over dozens of legal pages was supposed to
be typed into a draft suitable for submission to a thesis adviser.
In addition, Accutype never held itself out as an editing service.
She is not sure enough of her own spelling and punctuation skills
to take on that sort of responsibility; what is more, such
corrections would be so time consuming that there would be no way
for the business to turn a profit without charging an astronomical
rate per page. Moreover, it might be simply cheating to do this
sort of work for graduate students. Should they be able to get
degrees without mastering such basic skills?

       Assignment: Write a response to Telleman's
       letter. Try to regain his good will and make a
       sensible statement of policy. Don't offer to
       refund the money, which is needed to begin paying
       off the cost of the word processing equipment.

Carol's business grows rapidly, and by the end of the first semester, she is beginning to turn a profit. One day the mail brings her ads for the following software products:

SpellSwell--the best spelling checker on the market today. At the press of a key, this program will check your text against a lexicon of 40,000 words. Misspelled words will flash on the screen and possible correct spellings will appear beside them. Or you can print out your text with misspelling in boldface and possible alternatives in italics.

GrammarWhammer--a dream for those who always found English classes hard. Spots subject/verb and noun/pronoun agreement errors, improper uses of capitalization and punctuation, fragments, fused sentences. Errors flash on the screen or can be highlighted in printed text by a shift to red ink.

Carol sees a great money-making opportunity here, since she can obviously charge more for copy corrected by these programs. It also seems to her that since the correction is done mechanically, the process doesn't <u>seem</u> quite so much like cheating. But she is still a bit uneasy about the ethics of the situation, and finally decides that she should write to the ultimate authority-- E. J. Wilson, the dean of the graduate school--for a statement of the school's policy,

<u>Assignment</u>: Write the letter. Assume that you are enclosing the brochure with the descriptions of the correction programs.

Dean Wilson quickly discovers that the graduate school has no policy on this issue, though she finds two faculty resolutions that seem pertinent. One passed in 1975 says that "the sense of the faculty is that no student should receive a graduate degree from this institution without mastering the fundamental writing skills that indicate an educated person." One passed in 1983 says that "in such an age of technological advance, the faculty should make every effort to enhance students' understanding and use of the benefits of computer technology." The Dean sees that this will be a complex issue, but hasn't time to deal with it herself. She sends the memo shown on the next page.

INTER-OFFICE CORRESPONDENCE

TO James Anderson, special assistant   DATE 2/3/83

FROM E. J. Wilson, dean of Graduate School

SUBJECT Policy on computer correction of student
         writing

Attached you'll find a letter from Carol Johnson,
a brochure from a computer software company, and
two faculty resolutions. Collectively, they have
landed me in a fine pickle. You've got a good
head for these ethical dilemmas. See if you can
draft a memo outlining a sensible policy by the
time I get back from Barbados next Wednesday.
Warn me about possible pitfalls, consequences,
and impact on faculty and students.

Assignment: Write Anderson's memo

SENTENCE STRUCTURE

S 1   Review of Sentence Elements

Basic Elements   (p. 600)

      S   V   O   S   V
1. They tried it and it worked.

      S   V   O   S   V   C
2. Nobody likes her; she is too sarcastic.

                   C
3. That dog looks vicious.

             S   O
4. Those who trust you will not need an explanation.

                 O   O
5. I doubt that he will go, but I'll ask him.

          S   O
6. Did you get the tickets?

            S   C
7. Part of the sentence is illegible.

         V   O
8. They paid you a compliment.

            S   C
9. The trouble with Bill is that he is too sensitive.

                        O
10. We discovered that it was our fault.

Subordinate Clauses (p. 602)

```
                       O
1.  I will do (whatever you say).


            S
2.  (What he told me) is none of your business.


                  M
3.  The book (that I bought) cost eight dollars.


                        M
4.  The man (who is wearing the plaid shirt) is his uncle.


          M
5.  (If that is how you feel,) why don't you leave?


                  M
6.  The people (who lived in that house) moved to Minnesota.


                   O
7.  He said (that he was terribly embarrassed).


                      M
8.  This is the book (that I want).


                  O
9.  I would like to know (why they did it).


          M
10. (When you are ready,) call me.
```

Verbals (pp. 603-604)

1. <u>to tell</u>: infinitive, used as object
2. <u>thrilling</u>: participle, used as modifier
3. <u>reading</u>: gerund, used as object
4. <u>to play</u>: infinitive, used as subject
5. <u>drunken</u>: participle, used as modifier
6. <u>disappointed</u>: participle, used as modifier
7. <u>screeching</u>: participle, used as modifier
   <u>jarring</u>: participle, used as modifier
8. <u>thinking</u>: gerund, used as object
9. <u>to have invited</u>: infinitive, used as subject
10. <u>feeling</u>: gerund, used as subject

S 2 Period Fault and Sentence Fragments (p. 605)

1. . . . one ambition, to play . . . .
2. . . . this far, we must . . . .
3. . . . the whole audience, not just . . . . .
4. . . . with much difficulty, slipping . . . .
5. . . . the top twenty, we forgot . . . .

6. I believe our new member of Congress will successfully meet
   whatever challenge . . . .
7. . . . a stand," I began . . . .

S 3 Fused Sentences (p. 606)

1. . . . in the play-offs. When the game . . . .
2. . . . this matter. There is . . . .
3. . . . must be investigated. Unless better food . . . .
4. . . . when we punctuate. We use . . . .

   or

   . . . what we mean. When we punctuate . . . .
5. . . . to be helpful. In the last half . . . .
6. . . . in such a way. That is . . . .
7. . . . will refuse it? What do you hope to gain?

   or

   . . . such an offer? If you know . . . .

S 4 Run-on Sentences (pp. 606-607)

1. Because I was not sure which flight Jim would arrive on, I met
   all the planes coming in from Atlanta. When he was on none of
   them, I decided that I was wrong about which day he was coming.

2. Since we both object to being misled, we should be able to find
   a common ground for agreement.

3. After examining all reasonable transportation possibilities, I
   concluded that indeed I was stranded. I called my professor
   whose exam I was to take next day and told her that I would
   probably be absent. Then I started to hitchhike back to school.

4. Interested in learning about Thomas Wolfe's method of writing
   autobiographical fiction, I read his first novel and then the
   section of the Nowell biography dealing with his early life.
   The comparison was fascinating.

5. John Malcolm Brinnin wrote a book called Dylan Thomas in
   America, of which Mrs. Thomas disapproved. She insisted that a
   statement from her expressing her disapproval should appear at
   the beginning of the book.

6. When our freshman writing instructor told us about various
   theories for teaching writing, we asked him what scholarly research had to say about the matter. After explaining the difficulty of conducting research on the subject, he said, "There's
   not much that is conclusive."

S 5   Comma Splice (pp. 608-609)

Only one answer for each problem is given below. The period
can replace the semicolon or vice versa. The writer will decide
which to use, according to the desired degree of separation of the
main clauses. Also, the writer can restructure the sentence by
subordinating one of the present main clauses to the other.

1. . . . late tonight. Coach . . . .
2. . . . the reader; it is . . . .
3. . . . it today. All you . . . .
4. . . . a professional meeting. Moreover, he . . . .
5. . . . at the time. Looking back . . . .
6. Pay attention; before you . . . .
7. . . . Luke's integrity; strange as it now seems, we . . . .
8. . . . to the Senate; because it . . . .
9. . . . emergency meeting. Although there were others . . . .
10. . . . wasn't; enjoying their memories . . . .

S 6   Faulty Parallelism (pp. 610-611)

1. In high school we were asked to write legibly and accurately.

2. The evangelist ended the sermon with a hymn and a call for sin-
    ners to repent.

3. Sentence elements that perform parallel functions but are not
    written in parallel grammatical form should be revised.

4. The article cites three main causes for the energy crisis: the
    greatly increased demand for oil in industrialized countries,
    the failure of the big oil companies to build new refineries to
    meet this demand, and the influence of an increasingly unstable
    political situation on the supply of oil.

5. The narrator in Invisible Man was idealistic, intelligent, and
    active in advancing the cause of black people.

    or

    The narrator of Invisible Man was idealistic and intelligent,
    and he tried to advance the cause of black people.

6. By studying newspaper files and magazine articles and by inter-
    viewing knowledgeable people, I was able to gather the informa-
    tion I needed.

7. The executives of a corporation must be concerned with keeping
    the price of their product competitive and with making a
    reasonable profit for the stockholders.

8. In the President's first two years in office, his main chal-
    lenges were to persuade Israel and the Arab nations to reach a
    peace agreement and to find a way to control inflation in the
    United States.

9. Manipulative commercials encourage people to want things they
    do not need and to buy things they cannot afford.

10. Because he has always had both wealth and indulgent parents,
    he has never been forced to accept responsibility.

S 7 Dangling Modifiers (pp. 612-613)

1. Although I worked steadily each day, time ran out before I
    could complete the job.

2. The committee requires that candidates have perfect attendance
    to qualify for the award.

3. When I was a senior in high school, my English teacher had so
    many students that he was not able to give close attention to
    individual students' writing problems.

4. Having heard the weather report, we postponed our trip.

5. If the story is told in the first person, the reader is more
    likely to grant the narrator's credibility.

6. In order to study the effect of exercise on pigs' hearts,
    scientists are having pigs jog up to five miles.

7. Because I have quoted two authoritative sources, my reader
    should realize that my information is trustworthy.

8. Chaucer's work became more meaningful to us as we studied
    about life in the Middle Ages.

9. Secure in the knowledge that we had finally arrived safely, we
    welcomed a good night's sleep.

10. Just as I heard a sharp click, the suds subsided and the dial
    on the top of the washing machine read "drain."

S 8 Shifts in Subjects and Verbs
     Shifts in Person and Number (pp. 613-614)

1. When you get through a three-hour examination, you are ex-
    hausted.
    (A consistent use of third-person pronouns would also be
    acceptable.)

    or

    Taking a three-hour examination exhausts a person.

2. I tried to learn quadratic equations, but there is a limit to
    how much math I can learn.

3. In a situation like that, so many things can happen that we
    cannot foresee them all. All we can do is decide on a plan and
    then make whatever changes we have to.
    (A consistent use of you or one would also be acceptable.)

4. Loyalty means having complete confidence in someone, even if
    that person is under suspicion.

5. The book says the battle took place in 1847, but the book is
    wrong.

Shifts in Subject (p. 614)

1.   Students stop worrying about entrance examinations before
    they depart for the campus. They spend the last days shopping
    for clothes during the day and partying with friends at night.
    They give their families little attention, and they no longer
    think of entrance examinations.

2.   I often have difficulty writing the first draft of a paper.
    I have trouble finding a main idea to write about, and so face
    a blank page with a blank mind. When I do think of possible
    topics, I can't work them out. After writing a few sentences
    or a paragraph, I have nothing more to say; so I begin to fill
    up the wastepaper basket with discarded sheets. Thus I show a
    lack of concentration, the main weakness in my writing.

Shifts in Forms of Verbs (pp. 615-616)

1. The more we learned about the proposal, the clearer the issues
    became.

2. We spent the whole class hour discussing that question, but we
    arrived at no agreement.

3. I wrote inviting her to the party, but I have received no
    answer.

4. When we discussed the problem in class, it became quite simple.

5. As Douglas talked, I reminded myself that we would have to
    reserve judgment about him but that he would have to prove
    himself.

6. One behavioral scientist has said that he believes permissive-
    ness in the schools leads to student contempt for the schools.

7. Professor Wallingford said that she would return our papers at
    the next class session.

    or

    Professor Wallingford said, "I will return your papers at the
    next class session."

8. The rescue party worked for hours to extricate the child from the wreckage, and finally they succeeded.

9. He said we would be late for class anyway, so we should finish our Cokes and not worry.

   or

   He said, "We'll be late for class anyway; so let's finish our Cokes and not worry."

10. In choosing a mate for the rest of your life, you should look for certain qualities.

S 9 Incomplete Constructions (pp. 617-618)

1. We studied the subject as carefully as our opposition did.

2. I question the premise on which the argument depends.

   or

   I question the premise which the argument depends on.

3. I scribbled and outlined until I had exhausted my imagination, but I produced no satisfactory result.

4. Jason Compson, in The Sound and the Fury, is one of the most despicable characters in all of Faulkner's fiction.

   or

   Jason Compson, in The Sound and the Fury, is at least as despicable as any character in all of Faulkner's fiction.

   or

   Jason Compson, in The Sound and the Fury, may be the most despicable character in all of Faulkner's fiction.

5. Senator Benson has spoken more convincingly against the denial of civil rights than his opponent has.

6. We have insisted, and will continue to insist throughout the campaign, on equal opportunity for every ethnic group.

7. I sometimes think our professor has a better understanding of Macbeth than Shakespeare had.

8. One of the most valuable recommendations that the steering committee received came from a housewife whom the committee chairman inadvertently failed to mention.
   (Other revisions are possible. See 4 above.)

9. Our expectation is that the proposal will be rejected at the polls.

10. In the last quarter State launched a furious passing attack and won its fifth straight victory.

DICTION

D 1 Using a Dictionary (p. 621)

This exercise can provide the basis for an interesting class discussion if you will ask your students to bring their dictionaries to class on the day you work with it. The exercise itself will not require much class time, for the students will have learned, as they answered the questions, what the exercise is intended to teach. Item 4 can lead into other questions that you raise and that the students respond to as they check their dictionaries. The purposes of this part of the session will be to (1) help the students become still more knowledgeable about how to use dictionaries and (2) show them that even very good dictionaries have significant differences. This second purpose need not be a source of confusion: as the students learn about inconsistencies, they should discard naive ideas about what the dictionary says.

In the material below, three standard desk dictionaries often used by students are cited: The American Heritage Dictionary of the English Language (AH), Webster's New Collegiate Dictionary (WNC), and Webster's New World Dictionary of the American Language (WNW). The information from these three widely used dictionaries will help you to anticipate the kinds of responses that will emerge in class discussion. (The first item below is related to item 4 in the exercise.)

Order of definitions Some students become confused when the first definition is not the one they need, for they do not know that some dictionaries (including WNC and WNW) list definitions from earliest to most recent meanings. But not all dictionaries do that; for example, the editors of AH have tried to present meanings in "psychologically meaningful order, with one subgroup leading into another" (page xlvi). If you ask your students to turn to shambles in their dictionaries, you can make the point about order of definitions. Here are what WNC, WNW, and AH give:

WNC: 1. archaic : a meat market 2 : SLAUGHTERHOUSE 3a : a place of mass slaughter or bloodshed b : a scene or a state of great destruction: WRECKAGE c : a state of great disorder or confusion

WNW: 1. [Archaic exc. Brit. Dial.] a place where meat is sold; butcher's stall or shop 2. a slaughterhouse 3. scene of great slaughter, bloodshed, or carnage 4. any scene or condition of great destruction or disorder [rooms left a shambles by conventioneers]

<u>AH</u>: 1. A scene or condition of complete disorder or ruin: <u>The brawlers left the bar in a shambles</u>. . . . 2. A place or scene of bloodshed or carnage. 3. A slaughterhouse. 4. <u>British</u>. A meat market or butcher shop. . . .

<u>Spelling</u> If you will ask your students to locate the following words in their dictionaries, an informative discussion about spelling can develop. They can begin to develop criteria for determining whether a particular spelling is appropriate in their writing.

<u>judgment</u>: In <u>WNC</u>, <u>WNW</u>, and <u>AH</u>, <u>judgment</u> is listed first and <u>judgement</u> second. There is no notation about the <u>e</u>'s being primarily British. A student need not be troubled, then, by whether to include or omit the <u>e</u>, as long as the same spelling is used throughout the paper.

<u>benefited</u>, <u>benefiting</u>: WNC spells these words with both the single and the double <u>t</u>; neither <u>WNW</u> nor <u>AH</u> gives the double <u>t</u> spellings. You can explain that the double <u>t</u> spelling has come into usage because in so many verbs the final consonant is doubled before a suffix beginning with a vowel: <u>stopped, committed</u>, <u>controlled</u>. Such verbs normally are either one-syllable words or words of more than one syllable with the accent on the final syllable. (See page 686 in the text for more complete information.)

<u>alright</u>: WNC merely lists <u>alright</u> as another spelling for <u>all right</u>, with no comment. <u>WNW</u> says, "a disputed var. sp. of <u>all right</u>." <u>AH</u> says, "a common misspelling." The student is well advised to use <u>all right</u>, but an instructor should be slow to condemn <u>alright</u> severely. (If you can take an old dictionary to class, you can show that <u>alright</u> is not listed in it. The students may enjoy speculating about whether all dictionaries will accept the spelling one or two decades from now.)

<u>alot</u>: None of the three dictionaries lists this widely used misspelling. This sort of evidence should warn the student against its use.

<u>Usage and usage labels</u> The following quotations about criteria for determining acceptable usage show that the three dictionaries take similar, but by no means identical, stances on the subject of usage.

<u>WNC</u>: Three types of status labels are used in this dictionary—temporal, regional, and stylistic—to signal that a word or a sense of a word is not part of the standard vocabulary of English (page 15a).

<u>WNW</u>: . . . usage varies among groups of people, according to locality, level of education, social environment, etc. . . . usage varies for an individual in any given day depending upon the particular situation . . . and the purpose his language must serve. . . . None of the modes of using language in the cases cited is in an absolute sense more correct than

190

any of the others. Each is right for its occasion . . .
(page xiii).

AH: The makers of [this dictionary] accept usage as the authority
for correctness, but they have eschewed the "scientific" de-
lusion that a dictionary should contain no value judgments.
. . . good usage can usually be distinguished from bad usage
. . . . The best authorities, at least for cultivated usage,
are those professional speakers and writers who have demon-
strated their sensitiveness to the language and their power
to wield it effectively and beautifully (page xxiii).

Though there are some differences in temporal and regional
labels, the similarities are conspicuous: all use obsolete,
archaic, dialect or regional, and British.

But the stylistic usage labels, the ones that are most important to writers, are interesting because of their differences. WNW
does not list nonstandard; AH and WNC do, but with quite different
meanings (see page xliv in AH and page 16a in WNC). WNC is the only
one of the three to use substandard as a label (16a), though WNW
uses the term in explanatory notes. AH is the only one to use
informal (xliv) and vulgar (xlv). Only WNW uses colloquial (xiv).
But all three use the label slang (xliv-xlv in AH, 16a in WNC, xiv
in WNW).

Here are some words that the three dictionaries label differently. Ask your students to see what their dictionaries say about
them. (You may as well begin with ain't, for the students are
going to mention it anyway. All three dictionaries contain discussions of ain't; the one in AH is rather lengthy.)

ain't

WNC: substandard when used to mean have not or has not
WNW: colloquial for am not; dialectal or substandard when it
means is not, are not, has not, or have not
AH: nonstandard (see the usage note)

nowheres

WNC: chiefly dialect
WNW: dialect or colloquial
AH: nonstandard

irregardless

WNC: nonstandard
WNW: (no label--explanatory note that it is substandard or humorous)
AH: nonstandard (But remember that nonstandard does not have the
same meaning in AH and WNC.)

Class discussion of matters relevant to the material presented
here should convince the student that (1) he or she must become
well acquainted with the particular dictionary being used in order

© 1984 by Houghton Mifflin Company

to get full service from it and (2) there is no point in speaking
of what <u>the</u> dictionary says on controversial matters about language
as if there were only one correct answer to any particular question.

WORD ORDER

<u>WO 2 Ambiguous Order</u> (p. 626)

1. My mother planted in her garden the rosebush that I gave her
    on Mother's Day.

2. The children watched with shining eyes while the magician
    drew out a rabbit.

3. No boy, unless he was spiteful, would treat his father like
    that.

4. The list of expenses tells quickly and clearly the story of
    the man who wrote it.

5. Tonight in the student lounge there is a panel discussion
    about drug addiction.

6. Bill promised to pick me up on his way home.

7. When I met her I was so surprised that I forgot what I intended
    to say to her.

8. His neighbors said that at one time he had been in jail.

9. Richard Burton played superbly the part of the man who was cor-
    rupted by power.

10. There was a noisy disturbance at the back of the hall when the
    speaker said that.

11. The car that he wrecked is in the garage.

12. They talked frequently about going on a second honeymoon but
    never did.

<u>WO 4 Unemphatic Order</u> (p. 629)

.1. In the coroner's judgment, the cause of death was not drowning
    but heart failure.

2. Even her parents do not know where she is.

3. The challenger shocked the crowd when he knocked down the cham-
    pion six times in two rounds.

4. Although the plane's tires had been riddled by FBI marksmen who
    were there to prevent a hijacking, it made a successful take-
    off.

5. According to the late news last night, the Supreme Court refused to consider the appeal.

6. I think Wayne's personality will irritate other members of the council; however, I'll have to vote for him.

7. Since there was no objection to the minutes, the chairman said they would be accepted.

8. I firmly believe that the best argument for democracy is to consider its alternatives.

9. After much pleading from the students, the instructor promised that she would give the class some sample questions to study for the exam.

10. If you will examine the evidence carefully and impartially, you will see that it shows that the National League plays the best baseball.

11. I neither support nor oppose the bill.

GRAMMATICAL FORMS

GF 1 Principal Parts of Verbs (p. 633)

1. lay
2. raise
3. raise
4. sit
5. rose
6. lying
7. lay
8. setting
9. raised
10. lying

GF 2 Tense Forms (p. 636)

1. had planned
2. OK
3. Having practiced
4. had had
5. to pack
6. Two possibilities: either change is lucky to was lucky or change to find to to have found
7. had sensed
8. Having finished
9. to submit
10. went . . . had intended

GF 3 Case (pp. 640-641)

1. OK
2. OK
3. We . . . OK
4. I
5. OK
6. our
7. OK
8. OK
9. whom
10. us . . . me
11. whoever
12. OK

GF 4 Subject–Verb Agreement (p. 647)

1.	were	6.	are
2.	plans	7.	is
3.	was	8.	is
4.	has	9.	is
5.	plan	10.	are

GF 5 Pronoun–Antecedent Agreement (p. 650)

1.	his	6.	its
2.	himself or herself	7.	is . . . its
3.	one has	8.	his or her
4.	its . . . it	9.	who
5.	that	10.	they want

GF 6 Vague Pronoun Reference (p. 651)

The sentences can of course be revised in various ways. In several of the solutions below the writer has merely removed the vague pronoun and substituted its understood referent.

1. The defendant was visibly upset. At that very moment the jurors were in the next room deciding his fate.

2. Our having overspent our budget for the play is a major problem, for we need still more money for props and set construction.

3. In revival meetings it is customary for the worshipers to offer testimonies.

4. Hunters should be careful about how they carry loaded guns.

5. Because Mark Twain did not like his early work on <u>Huckleberry Finn,</u> he considered destroying the partially completed manuscript.

6. The figure skaters anxiously awaited the decision as the judges tabulated their score cards.

7. That Fred and Sue have agreed to have a church wedding pleases their parents.

8. My mother was pleased because my job in New York was only three blocks from my apartment and because the working hours were during the daytime.

9. Kemper's sketches of birds and trees showed where his interests lay.

10. Students living in an apartment will spend some of their time doing their own cooking and cleaning.

GF 7 Faulty Complement (p. 654)

Alternate solutions to several of the problems would be entirely acceptable.

1. My only preparation for college chemistry was a junior high school course in general science.

2. I feel bad about having caused you so much trouble.

3. Forgery is the offense of signing another person's name to a document.

4. I heard on last night's news that flooding has reached disaster proportions in some sections of the country.

5. In basketball, goal tending is the act of blocking an opponent's shot after it has begun its downward path toward the goal.

6. We reached complete accord in our conference.

7. The most unusual food I have ever eaten was a serving of boiled snails.

8. In tennis a double fault occurs when the server fails twice successively to hit the ball into the appropriate part of the opponent's court.

9. The boxer's chief disadvantage is that his opponents have learned that he has a "glass chin."

10. The judge explained that perjury is the crime of lying under oath.

GF 8 Confusion of Adjective and Adverb (p. 655)

1.	gently	6.	really
2.	surely	7.	happy
3.	horrible	8.	safe
4.	securely	9.	carefully
5.	calmly	10.	considerably

PUNCTUATION

P 1 Uses of the Comma

Commas to Separate Elements (p. 659)

1. The largest city in the world is Jacksonville, Florida, if you judge by area, not population.

2. I'll have orange juice, waffles with maple syrup, and black coffee.

3. When we finished sanding and staining, the desk looked beautiful.

4. "But the name is Manson, not Mason," said Aunt Lois.

5. After all, it was not such a difficult shot for a professional.

6. The yard was strewn with empty cartons, newspapers, scraps of lumber, and discarded tires.

7. Throughout, his speech was a masterful exhibition of how to talk around a question without answering it.

8. Father went to the airport to meet his sister, and Mother came with me to the reception.

9. Lyndon Baines Johnson, thirty-sixth President of the United States, was born near Stonewall, Texas, on August 27, 1908, and died on January 22, 1973.

10. No, I cannot wait any longer, for the train leaves in ten minutes.

Commas to Set Off an Interrupting Construction (pp. 663-664)

1. Dad, did you know that Dr. Jones, our chemistry professor, once played professional hockey?

2. Mary asked, "Joe, why don't you talk to the man in charge, the managing editor?"

3. Yes, her mother is a doctor--not, however, of medicine, but of philosophy.

4. No commas required.

5. The man, whoever he is, must be found.

6. No commas required.

7. Fred asked me, when he called last night, if we were still going to have the picnic. (In a particular context "when he called last night" might be restrictive and would therefore not be set off by commas.)

8. The children, looking very disappointed, thanked us anyway.

9. The instructor said, in addition, that some of the test answers were illegible.

10. No commas required.

11. Dad, you said we could go if we had finished our work. You promised, moreover, that we could use the car, even though the direction signal is not working.

12. A radio report, which may or may not be true, states that John Whalen, our line coach, has an offer from a professional team that he will probably accept.

13. The challenger, who was clearly the underdog before the match, made his defeat of the champion look so easy that the sportswriters began to hail him as one of the truly great champions.

14. However, the wig that she bought in the bargain basement was the best of the three.

15. The bus driver, Mr. Peterson, who is usually an easygoing person, was in a bad mood today, scolding the children at the slightest provocation.

Commas to Mark an Inversion (p. 665)

1. Whatever he says, take it with a grain of salt.

2. No commas required.

3. If he is going to fly off the handle like that at the slightest provocation, I think you should stop dating him.

4. As far as I know, they plan to stay here this summer.

5. Whatever the merits of the proposal, it comes too late to be considered.

6. Whether you like it or not, this is the final decision.

7. No commas required.

8. Since he has not answered any of our letters, even those we sent by registered mail, we must assume that he is not interested.

9. Knowing that his only chance to win might depend on stealing second base, the manager sent in a runner for Milney.

10. Confused and hurt by her parents' attitude, the girl ran sobbing to her room.

Review Exercise in Punctuation (pp. 679-680)

1. Mr. Reynolds, the insurance agent, had not arrived by nine o'clock.

2. "I wonder what's keeping him," Dad grumbled. "Are you sure that he said he would call at eight o'clock?"

3. "Yes, quite sure," I replied. He said to me, "Tell your father I will call at eight o'clock."

4. I have not seen Mrs. Manlin for some time; since her husband was killed she spends a lot of time at her mother's place.

5. Gutenberg, the inventor of movable type, was motivated by a desire to make the Bible more widely available.

6. OK

7. The speaker, who was obviously embarrassed, said that he did not answer questions of such a personal nature.

8. No wonder her hair looks different; she's wearing a wig.

9. Some of the shutters had fallen to the ground, others were hanging from one corner, and a few were firmly locked in place across the windows.

10. Seated at the speakers' table were Fred Hanley, Superintendent of Schools; Dr. Mason, Dean of the College of Education; Mrs. Helen Loftus, President of the Parent Teachers Association; and the chairman, Professor Robbins.

11. The girl who received first prize, a silver cup, was our neighbors' daughter.

12. OK

13. However important these facts may have been eight years ago, they have no significance today.

14. Trevino, despite the pressure he was under, continued to joke with the gallery.

15. He said, when I asked him, that he expected to take a brief vacation.

16. She said, "When I asked his opinion, he answered, 'If you want legal advice, I'll be glad to talk with you in my office.'"

17. Donald said, if I remember correctly, that he would be out of town for the next three or four days.

18. Where the old ice house used to be, there is now a little stone cottage with a white picket fence around it.

19. Giggling almost hysterically, the children either could not or would not explain what had happened.

20. Mules, though less speedy than horses in open country, are both faster and surer on those narrow mountain tracks.

Review Exercise in Punctuation (p. 681)

The punctuation provided here is that of the Newsweek story from which the passage was taken. Alternative punctuation would be possible at some points.

The plight of a normal person who finds himself committed to a mental institution and unable to convince anyone he is not insane is a standard plot for horror fiction. But in a remarkable study last week, Dr. David L. Rosenhan, professor of psychology and law at Stanford University, and seven associates reported just such a nightmare in real life. To find out how well psychiatric professionals can distinguish the normal from the sick, they had themselves committed to mental institutions. Their experiment, reported in the journal Science, clearly showed that once inside the hospital walls, everyone is judged insane.

The "pseudopatients,"[1] five men and three women, included three psychologists, a pediatrician, a psychiatrist, a painter and a housewife, all of whom were certifiably sane. In the course of the three-year study, the volunteers spent an average of nineteen days in a dozen institutions, private and public, in New York, California, Pennsylvania, Oregon and Delaware. Each pseudopatient told admitting doctors that he kept hearing voices that said words like "empty," "hollow" and "void," suggesting that the patient found his life meaningless and futile. But beyond falsifying their names and occupations, all the volunteers described their life histories as they actually were. In so doing, they gave the doctors every chance to discern the truth. "I couldn't believe we wouldn't be found out," Rosenhan told Newsweek's Gerald Lubenow. But they weren't. At eleven hospitals the pseudopatients were promptly diagnosed as schizophrenic and, at the twelfth, as manic-depressive.

As soon as they had gained admission, the volunteers studiously resumed normal behavior. They denied hearing voices and worked hard to convince the staff members that they ought to be released. But such efforts were to no avail; doctors and nurses interpreted everything the pseudopatients did in terms of the original diagnosis. When some of the volunteers went about taking notes, the hospital staff made such entries in their records as "patient engages in writing behavior." The only people who realized that the experimenters were normal were

1. Note that the writers follow Newsweek policy of writing a coined word within quotation marks the first time it appears in the article, but not afterwards.

some of the patients. "You're not crazy," said one
patient. "You're a journalist or a professor.
You're checking up on the hospital." (Copyright
Newsweek, Inc., 1973, reprinted by permission.)

MECHANICS

In this section, while you are discussing spelling difficulties and methods of improvement, it might be helpful to emphasize to students the usefulness of the two lists of words frequently confused or misspelled (pp. 686, 687-691). Here they are collected for convenient reference when a student is in doubt about their spelling.

Review Exercise in Mechanics (pp. 701-702)

1. Dr. Lindon . . . professor . . . University . . . .

2. Columbus discovered America in A.D. 1492 (or 1492 A.D.).

3. Four days . . . .

4. Her father is a lieutenant colonel in the Army of the United States.

5. Lower case spelling for senior, sophomores, juniors, and instructor's. Freshman is capitalized only because it begins a sentence.

6. Capitalize Father's Day.

7. Small n in navy.

8. . . . five days

9. . . . "Spotted Horses," . . . The Hamlet.

10. Capitalize New Year's Day.

11. . . . 71 Grand Ave. (or Avenue.)

12. No capital for mother-in-law.

13. . . . January 31 at 11:05 P.M. (or p.m.)

14. No correction needed.

15. . . . Bible . . . Biblical scholars.

16. Seventy-eight . . . .

17. Italicize pas de deux and tour jeté.

18. Italicize, or put quotation marks around, concave and convex.

19. Capitalize <u>American</u> and <u>European</u>. Italicize the titles of all these movies.

20. Capitalize <u>Democratic</u>, <u>Vice Presidents</u>, <u>Presidency</u>, <u>President</u>, <u>Chief Executive</u>, <u>Presidents</u>.

SELECTED BIBLIOGRAPHY

by Barbara Weaver

Anderson College

Works cited here have been selected for two purposes. First,
they articulate the philosophical and theoretical foundations of
Writing With a Purpose. Second, they suggest complementary
strategies for teaching and evaluating writing. Part I includes
general resources—bibliography, theory, pedagogy. Part II addresses planning, drafting, revising, and the notions of purpose
and audience that guide the writing process. Part III offers information on development, arrangement, style, and persuasion.
Part IV supplements instruction in writing about literature, developing the research paper, and writing for business.

I.   TOWARD PURPOSEFUL TEACHING

Before the First Word. Learning Designs and Educational Broad-
      casting Corporation, 1982. A 29-minute 16mm sound film or
      videocassette available for purchase or rental from Ency-
      clopedia Britannica Educational Corporation, 425 North
      Michigan Avenue., Chicago, Illinois 60611. Accompanied by
      "Teaching Notes" by Alice Trillin and Jane Garmey. The
      film follows two students and a professional reporter as
      they investigate New York's Sullivan Street for their writing
      assignments; it illustrates the process of finding a story
      through active inquiry—observing, interviewing, thinking,
      writing. Teachers' supplement suggests classroom activities
      and writing assignments.

Connors, Robert J. "The Rise and Fall of the Modes of Discourse,"
      College Composition and Communication, December 1981. Winner
      of the Braddock Award for the best CCC article in 1981,
      Connors traces the history of the modes as an organizing
      principle for composition instruction, citing the first edi-
      tion of Writing With a Purpose in 1950 as a breakthrough for
      making purpose the controlling idea. Connors argues that
      contemporary classification schemes by Moffett, Kinneavy,
      and Britton have in common their location in the writer's
      purpose rather than the written discourse.

Foster, David. A Primer for Writing Teachers: Theories, Theor-
      ists, Issues, Problems. Upper Montclair, New Jersey:
      Boynton/Cook, 1983. Foster presents a historical perspective,
      classifies rhetorical theories, analyzes sensitive issues,
      and suggests course planning and teaching strategies.

Irmscher, William. Teaching Expository Writing. New York: Holt,
    Rinehart, and Winston, 1979. In a clear and practical guide,
    Irmscher describes the writing process and suggests methods
    of teaching invention, structure, diction, mechanics, and
    style. His chapter on evaluation provides a succinct state-
    ment of criteria that can guide the grading of finished
    products; he illustrates evaluation with annotated student
    essays.

Kinneavy, James L. A Theory of Discourse: The Aims of Discourse.
    New York: W. W. Norton, 1971. Kinneavy classifies discourse
    by purpose, associating emphasis on the writer with expres-
    sive discourse, the reader with persuasive discourse, the
    content with reference discourse, and the text with literary
    discourse. Each purpose is analyzed in terms of its nature,
    its logic, its organization, and its styles.

Lindemann, Erika. A Rhetoric for Writing Teachers. New York:
    Oxford University Press, 1982. For the new teacher or the
    pro, Lindemann offers a substantive, well-documented dis-
    cussion of the sources of contemporary composition theory--
    research on composing, linguistics, cognition, classical
    rhetoric, discourse theory--and a set of approaches to course
    design, teaching practices, and evaluation.

Murray, Donald M. "Teach Writing as a Process not Product." In
    Rhetoric and Composition: A Sourcebook for Teachers. Ed.
    Richard Graves. Rochelle Park, New Jersey: Hayden Book Co.,
    1976. This well-known article cites ten implications for
    teaching when writing is envisioned as a process. Murray
    suggests that writing assignments, classroom styles, and
    evaluation techniques should enable students to learn a writ-
    ing process.

National Council of Teachers of English. Classroom Practices in
    Teaching English 1979-1980: How to Handle the Paper Load.
    Urbana, Illinois: National Council of Teachers of English,
    1979. This collection offers evaluation strategies that
    are more pedagogically defensible and less demanding of
    teachers' time than the traditional "red pen" response of
    the teacher-as-editor. Methods include peer evaluation, self-
    editing, non-graded writing, selective responses, and
    focussed feedback.

Tate, Gary, ed. Teaching Composition: Ten Bibliographical Essays.
    Fort Worth, Texas: Texas Christian University Press, 1976.
    Essays discuss the issues and review the literature on topics
    relating to composition. Of special note are essays by
    Richard Young on invention, Richard Larson on form, Edward
    Corbett on style, Frank D'Angelo on modes of discourse, Mina
    Shaughnessy on basic writing, and W. Ross Winterowd on lin-
    guistics.

SELECTED BIBLIOGRAPHY

Trimmer, Joseph F. "One O'Clock Jump." Journal of Teaching
    Writing, Spring, 1982. Trimmer's narrative of discovery as
    a writing teacher, influenced by his teachers Jonathan, the
    Romantic guru who taught writing as an art and "the Earl,"
    the classical scholar who taught writing as a craft, illus-
    trates the assumptions, methods, and standards of two ap-
    parently contradictory philosophies of composition. He
    suggests that teachers and students are part of a community
    of writers who attend both to process and product as they
    write and rewrite.

II. THE WRITING PROCESS

Eckhardt, Caroline D. and David H. Stewart. "Towards a Functional
    Taxonomy of Composition." College Composition and Communica-
    tion, December 1979. The authors suggest three benefits of
    a writing course organized according to the writer's purpose:
    (1) a closer approximation to "real writing," (2) a sense of
    progress in writing as the awareness of purpose broadens,
    and (3) an emphasis on first principles--stating goals en-
    ables writers to address their appropriateness.

Ede, Lisa S. "On Audience and Composition." College Composition
    and Communication, October 1979. Ede argues that students
    can create their own contexts for writing if teachers engage
    them in "purpose-oriented analysis" and devote continuous
    attention to audience, purpose, and content throughout the
    writing process.

Emig, Janet A. "The Uses of the Unconscious in Composing."
    College Composition and Communication, February 1964. Cit-
    ing evidence from professional authors and music composers,
    Emig argues for teaching methods that permit students to
    develop the rituals and habits conducive to thoughtful writ-
    ing. These methods allow more writing time, offer greater
    flexibility, and tolerate some idiosyncracy among student
    writers.

Flower, Linda S., and John R. Hayes. "Problem-Solving Strategies
    and the Writing Process." College English, December 1977.
    Flower and Hayes present a set of heuristics for analytical
    writing to help writers generate ideas and construct them in
    writing for a reader. They offer specific techniques for
    planning, generating, constructing, and arranging, supple-
    mented by advice about teaching and using heuristics.

SELECTED BIBLIOGRAPHY

Harris, Muriel. "Evaluation: The Process for Revision." Journal of Basic Writing, Spring/Summer, 1978. Harris outlines methods of teacher evaluation and peer evaluation, emphasizing that different kinds of responses are appropriate at different stages of the writing process. She argues that evaluation practices should model the self-evaluation strategies that student writers must learn.

Journal of Basic Writing, Fall/Winter, 1981. This issue collects essays on the theory and practice of revision, defined as the way in which writers discover what they think, experiment with form and style, and construct a meaningful piece of writing. Authors include Ann Berthoff, Donald Murray, Nancy Sommers, and Linda Flower; Alice Trillin's interview with Calvin Trillin illuminates the process of a professional writer as he progresses from information gathering to private draft to public product.

McCrimmon, James M. "Writing as a Way of Knowing." In The Promise of English: NCTE 1970 Distinguished Lectures. Urbana, Illinois: National Council of Teachers of English, 1970. Rpt. in Rhetoric and Composition: A Sourcebook for Teachers. Ed. Richard Graves. Rochelle Park, New Jersey: Hayden Book Co., 1976. McCrimmon argues that writing as knowing is as important as writing as telling. Whereas emphasis on the telling involves students with style, emphasis on the knowing involves them with content. Methods of invention should lead the writer back to the "problem of deciding what the subject means to him."

Meyer, Bonnie J. F. "Reading Research and the Composition Teacher: The Importance of Plans." College Composition and Communication, February 1982. The psychology of planning, derived from research in reading, demonstrates how plans help writers to achieve their purposes. Plans enable the writer to find and arrange ideas, to emphasize major ideas, and to articulate the mixture of old and new ideas for the benefit of an audience.

Sommers, Nancy. "Responding to Student Writing." College Composition and Communication, May 1982. Analyzing teachers' comments on student papers, Sommers argues that two kinds of comments are inappropriate: those that confuse teachers' purposes with students' purposes, and those that are not specific to the text at hand. She suggests that teachers learn to write comments that offer students reasons to revise.

SELECTED BIBLIOGRAPHY

Winterowd, W. Ross. "Invention." In his Contemporary Rhetoric: A Conceptual Background with Readings. New York: Harcourt Brace Jovanovich, 1975. Winterowd discusses the kinds of sytematic inquiry that "help writers work with ideas." Demonstrating that all "topics" (invention systems) are either finite or non-finite and either content-oriented or form-oriented, he classifies heuristics proposed by Aristotle, Kenneth Burke, Alton Becker, Francis Christensen, Frank O'Hare, and others.

III. THE EXPRESSION OF IDEAS

Booth, Wayne C. "The Rhetorical Stance." College Composition and Communication, October 1963. Booth argues that persuasion "presupposes that one has a purpose concerning a subject." He urges teachers to help students acquire the "rhetorical stance," a balanced position that considers audience, purpose, and subject.

Christensen, Francis. Notes Toward a New Rhetoric. New York: Harper & Row, 1968. Christensen offers a theory capable of uniting, in his view, modern grammar and modern rhetoric: a "generative" rhetoric of sentences and paragraphs. Christensen's method of teaching the "cumulative" sentence as a mark of mature style is an alternative technique to sentence combining.

Corbett, Edward P. J. Classical Rhetoric for the Modern Student. 2nd ed. New York: Oxford University Press, 1971. Corbett has compiled a history of classical rhetoric, a description of its theory, and an application of its techniques to composition and to literary and textual analysis. Chapters on arrangement and style are particularly useful.

D'Angelo, Frank. A Conceptual Theory of Rhetoric. Cambridge, Massachusetts: Winthrop, 1975. D'Angelo argues that paradigms for the arrangement of material (e.g., the methods of exposition) represent structures of thought as well. He reconstructs Aristotle's "topoi" as both a system of invention and a model of arrangement.

Lunsford, Andrea. "Cognitive Development and the Basic Writer." College English, September, 1979. Lunsford believes that many students have trouble analyzing and synthesizing information because of their level of cognitive development. Suggesting that writing classes can facilitate a student's ability to conceptualize, she offers sentence exercises and writing assignments for that purpose.

SELECTED BIBLIOGRAPHY

Markels, Robin Bell. "Cohesion Paradigms in Paragraphs." College English, September 1983. Although most current research describes cohesion (unity) as a semantic feature of language, Markels argues that cohesion is attained in a text by both semantic ties and syntactic structures. She was awarded an NCTE Promising Researcher Award for the research reported in this article.

McQuade, Donald M., ed. Linguistics, Stylistics, and the Teaching of Composition. Akron, Ohio: Department of English, University of Akron, 1979. 2nd ed. Carbondale, Illinois: Southern Illinois University Press, 1984. Forthcoming. This collection features articles that discuss relationships among linguistics, style, and teaching methods; issues include error analysis, imitation, sentence combining, and "generative" rhetoric. Noteworthy essays by James Kinneavy, Joseph Williams, Donald Freeman, and W. Ross Winterowd highlight the collection.

Milic, Louis T. "Theories of Style and Their Implications for the Teaching of Composition." College Composition and Communication, May 1965. Milic discusses dualistic and monistic theories of style; i.e., can style be considered independent of content? He argues that "rhetorical dualism" is the only theory that offers the possibility of teaching stylistic techniques to inexperienced writers.

Strong, William. "Sentence Combining: Back to Basics and Beyond." English Journal, February 1976. Strong summarizes the theory and practice of sentence combining and argues for its place in a writing curriculum.

Warner, Richard. "Teaching the Paragraph as a Structural Unit." College Composition and Communication, May 1979. Warner demonstrates three ways to represent paragraph structures using the notational systems of transformational grammar: a "generative" rule describes a unified paragraph; a "transformational" rule illustrates variations of a basic pattern; a "rhetorical" rule relates the paragraph to the larger unit of discourse in which it appears.

IV.   SPECIAL ASSIGNMENTS

Geckle, George L. "Heuristics and Schemata: Some New Problems Concerning Texts and Readers." The CEA Forum, October 1982. Geckle uses recent research in "response to literature" as a basis for his argument that teaching interpretive techniques for literary study is an unnecessarily limited approach.

Students need a cultural framework in which the text can be interpreted, and they need to acknowledge their personal responses before they approach a work critically.

Goswami, Dixie, et al. _Writing in the Professions_. Washington, D. C.: American Institute for Research, 1981. Four members of the federally funded Document Design Project offer thorough and up-to-date advice on teaching business writing as a process. They address planning, drafting, revising, and evaluation and devote separate chapters to organization, graphic design, and peer review.

Jordan, Michael P. "As a Matter of Fact." _The Journal of Business Communication_, Winter 1978. Jordan believes that students of business writing should be taught to recognize and to differentiate facts, opinions, and assumptions. To this end he suggests techniques for reporting facts, stating opinions, and clarifying assumptions.

Judy, Stephen N., and Susan J. Judy. "Interdisciplinary Writing." In their _An Introduction to the Teaching of Writing_. New York: John Wiley and Sons, 1981. The unit suggests approaches to writing as an interdisciplinary enterprise and offers useful writing projects.

McCarron, William E. "In the Business World and in Academe: The English Teacher in the 1980's." _College English_, March 1980. McCarron sees business writing as problem-solving and argues that the problems facing businesses and government demand humanitarian as well as technological solutions. He suggests teaching literature and composition, from the perspective of classical rhetoric, to prepare business writers.

Moran, Charles. "Teaching Writing/Teaching Literature." _College Composition and Communication_, February 1981. Moran suggests that creative writing assignments based on literature study will promote improvement in expository and critical writing about the literature. He reports a classroom experiment and offers several writing assignments and student responses.

Petersen, Bruce T. "Writing About Responses: A United Model of Reading, Interpretation, and Composition." _College English_, September 1982. Petersen argues that the composition research conducted by James Britton and Linda Flower is compatible with reader-response theories of literature espoused by David Bleich and Louise Rosenblatt. From this unified perspective, Petersen defends the personal, "affective" response to literature as a necessary first step in the writing process; from there students proceed to expository and critical writing.

SELECTED BIBLIOGRAPHY

Petrosky, Anthony R. "From Story to Essay: Reading and Writing."
    College Composition and Communication, February 1982.
    Petrosky offers a model for teaching writing about literature
    that incorporates reference to the text with reference to the
    reader's associations derived from the text.

Swegler, Robert A., and Linda K. Shamoon. "The Aims and Process
    of the Research Paper." College English, December 1982.
    Analyzing the differences between students' and teachers'
    views of the purpose of research papers, the authors argue
    that the academic model of a research product and the struc-
    ture of the research process should be taught together, as
    "a process of thought and expression."

Tryzna, Thomas. "Approaches to Research Writing: A Review of
    Handbooks with Some Suggestions." College Composition and
    Communication, May 1983. Tryzna contrasts the way re-
    searchers really approach their tasks with the way typical
    college textbooks represent that approach. He argues that
    the text should teach critical thinking skills though
    hypothesizing, differentiating fact from opinion by attribu-
    tive style, and actual research methods through automated
    bibliographic searching, LC subject classifications, review
    indexes, and networking outside the library.

NOTES

NOTES

NOTES

NOTES

NOTES